PROCRASTINATE LATER!

PROCRASTINATE LATER!

How to Motivate Yourself to Do It Now

Dr. MICHAEL E. BERNARD

SCHWARTZ & WILKINSON

Schwartz & Wilkinson
is an imprint of

Information Australia
45 Flinders Lane
Melbourne VIC 3000
Telephone: (03) 654 2800
Fax: (03) 650 5261

ISBN 1 86337 038 2

Copyright © M. Bernard 1991

The National Library of Australia
Cataloguing-in-Publication entry

Bernard, Michael E. (Michael Edwin), 1950 -
    Procrastinate later.

    Includes index.
    ISBN 1 86337 038 2.

    1. Procrastination. I. Title.

155.232

First printed April 1991, reprinted April 1992

Cover design by Graphic Connection
Printed in Australia by Australian Print Group.

DEDICATION:

To Patricia, for her love and support

Also by Dr. Michael E. Bernard

Clinical Applications of Rational - Emotive Therapy (New York: Plenum Press, 1985) with Albert Ellis.

Inside Rational-Emotive Therapy: A Critical Analysis of the Theory and Practise of Albert Ellis (New York: Academic Press, 1989) with Ray DiGiuseppe.

Rational-Emotive Approaches to the Problems of Childhood (New York: Plenum Press, 1983) with Albert Ellis.

Rational-Emotive Therapy: with Children and Adolescents (New York: Wiley, 1984) with Marie Joyce.

Reading Resue: A Parent's Guide to Improving Their Child's *Reading* (Melbourne: Australian Council for Educational Research, 1989, 2nd edition) with Susan Gillet.

Staying Rational in an Irrational World (Melbourne: McCullough, 1986).

You Can Do It! What Every Student (and Parent) Should Know About Success in School and Life (Melbourne: Collins Dove, 1987) with Darko Hajzler.

You Can Do It! Video Program (Melbourne: Seven Dimensions, 1990) with Eve Ash.

Contents

About the Author

Preface

Chapter 1.   Why Procrastinate? 1

What Exactly is Procrastination? 3
A Magnetic Theory of Procrastination 4
How Big a Procrastinator Are You? 8
Membership in the Born Procrastinator's Club 15
The Procrastinating Personality:
What We Now Know! 17
Actions Speak Louder Than Words 22

Chapter 2.   Addictions, Fantasies And Lies 25

Addictions 28
Fantasies 31
Lies 36
Why the 'Cover Up'? 45
Actions Speak Louder Than Words 49

**Chapter 3.   The 10 "Real Reasons"
                       You Procrastinate** 51

No. 1 Anxiety 58
No. 2 Self-Depreciation 60
No. 3 Low Discomfort Tolerance 62
No. 4 Pleasure Seeking 64
No. 5 Time Disorganisation 66
No. 6 Environmental Disorganisation 68
No. 7 Poor Task Approach 70
No. 8 Lack of Assertion 72
No. 9 Hostility with Others 74
No. 10 Stress and Fatigue 76

Summary Profile of Your Check Up from the
Neck Up 77

Actions Speak Louder Than Words 80

**Chapter 4.   25 Of The 'Best' Procrastination Bypass
Techniques.** 83

No.   1 Knock Out Technique .84

No.   2 Worst First Approach 85

No.   3 Remember-Forgetting Approach 85

No.   4 Bits & Pieces Approach 86

No.   5 Salami Technique 86

No.   6 Five Minute Plan 88

No.   7 Switching 89

No.   8 Referenting 89

No.   9 Premack Principle 91

No. 10 Getting a 'Round Tuit' 92

No. 11 Face the Music 93

No. 12 Swap Out Technique .93

No. 13 Peak Performance Time 94

No. 14 Do It, Delegate It, Ditch It 95

No. 15 Establish Priorities 95

No. 16 Establish a Set Time .96

No. 17 Change Your Environment 97

No. 18 Isolation 97

No. 19 Visible Reminders 98

No. 20 Monitoring 99

No. 21 Guided Imagery 99

No. 22 Rational-Emotive Imagery 101

No. 23 The Catastrophe Scale 102

No. 24 Paradoxical Intention 103

No. 25 Behavioural Self-Control 104

Actions Speak Louder Than Words 107

Chapter 5. Managing Your Anxiety And Self-depreciation 109

The ABC's of Anxiety and Its Management 110

Getting in Touch with your Anxiety:
Self-Awareness 112

Fear of Failure and Perfectionism 116

Fear of Disapproval 123

Fear of Success 127

Putting an End to Self-Depreciation 130

Self-Talk to Reduce Anxiety and
Self-Depreciation 135

Actions Speak Louder Than Words 138

Chapter 6. Discomfort Tolerance: The Key 141

Sensation Sensitivity 143

Low Frustration Tolerance and Discomfort
Anxiety 145

The 'Lining Up' Technique 151

Long-Term Hedonism and Delay of Gratification . . . 153

Relaxation 156

Stress Innoculation Training 162

Attitudes to Increase Discomfort Tolerance 167

Actions Speak Louder Than Words 169

**Chapter 7. Getting Organised,
Getting Started** 171

Time Disorganisation 172

Environmental Disorganisation 185

Poor Task Approach 190

Actions Speak Louder Than Words 195

**Chapter 8. Managing Hostility And
Lack Of Assertion** 197

Dealing with Difficult People 199

Managing Your Anger 201

Your Assertive Option 208

Different Kinds of Assertion 211
Specific Assertiveness Techniques 214
Actions Speak Louder Than Words 219

Chapter 9.   Managing Stress And Fatigue 221
Will Power 222
What is Stress? 225
Stress and Fatigue-Creating Stressors 226
How You Influence Your Stress and Fatigue 235
Life Style Management 238
Diet 238
Exercise 245
Recreation 249
Actions Speak Louder Than Words 254

**Chapter 10. How To Get Others To
                    Procrastinate Later** 255
Self-Control: Without It You Will Fail 257
Work on Changing the 'Real
Reasons' for Another's Procrastination 260
Behaviour Modification: Rewards and Penalties 264
Contracting 270
The 'One Minute Manager' 273
The Quarry Method of Performance Appraisal 275
Actions Speak Louder Than Words 281

About the Author

Dr Michael E. Bernard is a Reader and Psychologist in the School of Education at the University of Melbourne, Victoria. He is the founder of the Australian Institute for Rational Living and is currently the Director of Rational Effectiveness Training Systems (Australia), an organisation concerned with the improvement of managerial and employee performance, productivity and working life. Over the past decade, Dr Bernard has worked with numerous organisations (e.g., AMP, Collingwood Football Club, Attorney-General's Office, Australian Institute of Management, Rosehill International Hotel).

A close colleague of and collaborator with Dr. Albert Ellis, the founder of rational-emotive therapy (RET), today Dr Bernard is Australia's foremost authority on the ways in which rational thinking and attitude-change skills can be used to increase confidence and persistence in the work force as well as improve the quality of one's work and personal life. He has helped numerous individuals to overcome barriers to self-development, achievement at work, a smooth-running home life and in work and personal relationships.

One of Australia's leading trainers and consultants to business, government and education, Dr Bernard has developed a sound professional reputation for providing stimulating and skill-enhancing workshops.

He has written numerous research articles, chapters of books, and best-selling books, including *Staying Rational in an Irrational World* (McCulloch Publishing) and *You Can Do It! What Every Student (and Parent) Should Know About Success in School and Life*. He is the producer (with Eve Ash) of the popular international award-winning motivational program for students *You Can Do It!*.

In 1990, Dr Bernard had published the most comprehensive book ever written on teacher stress *Taking the Stress Out of Teaching* which summarised not only the main factors causing modern-day teacher stress, but also out-lined the most current methods which teachers can use to reduce stress and increase work satisfaction.

Preface

I have always been fascinated with the topic of procrastination for a number of reasons. To begin with, procrastination is one of the main causes of people not performing to the fullest of their native potential as well as people not living life to its fullest. At work, it is linked to under-achievement, work dissatisfaction and even to a lower than necessary salary. In personal relationships, procrastination can be seen as a major cause of unsuccessful dating and mating. If you are a student, putting off various aspects of your studying will not only add to your stress, it can also frequently lead to poor achievement or failure to complete a course. And if you procrastinate at self-development tasks, your inner life will be impoverished.

As well, the 'real' reasons for procrastination are by no means obvious. This is partly because many people do not like to admit to procrastination. Many of us make up rationalisations to justify to ourselves and others why we are putting things off ("I'll do it tomorrow when I have more time."). By denying we procrastinate, we cover up the real reasons we procrastinate.

Of particular interest is that just about everyone procrastinates. It is, therefore, not really abnormal behaviour - except in its very extremes - and as such reveals some interesting characteristics of human beings.

Procrastination is also something that everyone on their own can do something about. Whereas certain psychological problems such as depression and anxiety are harder to resolve without professional help, you can, by reading books such as this one, do something about your procrastination.

In fact, I would go so far as to say that if you are able to pinpoint exactly what you would like to start doing in no uncertain terms, then without a doubt you will be able to use ideas in this book to do what up until now, you've tended to put off. I can say without hesitation that the ideas in this book have helped countless people to make significant changes in their behaviour.

So while the numbers of people who procrastinate can make us somewhat pessimistic about our ability to achieve what we set out to do, the optimistic news is that each one of us can take control over those factors which cause us to procrastinate and then to make changes which will help us do what we want to do.

The material in this book comes from my own thorough review of research into the 'causes' and 'cures' of procrastination. The 10 reasons I propose to underly procrastination stem not only from what other investigators have found, but also from my own research with many different groups of people. Similarly, the techniques for overcoming procrastination are the ones which leading scientists and practitioners have found to help people stop procrastinating.

I would like to acknowledge the following contributions to this book.

Albert Ellis who, along with William Knaus, wrote the first major book in this area Overcoming Procrastination. In particular, their seminal ideas on 'rationalisations' formed the background to and provided some of the content of my own material presented in Chapter 2. Albert Ellis' theory of rational-emotive therapy greatly shaped my understanding and approach to this problem.

Material from the following authors and books aided in the preparation of certain sections of this manuscript and is gratefully acknowledged:

Edwin C. Bliss' Getting Things Done (Futura, 1976) and Doing It Now! (Futura, 1983) for his discussion of some of the techniques I have included in Chapter 4 on "Procrastination Bypass Techniques".

Michael Le Boeuf's How to Motivate People (Putnam, 1985) for ideas on rewards in the workplace.

William J. DiRisis and George Butz's Writing Behavioral Contracts (Research Press, 1975) for their guidelines on how to write contracts.

Bob Montgomery and Lynette Evans' You and Stress (Nelson, 1984) for their insights into life style management.

My own book <u>Taking the Stress Out of Teaching</u> (Collins-Dove, 1990) was useful for providing material used in this book on stress and assertion.

Michael Wilkinson, co-publisher of <u>Procrastinate Later!</u>, for his support in writing this book over the past 12 months.

Morrie Schwartz, co-publisher of <u>Procrastinate Later!</u>, for his enthusiasm for the project and for providing the title of the book before it was even written.

Sally Matheson, editor and publisher of <u>Successful Selling and Managing</u>, who over lunch one day told me to 'do it'.

Jon Pearce, Division of Chemistry and Physics, School of Science and Math Education, University of Melbourne, for his review of my discussion on the <u>Magnetic Theory of Procrastination</u>.

If you want some effective and simple techniques for how to stop procrastinating, you can turn directly to Chapter 4. The material which precedes and follows Chapter 4 is designed to help you gain awareness of why you procrastinate and offers additional skills for overcoming these basic causes.

I am sincerely hopeful that you will find more than one idea in this book which you will find useful in your desire to procrastinate later. When you do, I will be well rewarded for my efforts in writing this book.

Dr. Michael E. Bernard.

1

Why Procrastinate?

"Procrastination...to put off intentionally and habitually and for a reason deemed to be reprehensible such as laziness or indifference to responsibility."

Webster's Third International Dictionary

When was the last time you put off doing something which was important to do and only got around to it in the final minutes before it had to be done - or not at all? Was it filing last year's tax return. How about finishing paperwork, tidying your office, applying for a better or new job? What about things you've been putting off at home like the gardening, painting, paying the bills or doing spring cleaning? What about in your personal relationships? Have you been putting in the time on maintaining your friendships? How about settling a long-standing argument, getting out of a 'bad' relationship or simply meeting new people? And how about in the area of your own self-development? Have you been putting off exercising regularly, giving up smoking or drinking to excess, taking up a new or old hobby, further education or simply setting time for yourself to relax?

I want to emphasize right from the start that everyone procrastinates. It doesn't matter if you are the chief executive officer of a giant international corporation, publisher of a major book company, bus driver, hair dresser, real estate agent, student, housewife or househusband. It doesn't matter if you are rich or poor, young or old, white, black or any other colour. People from all backgrounds, experiences and ages procrastinate.

Some people find it hard to admit to themselves they are procrastinating. Instead, they make up what are called 'rationalisations' which are reasons that are superficially acceptable to explain why they are putting off doing something important. We'll examine common rationalisations in Chapter 2.

Sometimes we fail to recognise our procrastination because we've never thought of a particular type of avoidance behaviour as an instance of procrastination. Failing to give up smoking or to exercise regularly can be examples of procrastination if you have decided to give up the bad habit but still smoke and exercise only occasionally. Not asserting yourself with an intrusive family relative or an aggressive boss can also be considered procrastination.

If you look at yourself from all angles you will probably find that there are things you should be doing for some good reason but are simply not. In fact, one of the keys to overcoming procrastination - breaking bad habits - is to honestly admit that you are procrastinating and not get too cut up about it. I have found that simply knowing that procrastination is universal can make it easier for you to accept areas in your life where you are procrastinating, look into the reasons for your procrastination, and do something about them.

Now the reason that everyone procrastinates - whether they admit it or not - is that it is part of human nature. Human beings are not genetically programmed for perfection. And no matter how hard we try to be effective in our lives by accomplishing what we've set out to do, we will sometimes fall short. We will not get everything done. I don't mean to sound pessimistic; merely realistic. I wouldn't have written this book if I thought that we were doomed to be slaves to our biolgical make-up and, therefore, forever mired in procrastination. On the contrary, because of our unique capacity for reflection and self-analysis, we can overcome the causes of our procrastination and do what we set out to do.

What Exactly is Procrastination?

One can do it when one will, and, therefore, one seldom does it at all.

Earl of Chesterfield

Procrastination involves you deciding that it is in your best interest to do something and you delay doing it even though you can see the disadvantages in the delay.

Using this definition, procrastination seems a crazy thing to do. Bizarre! You decide that it would be a good thing for you to do something and yet you can't seem to motivate yourself to do it. No one is standing over you with a whip threatening you that if you do what you have decided to do you will be beaten. As I will discuss, you are the one who is ultimately determining whether you perform the tasks which will get you what you want.

Procrastination is a bad habit

When you procrastinate, you prevent yourself from getting what you want. An example? You've decided to spend more time with the kids but because of other committments, you never quite get around to it. And who loses out? Not only them, but you. In this situation, you have gotten into the bad habit of over-committing yourself to other activities which makes it literally impossible for you to achieve what you've set out to do with the kids. Fortunately, as with most bad habits, you can break your habit by, in this example, learning new habits of priority setting across the different areas of your life (work, home, self-development).

Now as you know, breaking bad habits is not easy. If it was, this book and others like it would not need to be written. Over the years, psychologists and other professionals interested in the area of human learning and motivation have developed proven techniques for overcoming different bad habits. And the technique which will work for you will depend partly on the causes of your procrastination and partly on the type of person you are. You will find certain habit-breaking techniques useful while others you will find frustrating and a turn-off. The trick is to find what works best for you.

Not all procrastination is bad

Sometimes, it is wise not to do something. For example, you may have a certain amount of money to invest and may be delaying the decision about which way to go. Should you put all your eggs in one basket? Should you safely invest in a plan offered by your bank at lower interest, put your money in a blue chip stock or take a 'safe' risk by going with a plan promising higher gains (and possible losses) on your investment. Rather than impulsively rushing to make a decision, it would be wise to, in a sense, procrastinate until you've received advice from different 'experts'; until you have all the facts.

Sometimes it can be wise to procrastinate as a way of resolving interpersonal hassles. For example, you may, after being dealt with harshly by one of your work colleagues, choose to do nothing rather than be confronting. By not pouring fuel on the fire, you may diffuse the situation. Now I'm not saying avoiding conflict is generally the best policy. If the problem is recurrent and disruptive, procrastination will not help resolve the issue. However, experience does show that, in some cases, the passage of time is a wonderful healer.

A Magnetic Theory of Procrastination

I have developed what I call a 'magnetic' theory of procrastination because it seems to me that when you procrastinate at doing some task, as you think about or actually start to make motions of doing it, you find yourself almost being pulled away from doing what you've set out to do. It is almost as if some unseen magnetic force is both repelling you away from what you've decided to do and drawing you towards other activities. A simple example can be procrastinating at writing a letter to a relative you haven't seen for a while. As you think about getting started, you seem to get pulled away from the task by what almost seems to be a strong magnetic force over which you have little control.

To understand this theory let me refresh your memory about the properties of magnets. Very briefly, most magnets that you are accustomed to seeing have both a north and south pole. Surrounding each pole is a magnetic field. Of particular interest is that a magnetic field surrounding a north pole in one magnet is attracted to the magnetic field which surrounds a south pole of another magnet. Of equal importance is knowing that if you bring two magnets together so that either the south pole of one is oriented towards the south pole of the other or the north poles of each magnet are brought together, the magnets will repulse one another.

Simply put, the magnetic theory of procrastination says that there are many opposing forces which stand between you and what it is you have set out to do. These opposing force fields act to repel you away from your chosen task. This effect is similar to the way in which magnetic force fields can repel one another. The number and strength of opposing forces explain why you are procrastinating. In order to overcome your procrastination, you will need to understand what these forces are and take steps to reduce their repelling power.

In real life, there are a variety of different forces which can come between your decision to do something which will help you achieve what you want and you acting on that decision. Many of these somewhat mysterious forces turn out to be things in yourself such as anxiety about doing the task, low tolerance for the discomfort of having to do the task, your level of hostility in having to do the task, your ability to organise your time so that you can fit in what's possible and your level of stress and fatigue. Other forces have to do with things outside you such as how disorganised your world is including your work area. These are some but not all of the real reasons why you procrastinate and will be discussed in detail in Chapter 3.

Let me describe how this theory applies to you. Suppose you are a flat, round, metal magnet with your north pole on top and your south pole on the bottom. You are attracted to the idea of doing something which can also be represented as a magnet except that its south pole is on top and its north pole is on the bottom. As your magnetic force field (north) approaches the other magnet's force field (south), the magnets will gather increasing momentum until you and the task you've set out to do connect together.

Procrastination begins with you represented by a magnet being attracted to some task represented by another magnet. However, in procrastination, as you move closer to the task you wish to accomplish, additional magnetic fields come between you and what you want to achieve. As the magnetic field surrounding your north pole come in contact with the force fields surrounding the north pole of these other magnets, your magnetic field becomes repelled by these other magnetic fields away from the task you want to accomplish. The more you try to get closer, the more you are repelled by these other fields which stand between you and your destination.

You can see this relationship depicted in the following illustration. 'You' are represented by a magnet at the bottom of the drawing. At the top of the drawing is another magnet which represents the task you want to accomplish. 'You' as a magnet have a magnetic field surrounding your north pole which will be attracted to the force field which surrounds the south pole of the task you've set out to do. Between your magnet and the other magnet are a host of magnets which can repel you away from the task and attract you to other less important activities. There are 10 magnets which represent the 10 'real' causes of your procrastination. The question marks beside each of the magnets indicate that the identity of the real reasons you procrastinate is sometimes obscure. In Chapter 3, I will label and describe the 10 'real' reasons you procrastinate.

The Magnetic Theory of Procrastination

**TASK YOU WANT
TO ACCOMPLISH**

YOU

Sometimes you can spend your whole life attempting to do something positive for yourself only to be continually repelled by these magnetic fields which you have a hard time seeing, do not understand, are seemingly beyond your control and which prevent you from getting you where you want to go. Sometimes, you reach a point where you can give up trying because the forces of resistance appear too strong and overwhelming.

The good news is that, just as in physics you can de-magnetize the strength of force fields surrounding magnets, so too can you in real life take control of those factors which are causing your procrastination. In physics, through a process known as 'heating', you can reduce the repulsive strength of magnetic fields. This book presents a vast array of psychological 'heating' techniques designed to neutralize those factors responsible for your procrastination. Further illustrations of the magnetic theory of procrastination will be presented in Chapter 3.

How Big a Procrastinator Are You?

I think it is very difficult to judge relative to other people the extent to which you procrastinate. This is partly because you do not normally keep a running log on the numbers of tasks and activities you are putting off. In addition, you normally are not all that vitally absorbed in the life of someone else to keep tabs on their procrastination. There is another factor which can distort the extent to which you procrastinate; namely, your attitude towards your procrastination. If you are someone who believes you should never procrastinate and that it is terrible to put off doing important things, it is likely that you may exaggerate the extent to which you procrastinate. I find a number of people who attend workshops I conduct on procrastination relieved to find out by the end of the workshop that compared to others, they really didn't procrastinate all that often.

I have developed the following Procrastination Task Checklists with two purposes in mind. First, they offer you an opportunity to examine how often you procrastinate at doing things across different areas of your life. (Given our human tendency to dislike admitting we procrastinate, these checklists will be more challenging for you than they would at first seem). Second, the Procrastination Task Checklists will give you an opportunity to compare how often you procrastinate at certain tasks with people in general. I have given these checklists to hundreds of members of the general public. You will be able to compare yourself with the 'average' person to see exactly how extreme your procrastinating habits really are.

Procrastination Task Checklists

Directions: The following questionnaires are designed to examine the typical ways people procrastinate. By procrastinate, I mean putting off doing things you know you should be doing even though you see the disadvantages in delaying. That is, even though you know you should be doing the task or contacting a person, you delay doing it until a later time when the deadline approaches and you rush to get it done; or maybe it does not get done at all.

All people put off doing things they know they should be doing even though they see the disadvantages in delaying. Please indicate how often you put off doing things you think you should be doing.

Circle 1 if you almost never put it off

Circle 2 if you sometimes put it off

Circle 3 if you often put it off

Circle 4 if you almost always put it off

Circle NA if the questions does not apply to you

Work Tasks and Work Relationships

Directions: Indicate how often you put off doing the following activities.

	Almost Never	Some-times	Often	Almost Always	Not Apply
1. Returning an important phone call at work.	1	2	3	4	NA
2. Tidying your office/desk.	1	2	3	4	NA
3. Applying for a promotion or better job.	1	2	3	4	NA
4. Career advancement activities (taking a course at your own expense; in-service course; attending conference).	1	2	3	4	NA
5. Long-term planning for you or your company.	1	2	3	4	NA
6. Paper work, filing and/or updating reports.	1	2	3	4	NA
7. Returning an unimportant phone call at work.	1	2	3	4	NA
8. Public speaking.	1	2	3	4	NA
9. Asserting yourself with a negative or difficult co-worker or superior.	1	2	3	4	NA
10. Work which you take home to do.	1	2	3	4	NA

Home Tasks and Family/Personal Relationships

Directions: Indicate how often you put off doing the following activities.

	Almost Never	Some-Times	Often	Almost Always	Not Apply
1. Writing or calling a relative.	1	2	3	(4)	NA
2. Organising/attending family gatherings.	1	2	(3)	4	NA
3. Identifying quality time for your significant other(s).	1	(2)	3	4	NA
4. Resolving conflict/ disagreement with relative or friend.	1	2	(3)	4	NA
5. Asserting yourself in your significant relationships.	1	2	(3)	4	NA
6. Writing or calling friend.	1	2	3	(4)	NA
7. Home maintenance tasks (washing windows, repairs, painting, cleaning garage).	1	(2)	3	4	NA
8. Book-keeping/paper work (paying bills, filling out warranties, doing tax).	1	(2)	3	4	NA
9. Daily chores (tidying, ironing, cooking, cleaning).	(1)	2	3	4	NA
10. Setting up and sticking to home rules (delegation of responsibilities; curfew during week; amount of TV watched; who does shopping/cleaning).	(1)	2	3	4	NA

Self-Development

Directions: Indicate how often you put off doing the following activities.

	Almost Never	Some-Times	Often	Almost Always	Not Apply
1. Spending time on hobbies.	(1)	2	3	4	NA
2. Attending/participating in recreational activities (cultural, art, sporting).	1	2	(3)	4	NA
3. Further education.	1	2	3	(4)	NA
4. Taking a class which interests you.	1	2	3	(4)	NA
5 Exercising	(1)	2	3	4	NA
6. Dieting/improving your nutrition.	1	(2)	3	4	NA
7. Giving up/modifying smoking or drinking.	(1)	2	3	4	NA
8. Health maintenance activities (visit dentist, doctor, counselor, nutritionist).	1	(2)	3	4	NA
9. Finding time for yourself.	(1)	2	3	4	NA
10. Meeting new people.	1	2	3	(4)	NA

In looking over your answers to these three Procrastination Task Checklists, you might wish to consider whether you tend to procrastinate more often at tasks associated with your work, home or self-development. You may also want to look and see if there is any type of activity you tend to put off across the different areas such as 'boring' or 'anxiety provoking' tasks.

The 'average' score for members of the general population for each item on the above Procrastination Task Checklists is between 2 and 3. A 'rule of thumb' for knowing the extent of your procrastination is as follows. If you have circled a '3' indicating that you "often" procrastinate on three or more 'Work Tasks' and 'Work Relationships', you are an above average procrastinator in the work area of your life. As well, if you "often" put off doing three or more of the tasks listed in the Home Task and Family/Personal Relationships, you tend to be an above average procrastinator in this area. In terms of Self-Development, if you put off more than five tasks, you can consider yourself an above average procrastinator when it comes to activities surrounding your home and personal relationships.

You might be interested in knowing the 10 most frequently reported areas of procrastination. In order from most often put off, the list is as follows:

- home maintenance tasks
- dieting
- exercising
- writing to a relative
- further education
- applying for promotion
- long-term planning
- paper work and filing
- meeting new people
- writing/calling a friend

In case you are or have been a student and are interested in examining areas of your procrastination, here is the Procrastination Task Checklist for Study Tasks.

Study Tasks

Directions: Indicate how often you put off doing the following activities.

	Almost Never	Some-Times	Often	Almost Always	Not Apply
1. Attending class.	1	2	3	4	NA
2. Taking notes in class.	1	2	3	4	NA
3. Reviewing and revising notes.	1	2	3	4	NA
4. Getting started and/or finishing work you find boring.	1	2	3	4	NA
5. Doing 'extra' reading.	1	2	3	4	NA
6. Studying for exams.	1	2	3	4	NA
7. Getting started and/or finishing work you find hard.	1	2	3	4	NA
8. Asking instructor/tutor questions in class.	1	2	3	4	NA
9. Asking for extra help.	1	2	3	4	NA
10. Taking an exciting class or course because you know it will be hard and you might not get a top grade.	1	2	3	4	NA

On average, students report they "often" put off three of the above tasks. If you find that you put off five or more of the above study tasks, you can consider yourself an above average procrastinator when it comes to studying.

Membership in the 'Born Procrastinators' Club

I know quite a few people who believe they are 'born procrastinators'. They think this largely because they find it so easy to put off doing things which they want to do. However, it is also interesting to note that those people who readily admit to being 'born procrastinators' are frequently also likely to have extremely high self-expectations believing, as I've already mentioned, that they should always do what they've set out to do. It doesn't take too many instances of procrastination on their part for them to come up with the conclusion that they are 'born procrastinators'. 'Born procrastinators' are likely to blame themselves for their procrastinating behaviour rather than events beyond their control. I am frequently asked if there is such an animal as a 'born procrastinator'. This seemly simple question unfortunately involves a rather long series of explanations to answer it in full. It is the case that certain people have a personality make-up which makes it much more likely for them to procrastinate. In a moment, I'll refer to those personality characteristics which predispose people to putting off doing things they've set out to do. The issue, however, is whether people are actually born with personality characteristics which express themselves throughout their lives and, specifically, determine how efficient they are in doing things which they might not feel like doing.

You most likely have heard about the "nature-nurture" controversy which still today generates heated debate at professional conferences and after-conference cocktail parties. That is, are people the way they are because of their genetic make-up inherited from their near and far family members or do people turn out as a result of the ways their parents nurtured them? My belief is that your personality today is both a product of the basic biological-genetic structure you were born with and the teaching-loving of your parents.

I am particularly impressed with the results of different researchers who study early childhood temperament who have been able to discover a number of different dimensions of child temperament in children as young as six weeks old. For example, Chess and Thomas, researchers at Columbia University in New York have described a "difficult child temperament" which they apply to children who have high intensity reactions to negative events and who readily withdraw from any new situations. They also describe children who are easily distractible with short-attention spans who may experience pronounced negative moods. It seems to me that early childhood temperament which is largely governed by your genetic make-up gives rise to people's adult personality make-up and, in particular, those factors I discuss in Chapter 3 which are the real causes of procrastination.

I also have the opinion that one's personality - including those negative aspects responsible for procrastination - is shaped by the lessons provided by parents. For example, children born with 'difficult temperaments' are more likely to develop personality characteristics which can lead to widespread procrastination unless their parents set and enforce rules at home, are vigilant in monitoring their child's behaviour and expend a great deal of energy in helping their child develop self-discipline. That is, you are more likely to procrastinate if you have difficulty delaying gratification and tolerating the short-term frustration of not getting what you want or having to do what you don't want to do.

My own observations as well as research suggests that if your parents failed to expect, teach and reward you for both putting up with frustration associated with doing things you didn't feel like doing as well as for waiting to get what you want, you as an adult are more likely to put off doing tasks you find initially frustrating and more likely to be distracted by immediate pleasures. And if you were one of those children described as having a difficult temperament to begin with, the failure of your parents to teach you self-discipline skills will have increased your natural tendency to procrastinate. (The lack of success some parents have in teaching their children these skills frequently can have more to do with the difficult child's resistance and oppositional behaviour than it has to do with parental ignorance or negligence).

So, what about it, is there such a thing as a 'born procrastinator'? Taking the above into account I would say yes, by which I mean that as a result of temperament and parenting style some adults are more likely to possess certain attitudes and lack certain mental skills which will normally lead to a greater than average amount of procrastination.

How do you know if you are a 'born procrastinator'; meaning that you find it harder to do the things you've set out to do than other people because of the way you were born in combination with your parent's efforts? A simple way to start is to look back at the results of your Procrastination Checklist. Do you procrastinate more or less often than people in general? If you procrastinate less often, you are less likely to be a 'born procrastinator'. After all, to be eligible for the Born Procrastinators Club, you have to procrastinate more often than the average person. Also, you have to procrastinate at the more important things in life in comparison with others. So check and see if you are more likely to put off important activities such as returning important phone calls, asserting yourself, identifying quality time with your significant other, or exercising, or whether your procrastination centres on less important tasks such as returning unimportant phone calls, home maintenance tasks or taking a class which interests you.

The Procrastinating Personality: What We Now Know!

Your personality consists of a set of habits that characterise the way you manage your day-to-day living and which, under normal circumstances, is fairly stable and predictable. As you can imagine, different personality theorists have defined personality in different and overlapping ways (e.g., neuroticism, introversion-extraversion, self-esteem, ego strength). What follows now is a listing and brief description of personality characteristics which research has shown to be related to procrastination. You may want to ask yourself which of the labels and descriptions seem to apply to you. While this sort of self-appraisal will probably do little to help you to stop procrastinating, it may help you gain greater insight into yourself - not a bad place to begin the process of change. You may find one or more of these characteristics being applicable to you.

1. **Neuroticism/High Anxiety.** Neuroticism means that you have a tendency to emotionally react very quickly, intensely and for a long period when you are confronted with unpleasant events or stressful situations. And one of the most common of the negative emotional reactions is high anxiety. So, for example, highly anxious-prone people can perceive public speaking as so unpleasant and threatening that they avoid it altogether.

2. **Depression/Low Self-Esteem.** Some people have a tendency towards feelings of depression and low self-esteem. They hold themselves in poor regard. As a consequence, they do not believe they are really deserving of anything good in life and, therefore, they put off trying or give up very easily.

3. **Rebelliousness.** A connection has been found between people who resent authority and authority figures and their defiance in resisting what they have been asked or are required to do. Commonly observed in adolescents, the rebellious individual will avoid beginning tasks or showing up to school or work in spite of the fact that they can recognise that, in terms of what others see as important for their own welfare and future, their procrastination is doing themselves in.

4. **Pessimistic/External.** Some people who chronically procrastinate approach life with pessimism and a sense of helplessness. Their general attitude sounds somethings like: What's the point in really trying, there is nothing I can do to really change my life. If I succeed at accomplishing something I've set out to do, it is due to luck. Good things which happen to me are externally caused. I am a victim of circumstances.

This personality outlook not only frequently leads to depression, but also to ingrained tendencies to procrastinate at important activities.

5. **Irrational Beliefs.** People who take their desires for achievement and social approval to the extreme and believe they **must** always be successful and **need** approval are likely to experience high anxiety and low self-esteem surrounding their achievement and relationships. In a similar way, people who **demand** that others treat them fairly and considerately rather than rationally preferring consideration are likely to be hostile and rebellious. And people who **demand** that their life be exciting and easy and that they **need** comfort find they are less likely to put up with the frustration of hard work. Irrational beliefs activate high anxiety, low self-esteem, rebelliousness and low frustration tolerance, all personality characteristics leading to procrastination.

6. **Lack of Achievement Motivation.** Achievement motivation consists of three seperate dimensions. First, the need for acquiring knowledge and solving academic problems as ends in themselves. Second, using achievement as a source of ego-enhancement. Here the person's feelings of adequacy derive from his or her achievement and competence level. Third, achievement serves the purpose of bringing the person approval from important individuals or groups. By meeting other peoples' expectations for achievement, the person satisfies a need for affiliation. As is clear from this description, a lack of achievement motivation is clearly linked with the tendency to fail to initiate or complete tasks which require sustained learning or problem solving.

7. **Poor Self-Control/Impulsiveness.** Over the years, people learn mental habits which allow them to control their normal instincts and impulses. Unfortunately, some people fail to learn sufficient self-control to enable them to put in the effort on

tasks which they find frustrating, especially when it is
a sunny day and they'd rather be sailing.

8.   **Disorganisation.** Some people are by nature
disorganised. You may know this about yourself by
the number of times you are late for appointments,
forget to have on hand important resources and waste
time. Disorganisation along with anxiety is one of the
personality characteristics most likely to result in
procrastination.

If you are someone who regularly procrastinates, you may
find one or more of the above descriptions of personality
as applying pretty well to you. You'll know then that there
are good reasons why you are procrastinating! There are
habits you've inherited or acquired which make it harder to
get all the things done you've set out to do. This information
about yourself can help you challenge the idea that "I
shouldn't procrastinate". Granted that procrastination is
not so good and that you would prefer it if you got on with
things more immediately, it obviously doesn't make sense -
nor help you - to demand that you must not procrastinate.
This attitude will only increase your emotional turmoil and
make it harder to do what you've set out to do.

Now this book is not really about changing your personality.
Let's agree that this is a significant challenge not readily
accomplished. And, from the experience gained of working
with many people, I think the number of people who can
show dramatic changes in their personality are not that
large. However, the good news is that everyone - regardless
of personality characteristics - can learn to stop procrastinating. No exceptions. Here's the series of steps you will
follow in this book for learning to procrastinate later:

1.   Clearly describe for yourself what task or activity you
have been putting off and which you would like to
start to do.

2.   Clearly describe to yourself what you actually do
when you are putting off doing something (see
Chapter 2).

3.   Clearly describe to yourself any rationalisations you usually make up and fantasies you experience, which divert you from what you want to do (see Chapter 2).

4.   Clearly describe to yourself the 'real reasons' you are procrastinating (see Chapter 3).

5.   Select and put into practice one or more of the 'procrastination bypass' techniques to get moving (see Chapter 4).

6.   Work on, one at a time, the 'real reasons' you are putting off a particular task or activity (see Chapters 5 - 9).

Larry Lawrence looked into the mirror as he combed his hair. Larry, aged 42, was the head of a medium-sized and reasonably successful electronics firm. He sat down to tie his tennis shoes and wondered why he wasn't his normal cheery self. It was a perfect Saturday afternoon for tennis. Lovely blue sky, warm with almost no wind. Larry noticed he was a bit tight in his shoulder muscles and was feeling a bit unsettled in his stomach.

"Hey Larry," boomed Bill Cooper, "Whaddya say we have a bit of a wager on the match? You and Helen killed us last week, but that's because I was a bit over-done from the night before. What about it?"

Larry looked at his friend Bill who he'd known for 15 years now. Old Billy Boy was a bit of a sight. He'd put on about 20 pounds over the past few years and was starting to really show it around the sides.

"Not today, let's just have a hit."

"Hey, what's wrong with you, Larry? You look like I felt last week. Did you play up last night? Not with Helen I hope."

"No way. In bed at 10pm. I wouldn't lay a hand on your favourite graduate student no matter how gorgeous she is. Helen's safe - at least until after her exams are over. No, maybe it's something I ate."

"You're not still uptight about work are you?" persisted Bill. "Haven't you done anything about hiring someone to help you manage the overseas sales like you said you were going to; you know, so you'd have more time to do planning?"

"No, not yet. I'm still trying to get a bit more business in so that whoever I hire will have some business to handle. Otherwise, he'll be bored."

"Larry, it's not my business, but didn't you say last week that you can't get more business in until you have decided which way you want to go and that to do this you need some more time and someone who can take the pressure off you?"

"Yeah, I know. Anyway, what about this diet and exercise program you were supposed to be going on?"

"Hey, I'm on it. Started yesterday. It's working great. All I've had today are apples - as many as I could eat. I think somethings already happening."

"I hope it doesn't happen out there! Alright, five bucks a set. Bonus five if either takes all sets. I'm sure the 'apples' will give us the edge."

Actions Speak Louder Than Words

In the space provided, write down the specific activities, tasks and things you've been putting off that you would like to start doing. Refer to your Procrastination Checklist. Add anything else that occurs to you.

Work Tasks and Work Relationships

_____

_____

_____

_____

_____

_____

_____

Home Tasks and Family/Personal Relationships

_____

_____

_____

_____

_____

_____

_____

Self-Development

_____

_____

_____

_____

_____

_____

Study

_____

_____

_____

_____

_____

_____

_____

2

Addictions, Fantasies and Lies

The greatest victory is victory over self; to be conquered by self is of all things the most shameful and vile.

                                        Publius Syrus, Roman Poet

Procrastination begins with you deciding to do something and then, contrary to your decision, you end up not following through on your decision. Let's be crystal clear on how this looks.

Suppose you make a decision to become closer to one of your parents (or kids.) Perhaps you've had a history of fighting and unpleasantness where you have withdrawn from much contact. And let's suppose you have decided that you want to spend more time with your parent and, indeed, become more affectionate. It is now several months after you have made the decision to do things with your parent to become closer and you still have not done anything, even though opportunities were available for you to make closer contact.

Let's analyse what might lead to your procrastination. As you think about calling your parent up (or even giving them a hug), you start to experience unpleasantness and discomfort. It might be tension in your head, queasiness in your stomach, tightening of different muscles, shortness of breath or any number of different negative sensations particular to you. In other words you don't feel like contacting your parent. You've decided you want to do it, but you don't feel like doing it. And rather than contact your parent, you put off doing it until a later time.

At first, you think to yourself "I'll do it later when I feel more relaxed and confident." And when later comes, you think "I really need to finish a couple of important tasks at home and then I'll do it." As time passes on you begin to feel guilty about not having done anything. To escape your guilty conscience, you decide to buy the latest novel by your favourite writer and spend all your available time enjoying the book. And the more you put it off, the harder it gets, until you reach a certain point when you decide that because you haven't contacted your parent, either you didn't really want to do it because if you did you would have done it or it simply was not fated that you and your parent were meant to get closer. Sound familiar?

Even if you cannot relate to the particular example, you may notice some similarities in what you do when you avoid something you set out to do. Indeed, the above scenario illustrates a number of the basic principles of procrastination.

Principle 1. Most people have a tendency to put off doing things which they find unpleasant or frustrating.

Principle 2. Rather than doing things they don't feel like doing, people engage is some other activity which is less stress creating or more enjoyable. They may also engage in some form of fantasy which helps them escape from having to do something they don't feel like doing and which makes them feel good.

Principle 3. Most people dislike admitting to themselves that they are procrastinating. Most people feel ashamed or guilty. They make up rationalisations (excuses, justifications, explanations) which help them deny they are needlessly procrastinating.

Let's see how these principles apply in another example. Suppose you have decided to do a major re-organisation of your office and, in particular, file things away where you can find them. You decide this because, as of late, you've been slowed down by not being able to find important papers.

It is now three weeks since you've made the decision and your desk and files are still disorganised; that is, you've been procrastinating. You've been doing lots of other things such as writing an overdue report as well as spending more time at the gym over lunch getting fit, promising yourself you'll get to 'tidying' just as soon you take care of other current work. When questioned about not having followed through on your decision to get organised, you defensively point to the report you've written and how much fitter you feel. As you delay further and start to feel guilty, you spend more time reading the entertainment and society section of the paper, rather than tidying your desk.

Principle 1 says that the reason you are procrastinating at getting your office organised is that you find the task frustrating and unpleasant.

Principle 2 says that you will find some activity to divert yourself from getting organised and that the activity is one which reduces stress and makes you feel good. In this case you have chosen to do other work and to exercise. This principle also suggests that your reading of the society and entertainment pages is a type of escapist fantasy, once again, serving to divert you away from what you've set out to do and which, possibly, increases your enjoyment.

Principle 3 says that you do not like to admit that you are procrastinating and that your belief that "I am doing more important things" and "I'll do it as soon as I've done these other important things" is really a rationalisation which helps you cover up the fact that you are procrastinating.

As I'll mention in some detail in the next chapter, there are other important reasons why you may be procrastinating besides simply avoiding tasks you don't feel like doing. However, it is vital for your understanding of your procrastination to examine how these basic principles of procrastination explain some of the reasons you are putting off doing things. The most important principle is Principle 1. To procrastinate later, you have to learn to recognise the discomfort and frustration associated with tasks you put off and learn to either tolerate or reduce discomfort and frustration. (I will discuss how to do this in the following chapters.)

In this chapter, you'll have a chance to examine the most common addictions, fantasies and lies (rationalisations) which people employ to divert them from following through on important tasks and which block them from discovering the real reasons they procrastinate. You'll also have an opportunity to discover why people hate to admit they procrastinate and why they almost instictively cover up their procrastination with rationalisations. By admitting rather than denying your procrastination, you will be in a far better position to do something about it.

Addictions

Action diversions or 'addictivities' are frequently substituted for what must be done .... A person feels anxious about writing a report and finds chainsmoking, overeating, sleeping, playing solitaire, doing pushups - almost anything but doing the report- temporarily more rewarding. These activities are habitual responses to stress .... The concrete problem - writing the report - is artfully dodged for the moment through absorption into the addictivity.

William Knaus, Do It Now, 1979

One of the characteristics of habits is that you perform them without too much thought; they seem to happen almost automatically. This is especially true of procrastination. You don't generally go around thinking to yourself: "Hell, I've set out to do something, but, you know, I don't really feel like doing it. Rather than doing what I don't feel like doing, I'll make up an excuse that will allow me to do it later. Or maybe, I'll just have a few minutes of delightful fantasy before I start." Most of the time, before you have thought very much about it, you find yourself doing something else rather than what you initially set out to do.

One of the ways to become more aware of the automatic processes which seem to drive your procrastination is to discover what it is you typically do while you are putting off a particular task or activity. I call these diversionary activities 'addictions' to emphasise that they seem to you to happen automatically, you seem to be unable to resist doing them, and they help you to feel better about what it is you are putting off doing. Let's have a look at some of the most common 'addictions'. (Remember, these are things you seemingly choose to do when you are procrastinating.)

Lower priority activity addictions

When you put off doing something, you frequently select some other lower priority activity to do instead. You may convince yourself that the lower priority activity is actually more important than the important task you've been putting off (which it normally isn't). At work, if you have to get started on an important report or paper which is not due for awhile, you may instead elect to spend time organising your files, making unimportant phone calls or simply getting a coffee and visiting with a colleague you haven't spent much time with over recent times. At home, rather than discussing with your mate an issue of concern to you, you wash the floor. Or rather than fix the side gate or patch up a whole in the wall you made sixteen months ago while trying to hang a new print, you decide that you need to spend more time with the kids.

Health-related addictions

It is very easy for you to justify putting off doing something important if you instead elect to do some health-related activity. "Rather than getting started with the last six weeks of ironing, I'll just go for a brisk jog (or walk). It will do me the world of good. Then I'll feel more in the mood to iron"; "I think I'm ready to break my sit-up record; I'll go for 1,001". While doing something healthy for yourself is not something to put off, make sure that your frequent trips to the gym are not motivated out of you avoiding something which you do not really want to do such as resolving personal problems, finishing the house renovations or meeting new people.

Relaxation addictions

Some people use a variety of relaxation activities while they are procrastinating. You may be someone who is into yoga, meditation or other forms of physical and mental relaxation. You may also rely on soothing music or a good book to deliver you away from important tasks.

Recreation addictions

It is quite common to get hooked on certain recreational pursuits not only because of the intrinsic enjoyment they bring, but also because they represent for you a way out of doing things you really don't want to do but have to do.

You may be someone who is a golf-addict, skiing addict, gin rummy addict or a yachting-addict. Whatever your recreational addiction is, ask yourself whether you use the addiction as a convenient way out of doing things which you find unpleasant. Also, ask yourself whether your recreational addiction is something to control. Is it something you have to do and find yourself spending countless hours involved to the detriment of other important aspects of your life? Does your need for short-term pleasure drive you towards recreational activities and, therefore, away from other less exciting, time consuming yet important tasks?

Eating, drinking or smoking addictions

If you over-eat, repeatedly drink to excess, or are a chain smoker, you may well find that these addictions are behaviours which you compulsively engage in rather than doing other less desirable tasks. All of these addictions can not only divert you away from unpleasant tasks or encounters with people, they also serve to increase your pleasure. This latter quality is one of the reasons they are so hard to give up.

Socializing addictions

You may be a person who is hooked on people contact and use the enjoyment you get from socializing as a way of prolonging whatever it is you're procrastinating at. Highly anxious extraverts, in particular, can find themselves compulsively talking on the phone, organising dinner parties etc., rather than facing up to completing important tasks.

Spending money addictions

Rather than smoking, drinking, eating, exercising, recreating or socializing, you may find that the best way you know to dodge the discomfort involved in doing certain things is to spend money. And boy is it effective! Rather than write a long over-due report or letter, do the tax, clean the car, plan getting back to work or a career change, you use the excitement of a bargain or looking for a special 'used' car as a diversionary activity.

You may be less than enamoured with the idea that some of your favourite past-times serve more insidious motives than pure pleasure-seeking and, in fact, are addictions which you have little control over and which help perpetuate procrastination. Unfortunately, it is these addictions that not only make it hard to overcome procrastinatrion, they also prevent you from being aware of the real reasons you are procrastinating. For example, by spending all your available free time in your work room/study pursuing a hobby or interest, you may be dodging other tasks at home which have to be done or dodging sustained contact with one or more people. Now your hobby addiction covers up the real reasons for you not doing tasks at home (hostility with someone else, low discomfort tolerance) or for avoiding people contact (hostility or anxiety).

Fantasies

Phantasy life gives the illusion that wishes and aspirations have been fulfilled; it thinks obstacles away; it transforms impossibilities into possibilities and realities...It is a search for pleasurable sensations and an avoidance of everything likely to cause pain.

Varendonck, The Psychology of Daydreams, 1921

The fantasies of daydreams are often very pleasurable and fun. Unencumbered by the realities of your life, the fantasies you create often provide you with a wonderful outlet for doing and being what you want. And what is so fantastic about fantasies is that there are no limitations. You can soar to whatever heights of experience you so choose - without having to resort to drugs! Indeed, your life would be very much impoverished if your ability to fantasise was taken away from you.

However, there is a 'down side' to fantasies. And the downside involves too much of a good thing. When you employ fantasy as an escape from making or following through on decisions which can help make your life better, then fantasy becomes destructive. When you resort to fantasy as a way of diverting yourself away from approaching certain tasks, situations and people, fantasising becomes escapism and makes it much easier for you to procrastinate.

'Escapist fantasy' is a primary means by which you can reduce the discomfort and frustration you may feel in connection with a task you have set out to do. At this time, the fantasy diverts you from having to carry out some action. While you are fantasising, the discomfort you were anticipating becomes dissipated and replaced by the more pleasurable sensation invoked by your particular fantasy. As well, escapist fantasy can help alleviate the guilt you may experience while you procrastinate. Rather than thinking about what you haven't done and getting somewhat upset with yourself, you may well occupy yourself with images of you either having completed what you're putting off doing or enjoying yourself in some other way.

I recently worked with a graphic designer who put off getting started on some of her projects. She knew that to meet her committments, she had to start her drawings several days before they were due. Knowing and doing were, unfortunately, two different things. Of interest here was the amount of time this procrastinator spent daydreaming when she should have been working. She could spend over 30 minutes at her drawing table gazing away in space imagining many different pleasurable scenes from her being awarded a huge contract to do the Hallmark Christmas card designs to her last love-making session with her new boyfriend. By the time she came back from outer space, it was time for a coffee - and so went her day.

You might wonder in the above example why it was she felt the urge to daydream at a time when she really needed to work. Once again this has to do with how she felt while working on a particular project. As I'll discuss in the next chapter, her anxiety about the quality of her work was the main reason for her procrastination and served as the catalyst for her to start to daydream. As well, her ability to tolerate the discomfort she experienced at getting started was too low.

I have found that people vary quite a bit in terms of how often they use fantasy as a procrastinating diversion. If you are someone who has always been a daydreamer, even as a little child, you will be more likely to use escapist fantasy to relieve tension surrounding things you have to do. I have found that creative people - writers, actors, and musicians - seem to be prone to escapist fantasy.

Fantasies

Rather than actually performing the actions necessary for you to achieve a goal, fantasies have you imagining accomplishing what you've set out to do and more. The fantasy takes the place of, or is a substitute for, the real thing.

I recently spent some time working with a young actor who experienced very intense fantasies surrounding particular women to whom he was physically attracted. He seemed especially skilled in bringing his fantasies alive. He reported he could actually smell the perfume they were wearing and spent much time occupying himself with erotic fantasies. While I assured him that there was nothing wrong with his explicit heterosexual fantasies, I did ask him whether he used the fantasies as a way of diverting him from the task of initiating contact. After considering the point, he admitted that he would much prefer to convert some of his fantasy contact into reality contact. We then addressed the issues surrounding his avoidance of women.

Many people like this actor live many parts of their lives through their fantasies. They find it difficult to work towards achieving their goals and prefer the easier and more enjoyable substitute of fantasy.

Spectator fantasies

Another common type of fantasy involves you identifying with the lives of well-known personalities you see in the movies, on television or in the novels you read. Instead of facing up to the drudgery of your life circumstances and trying to achieve for yourself those experiences that you would find pleasurable, you let your life slip by and, instead, gain your pleasures from watching what others do.

Now once again, a certain amount of spectatoring is healthy, enjoyable, normal and, sometimes, helpful. Noticing how other successful people go about achieving their pleasures and happiness can, in some instances, provide a useful model for you in planning how to go about your life. I think autobiographies of well-known people do provide insight and realism about how people with particular talents have made a success (or failure) of their lives. As well, 'junk' movies, books and, yes, 'soapies', can offer welcome relief from the stresses and strains of your life.

When you use 'spectating' fantasies as a substitute for living your own life, you are likely to procrastinate at important things in your life that can bring you decidedly more pleasure and fulfilling experiences. The problem with spectating is that it is a very passive activity. And passivity means that while others you observe are making the conquests you desire, you remain the same. By relying on spectating fantasies, you only maintain the inertia in your life that keeps you in a rut.

Some people even delude themselves into believing they 'need' to have their fantasies. People who escape into music and books rationalise substituting escapism for fronting up to the tasks they have been putting off by thinking: "I am the kind of person who really needs to be surrounded by culture. Once I get my fill, I will be ready to do what needs to be done." Chronic procrastinators use this type of self-deception to avoid doing important tasks.

Rescue fantasies

Waiting around for something good to happen to you is another major cause of procrastination. You know the picture. It is quite common. It occurs in many areas of our lives.

Rescue fantasies can thwart you from achieving your goals in the area of dating and mating. Now the process of finding a partner or mate is often a very difficult one. Not only do you have to make the effort to make yourself presentable, but then you have to journey to places and meet new people where there is a high probability of either non-success or rejection. The rescue fantasy in this scenario can be described as the 'knight in shining armor'. Rather than putting up with the hassles of dating and mating, you convince yourself that not only will someone knock on your door or ring you up, but that this person will be your 'ideal' mate. This type of fantasy can also be seen as a form of rationalisation. After a certain period of time of sitting around and doing little to meet new people, you may start to experience feelings of guilt triggered by the thought "I really should do more than I am. I am a real 'zero' for doing nothing to meet someone." The fantasy of being discovered and spirited away not only temporarily removes the discomfort of loneliness, it also helps replace guilt with feelings of optimism and hope.

A variation of the 'knight in shining armor' fantasy is the 'cavalry to the rescue'. You'll be familiar with the cowboy and indian movies where a wagon train of settlers is being attacked and about to be destroyed. Just as all seems lost, a bugle is heard and the cavalry rides in to save the day. Many procrastinators seem to get caught up in this dream. Faced with having to hand in a report, file a tax return, take an examination or give a talk, the procrastinator wishfully imagines that he or she will be saved somehow from having to complete the important task or project. While sometimes a last-minute rescue does take place, more often than not the bell does toll and the goods have to be produced.

It is important to recognise 'rescue' fantasies for what they are; myths. Don't be deceived by what you see on television or in the movies. Even if you believe in a Grand Maker, he or she does not monitor your life to ensure that you are rescued from your loneliness or from fronting up to doing things you don't want to do. By learning to get on with doing

things you have typically put off until later, you will come to
see that you can rescue yourself.

As I've already suggested, many people do not admit they
are procrastinating needlessly. Some people do. As people
do not like to experience the shame and guilt associated
with putting off doing things, they make up white lies to
themselves so that it appears to them that they are not really
procrastinating. Before going into the reasons for why
people lie to themselves to cover up their procrastination,
let's examine what their excuses and deceptions commonly
sound like. (Many of the rationalisations described below
were first identified by Albert Ellis and William Knaus in
their ground breaking book Overcoming Procrastination.)

Lies

*Rationalisation was introduced into psychoanalysis by Ernest
Jones. It means justification, or making a thing appear
reasonable, when otherwise its irrationality would be evident
.... It is said that a person covers up, justifies, rationalises an
act or an idea that is unreasonable and illogical.*

Psychiatric Dictionary, Sixth Edition, 1989

Rationalisations help make your procrastination appear
justifiable or reasonable to yourself. Without them, you
would have to admit that you procrastinate and bear the
consequences of shame and guilt. However, and this is a
vital point, rationalisations work against your ambition to
get things done. They actually serve to drive you further and
further away from your chosen goal. In this sense,
rationalisations are very self-defeating in that they lead to
self-defeating behaviours. Let's examine the most commonly employed rationalisations and why they they don't hold
water, starting with the most poular one of them all: the
mañana attitude, which in Spanish means tomorrow.

**"I do not have time to do this today. It will be easier for me
to do it tomorrow."**

As I've indicated, people have a tendency to veer away from
doing tasks they find uncomfortable or frustrating - some

people more than others. Rather than doing the task in the present, you re-schedule it to a time in the future. Whether the task is letter writing, sitting down and learning how to use the computer you've just bought for mega-bucks or talking to a significant person in your life about an important issue in your relationship, the *mañana* attitude not only helps you avoid doing a task you find unpleasant, it also helps you rid yourself of any guilt or shame by promising that you'll do it soon. You look optimistically to the future without having to do anything in the present.

The Lie. Unfortunately, the *mañana* attitude doesn't really work. First of all, by putting off doing something, deep down you often experience nagging feelings of self-doubt and anxiety about ever getting the job done. The 'Big Lie' is of course that all too often, because the task is rarely easier to do tomorrow, you do not get around to doing the task at all? An example: Think of all your broken New Years' resolutions.

"I'll do it as soon as other things in my life have cleared up."

This is a variation of the *mañana* attitude and involves you again agreeing to do what you've set out to do at a later time. With this rationalisation, however, your decision to follow through depends on some other circumstance in your life changing.

For example, I recently was working with an attractive female who was putting off going out on dates even though she strongly desired to have an intimate and permanent relationship. Her rationalisation for not bothering to make the effort to show others she was interested and trying to meet new people was "I'll start to date more when I lose some weight." Being somewhat over-weight, it may have been true that her chances of finding the type of man she was after might be lessened. As she was also procrastinating at losing weight, she was creating real problems for herself by tieing her dating behaviour to a future set of circumstances which may never materialise.

Other examples of this rationalisation involve the self-deception around avoiding certain types of work because you don't feel more inspired, creative, relaxed or in the mood or until other things get done. "I can only do this work when my creative juices are flowing" is often a cop out for simply not feeling like doing it and can lead to big problems if you are someone who gets easily frustrated when getting started on a project. It is often only when you get past the frustration of getting into a project that your creativity is set free.

The Lie. As with the *mañana* attitude, this rationalisation gives you temporary relief but doesn't really lead to getting the job done. In fact, this attitude can do more harm than good. If you've put 'on hold' doing something until after things in your life have changed, and if what you need to have changed is not very likely to change, then you might never see the green light to take things off 'on hold'.

Suppose you would like to talk to your mate about not wanting to do so much of the housework and that you would like to work out a new, more sharing, arrangement. Because you get a bit anxious about opening up the topic, you decide that you'll wait until your mate shows some interest in what you've been doing and wants to discuss these issues with you. Your rationalisation "I'll wait until my mate seems receptive" helps you dodge the discomfort of making an assertive request. However, if your mate is not the listening nor observant type, you may, because of your rationalisation, never get what you want.

"Make hay while the sun shines."

This motto can make a lot of sense for the person who has a hard time having fun and who needs encouragement to take advantage of opportunities when they present themselves. However, the motto becomes a rationalisation if you invoke it at times when you are faced with doing something you don't feel like doing.

If you embrace this motto as a basic philosophy, many of your decisions to do certain things involving hard, tedious or sustained effort will be interrupted by your inclination to play and have fun. Rather than making the sacrifices needed to achieve certain long-term goals, you procrastinate and indulge in short-term pleasures because you want to have fun, fun and more fun and are scared that you might miss out. So short-term pleasure seeking can be rationalised by the belief that you deserve fun and can lead to you becoming one of life's real under-achievers. After all, if you're playing and avoiding doing the hard stuff which is almost always necessary in converting your potential into reality, how can you expect to be a success?

The Lie. There are a number of self-deceptions which surround this rationalisation. It is true that you will, by carrying through on a decision which involves you working hard and putting in sustained effort, miss out on a particular opportunity to enjoy yourself. It is, however, very unlikely that future opportunities of a similar kind will not come your way after you've completed what you've set out to do. Moreover, because people will actually look up to you because of making the sacrifice of short-term pleasure for longer-term gain, they will be more likely to invite you to partake of more pleasures than if you compulsively give in to your every impulse.

Another irrational aspect of this motto, when used unquestioningly to justify avoiding certain tasks, is the notion that because past or present circumstances in your life have been so bad, you deserve to have fun all the time. Deservedness implies that the Universe watches over everyone and decides that certain people, because of their circumstances and suffering, deserve fun. If that were so, then why do we have so many poor and unhappy people? What I'm suggesting is that if you have experienced significant pain in your life then that is bad for you and unfair. I guess you have to ask yourself whether always making hay when the sun shines helps you improve your life circumstances not only in the short-term but the long. If it honestly does, terrific. More often than not, it doesn't.

"Since I do my best work under pressure, I'll just postpone this until the pressure builds."

This rationalisation involves you defining the conditions surrounding you finishing a task as necessarily involving a

large amount of pressure. You start off with some task or
project which has to be completed by a certain date. When
you think about settling down to do it you experience an
intense amount of discomfort (why you feel so discomforted
about the task has to do with the 'real reasons' you procrastinate to be covered in the next chapter). Rather than admit
that you are postponing working on the task because once
again you don't feel like doing it, you convince yourself that
your work is far better when you do it at the last minute.

The Lie. Now it is true that a certain amount of anxiety and
pressure seems to fuel the intellectual machinery. Pressure
also seems helpful to overcome the inertia in starting certain boring or time-consuming tasks. However,
procrastinators carry this observation too far. They become
far too dependent on pressure. They become addicted to
larger and larger doses of pressure before they can get off
their behinds and start to work. This becomes a particular
problem when you've got multiple deadlines which coincide
with one another. At these times, the "I work best under
pressure" rationalisations really screws up you and your
results.

While it may seem that tasks are easier to complete when
you place yourself under pressure, in reality the tasks require the similar amount of effort whether you start them
sooner or later. What often happens when you do something at the very last moment is that you haven't taken the
time to assemble all the required materials, you rush
through the work, don't have time to check it out and it
doesn't turn out very well.

**"Once before I did something just before deadline and it
worked out well; I'll do it at the last minute again."**

This rationalisation is similar to the previous one and is
invoked when you have something to complete which you
find in a word, nauseating. The thought of doing it triggers
off an allergic reaction in you. All you want to do is put it
out of sight and mind. By convincing yourself that you can
still do a great job even when you attack the project at the

very last minute, you give yourself permission to procrastinate and not to feel bad about it.

The Lie. This rationalisation borders on magical thinking. I think all of us have had the experience of at least once in our lives having put off something until the last minute and 'fluking' a good result. However, only chronic procrastinators convince themselves that the probabilities of a repeat performance are close to 100 percent.

The Lie can also involve you deluding yourself into believing that what was just an okay performance or result was really an outstanding achievement.

"If I wait until the last minute to complete my work, I'll save myself lots of time and effort."

The self-deceptions you can come up with to justify putting off doing work can really be very amusing. If you can convince yourself that you can make a big saving in time and effort by doing things at the last minute, you will not only be more likely to procrastinate, but also feel good about procrastinating. After all, time is precious and if you can save some with a little procrastination, then maybe procrastination isn't such a bad thing after all.

The Lie. If it were true that you save time by putting things off to the last minute, then I'd start to become worried about the fact that I'm not procrastinating more often than I do! The fact is that you only save time if you rush your work at the last minute. If your concern is saving time, why not rush your work well before its due and see if you can maintain good quality. More often than not you cannot.

An associated problem with this Lie is that you can also experience nagging or gnawing feelings of panic while you are ostensibly saving time. The panic, of course, surrounds the issue as to whether you'll actually finish it or not.

"There's no point in starting if I don't know how to do the job properly."

This rationalisation is commonly invoked by people who have trouble sustaining the effort frequently required to get a project underway. In the next chapter I'll discuss this as one of the main causes of procrastination. It becomes a rationalisation when you invoke it to help you escape the frustration of getting started on a task.

The Lie. The truth is that there is every point in trying when you are having trouble getting into a project. Most probably you know enough to make a start and in so doing, you will discover how the job should be done. 'Trial and error' learning is frequently a very useful approach to getting into difficult projects. And if you really do not know enough, find out as quickly as possible what you need to know and then hop into it.

"How can I be expected to finish a project that I've lost interest in."

This rationalisation can help block you from ever completing a project that has extended over time. Here, you convince yourself that it is absolutely necessary for you to have an active interest in what it is you're doing to be able to work on it.

The Lie. It is sometimes the case that because a project has taken so long, you can lose much interest in it. Your interest in the final project may have changed, partly because of the amount of frustration and guilt you have experienced along the way. Indeed, your low interest may be a result of convincing yourself that the project is simply too hard and unbearable to complete. The Lie is that if and when you decide to get on and finish the project without procrastination you will finish the project with or without your original interest returning. More often than not, once you re-energise, you'll find yourself becoming re-absorbed in the project.

"I really don't want to do this anyway."

This is a real killer of a rationalisation. It tends to be used when you have decided that what you've been putting off doing is really too hard, too frustrating and too painful to achieve and, therefore, not worth doing. What accompanies this rationalisation are further self-deceiving reasons why you know longer wish to commit yourself to a particular course of action.

An example would be if you were interested in meeting an attractive stranger at a party. You catch sight of the person and you make an instantaneous or considered judgment that you would enjoy knowing more about the person. Perhaps, you feel chemistry. However, for reasons to be covered in the next chapter, you never get around to going up to the person. As opportunities continue to present themselves and as you start to predict that you'll probably never take the first step, rather then condemning yourself as a 'weak coward', you justify your procrastination with the thought: "I really am not that interested in meeting new people. It wouldn't have worked out. Surface appearances are often deceiving. Phew, I'm glad I didn't say anything!".

The Lie. The big Lie here is that deep down you really still want to accomplish the task that you originally decided before your procrastination and supporting rationalisations blocked you from achieving what you wanted. The big Lie is one big cover up of your inability to follow through on a decision to act which would bring you more enjoyment, pleasure, satisfaction and happiness. Rather than looking at the "real reasons" for your procrastination and working on them so that you get what you want, you fall back on one of the most basic and harmful self-deceptions of the lot.

It is sometimes very difficult to discover the specific rationalisation you use to divert yourself away from your chosen activity. They are often ingrained so deeply in your 'psyche' that it takes a real effort to tune into them. We are not trained to listen to our thinking. Moreover, much of our thinking happens so quickly and automatically that it takes a trained listener to discover which, if any, rationalisations are interfering with performance.

Edwin Bliss, author of <u>Doing It Now</u>, has provided a list of 40 of the most common excuses or reasons for procrastination. Some of these overlap with the one's I've just presented. Cast your eye on the list and see how many ring a bell.

Bliss' top forty cop-outs

1. It's unpleasant.

2. It's not due yet.

3. I work better under pressure.

4. Maybe it will take care of itself if I just don't do anything.

5. It's too early in the day.

6. It's too late in the day.

7. I don't have my papers with me.

8. It's difficult.

9. I don't feel like doing it now.

10. I have a headache.

11. Delay won't make much difference.

12. It may be important, but it isn't urgent.

13. It might hurt.

14. I really mean to do it, but I keep forgetting.

15. Somebody else might do it if I wait.

16. It might be embarrassing.

17. I don't know where to begin.

18. I need a good stiff drink first.

19. I'm too tired.

20. I'm too busy right now.

21. It's a boring job.

22. It might not work.

23. I've got to tidy up first.

24. I need to sleep on it.

25. We can get by a little longer as is.

26. I don't really know how to do it.

27. There's a good TV program on.

28. As soon as I start, somebody will probably interrupt.

29. It needs further study.

30. My horoscope indicates that it is the wrong time.

31. Nobody is nagging me about it yet.

32. If I do it now, they'll just give me something else to do.

33. The weather's lousy.

34. It's too nice a day to spend doing that.

35. Before I start, I think I'll take a break.

36. I'll do it just as soon as I finish some preliminary tasks.

37. My biorhythms are out of sync.

38. The sooner I fall behind, the more time I'll have to catch up.

39. I'll wait until the first of the year and make a New Year's resolution.

40. It's too late now, anyway.

Why the 'Cover Up'?

Naturally you may not find it easy to overcome your self-deception and your rationalisation about procrastinating. The main reason for deceiving yourself relates to your shame about frankly admitting your procrastination; and unless you rid yourself of this kind of shame, your incentive to use mañana and other rationalising excuses remains the same.

Albert Ellis and William Knaus
Overcoming Procrastination, 1977.

In Chapter 1, I provided a number of good reasons why people procrastinate. Once again, some of us have inherited dispositions which make it more likely that we will procrastinate. Some us have were never adequately taught the self-discipline skills necessary to tolerate frustration and delay gratification. As well, many people today procrastinate simply because they have too much to do and not enough time to do it. And put quite simply, all people are fallible some of the time. We are not robots which can be programmed to do everything that is on our plate. We sometimes - because of our humaness - goof up. It may well be very bad that we procrastinate at something important; however, it means no more or less that it is bad.

While this may seem sensible and hardly worth stating, many people do not think this way at times when they observe themselves needlessly procrastinating. At these times, people can take the sensible and make it quite irrational. Let's look at a common example.

Your New Years' Resolution was to get fit. You know what's required to get fit including eating and drinking in moderation, eating healthier foods and exercising. It is now August and you still look and feel like Tubby the Tuba. You have spent most of the year procrastinating. When you think about the fact that you are still eating the wrong foods, drinking to excess and not exercising, you tell yourself "I should be more self-disciplined. I really am a loser for not following through on my fitness program". These and re-lated thoughts will lead to extreme feelings of anger, shame and guilt. Given that you do not enjoy these feelings about yourself, you manufacture the rationalisation: "As soon as I get my last child off to school, I'll feel less stressed and will be more motivated to lose weight." ("So I might as well have another cupcake now while I still can"). The rationalisation provides you with an acceptable excuse for why you've been procrastinating (pressures of kids) and offers you the promise of better times.

The problem with the rationalisation in the above scenario is that the real reasons for your procrastination remain covered up; namely, your pleasure-seeking and the anger you have towards your mate for encouraging you in a rather negative way to lose weight.

In order to eliminate your 'need' to resort to rationalisa-tions so as to cope with the shame of procrastination, you have to reduce how stressed out your feel about your procrastination. One of the best ways to do this is to eliminate those irrational ideas about your procrastination and replace them with more sensible ones. The three thoughts which generally give rise to your shame and guilt are:

1.   I shouldn't procrastinate.

2.   It's awful to procrastinate.

3.   I am a real loser.

Given what you know about all people's tendency to procrastinate, it would be better to change the un-realistic expectation in the first thought to: "While it is strongly preferable for me not to procrastinate, when I do, I do. Now how can I change my approach so that I improve in this area?"

Given that most types of procrastination do not result in a catastrophe for you or others, it would be more sensible to change the second thought to: "While my procrastination is unfortunate and bad because it is stopping me from achieving what I want to do, it is hardly the end of the world and I can definitely cope with it."

And finally, rather than damning yourself as a total loser for procrastinating, it would be less stress-creating for you to accept that even when you procrastinate you are still an okay, all right sort of person. Procrastination, even where you are putting off something very important, doesn't take away the rest of your good qualities. The idea here is to accept yourself while disliking your procrastination and, once again, working hard to change your behaviour.

Learning not to be so hard on yourself when you procrastinate will reduce your shame and guilt. And once you feel less cut up about what it is you are not doing, then you'll be less likely to rationalise your procrastination and more likely to seek out the real causes of your procrastination and do something about them.

Denise waited for Helen to get her racket which she had left in the car. She was feeling especially good today. She had finally started to sort out a little bit of one part of her life. Finally, she had started to play tennis again and was feeling much trimmer. It had been a big struggle to organise her two kids, James and Andrea, so that she had some free time. Time for herself and for some recreation had become a real 'sore' spot for her. And she was pleased that she was able to get Bill to do something other than work. Tennis was a good start.

"Phew," Helen exclaimed, "I was worried that some- one might have stolen it. Let's not keep the boys waiting."

"It's really great that you could play again this week with Larry. We had a good hit out last week."

"Yeah", agreed Helen, "but I'm starting to feel a bit guilty. I've got some really big exams coming up in a few weeks and I should be studying. Denise, if I don't stop playing tennis and start studying, I'll be in real trouble!".

"I thought you liked your course," replied Denise.

"Oh, I mostly do. It's just that I have so much to do I don't know where to begin. Plus I've got that research proposal to do. I'm not really sure what the problem is." Helen looked a bit panicky.

"Would you like me to talk to Bill?" asked Denise, "He's a master of time management - especially when it comes to getting his work done."

"That'd be great Denise. Nice to see Bill up and around. He always seems to be working."

"It's a bit of a worry," sighed Denise, "He's been promising to work less but he always seems to have something else to do."

"Doing all the housework like you do, Denise, and looking after the kids doesn't leave much time for you. What does he say?"

"Bill hates it when I bring it up. He gets real defensive and angry. I suppose I should mention it to him again. I can never seem to find the right moment. But if I don't I'll never get out of the house —"

"Ladies. The wager has been accepted." Bill's voice cut across Denise's as they entered the court. "Larry and Helen versus Denise and myself. The big re-match. Five bucks a set!"

Bill," said Helen rather meekly, "five bucks is a bit steep for my graduate student budget. I think fifty cents a set would be more like it."

"Helen", said Larry, "Never mind. Today, we've got our own secret weapon. We'll suprise it on them."

"What is it?" whispered Helen as she and Larry walked to their side of the court.

"It's Bill. All he's eaten in the past 24 hours is apples. If we make sure we hit mostly to him, all that running around will not only short-wind him, but he'll have a hard time holding himself together. He won't know whether to run for the ball or the toilet. We'll kill 'em!"

Actions Speak Louder Than Words

1. Pick one specific and important task or activity you've been putting off doing (see Actions Speak Louder Than Words in Chapter 1). See if you can identify the lies (rationalisations), fantasies and addictions you typically employ which divert you.

Rationalisations

_____
_____
_____
_____

Fantasies

_____
_____
_____
_____

Addictions

_____

_____

_____

_____

2.   Do this same analysis for other tasks you've been
       avoiding.

       Notice any similarities and differences in the
       rationalisations, fantasies and addictions you employ.

3

The 10 'Real' Reasons You Procrastinate

For every thousand persons hacking at the branches of evil, only one person chops at its roots.

Thoreau

As I indicated in Chapter 1, when you procrastinate it is as if different opposing magnetic fields repel you away from the straightforward path towards an activity, task or person which you would normally be attracted to. Let me, again, illustrate my magnetic theory of procrastination by using the example of putting off writing an important report which is due at the end of the week. The report could be one requested by your boss, manager or chief executive officer in which you are to provide a statement of your goals for the next two years, new directions which you wish to undertake and the means by which you are going to achieve your goals.

I want you to imagine that you are a magnet positioned at one end of a room. At the other end is another magnet which is the task of writing the report. Your northpole is attracted to the task's south pole and under normal conditions, as you move across the room toward the other task, you would be strongly attracted to it and, therefore, get to working away on the report. What happens to cause you to procrastinate is that as you start across the room, many other large magnets appear between you and the task you want to accomplish and because of their force fields, you are repelled away from the task of writing the report.

The Magnetic Theory of Procrastination

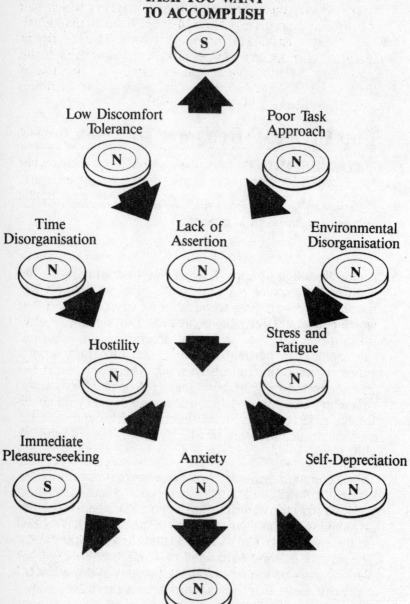

The drawing on the opposite page once again shows how these magnets obstruct your path and repel you away. As you can see, there are 10 different magnets which can obstruct your progress. Nine of them have similar north poles on top and actually repel you away. The identity of each of these opposing forces is written below each of the magnets. A tenth magnet, "pleasure-seeking", because of its south pole, tends to draw you towards it (remember, opposites attract, similar fields repel).

You can employ this analogy to any task you are avoiding doing. Imagine yourself as a magnet on one side of a room and on the other side is a magnet which represents what you want to do. It might be exercising, becoming intimate, asserting yourself, meeting someone new, giving a public talk or paying your tax.

If you are procrastinating, then it is likely that one or more of the 10 magnetic fields are repelling you away from your goal. The more magnets which obstruct your path, the harder it will be to get where you are going. If there are quite a few of the magnets in your way, is it any wonder that you have a hard time getting around to what you want to do?

People vary quite a bit as to which of these forces are operating to cause them to procrastinate. Chronic procrastinators tend to have quite a few of these forces operating in many areas of their lives, while other people have a fewer number. The stronger these magnets are relative to the force of the magnet which represents what you want to do, the harder it will be for you to get your magnet to connect with your chosen task.

In this chapter, you will have an opportunity to learn more about these 10 reasons why you procrastinate. Once you know how prominent they are in your life, you will be in a good position to do something about them so that you can become what you want to be, not just what you have to be!

Let me describe the full range of possible opposing magnetic fields which represent the 'Real' reasons you procrastinate. The reasons why you might procrastinate at one task (e.g., home maintenance) may be different from the causes of your procrastination at other tasks (e.g., applying for a better job). The 10 'real' reasons you procrastinate are:

- **Anxiety.** As you think about, or start to work, you find yourself becoming very worried about how the report will be received and evaluated by your superior. You anticipate that, given your late start on the report, it will be evaluated poorly. To escape the anxiety, you lose yourself in other thoughts.

- **Self-Depreciation.** You have a poor regard for yourself and are always ready to put yourself down when the slightest thing goes wrong. You really don't believe a goof-ball like you deserves a brighter future and, therefore, you have a hard time coming up with forward planning and challenging directions for yourself. As you procrastinate, you feel even more unsettled about yourself which makes it hard to do the job.

- **Low Discomfort Tolerance.** You find the thought of writing the report either frustrating, anxiety-provoking or both. Since you find it difficult to tolerate frustration and anxiety, you divert yourself from the task thereby reducing your discomfort.

- **Pleasure-Seeking.** You would rather be getting stuck into something more exciting at work than writing a boring report. You find yourself being drawn to other more challenging and fulfilling activities.

- **Time Disorganisation.** You haven't scheduled enough time to do this report along with everything else you have to do. This might also be revealed in you having difficulties setting priorities in terms of how you use your time to accomplish different tasks of varying importance.

- **Environmental Disorganisation.** Your work area is too noisy with too many distractions to enable you to concentrate. You may also be missing important resource and reference material that you need to complete the report.

- **Poor Task Approach.** Even when you finally settle down to do the work, you are put off by not knowing where to begin and being overwhelmed by the size of the task. You might tend to become blocked by not knowing how to get started.

- **Lack of Assertion.** You find it difficult to say "No" to requests made of you at work and find yourself with so many different things that you have committed yourself to that you really do not have enough time to get your report done and honour all your committments.

- **Hostility with Others.** You might be very angry about having to do the report in the first place. What a waste of time. As well, it might show a lack of confidence in you by the 'higher ups.' You feel like showing them by refusing to submit the report.

- **Stress and Fatigue.** You might be tired and spent from other work demands, hassles at home or simply that you are out of shape. You might be lacking fuel.

Now there is both good and bad news in this analysis of why you procrastinate. The bad news is that for you to show a large improvement in the number of things you procrastinate at now and in the future, you will need to tackle each of the different causes of your procrastination and work at making changes in yourself and in your world so that you effectively minimise or remove the cause from interfering with what you wish to do.

For example, if you believe that one of the major causes of your procrastination is time disorganisation, for you to procrastinate less, you will have to become a better time manager. Or if one of the main reasons you avoid doing certain things is anxiety including fear of failure and fear of disapproval, then you will need to learn how to manage your anxiety. This can be seen as bad news insofar as you'll probably realise that changing yourself in these areas will most probably be a slow, difficult and frustrating process. It might even seem that, given how many negative forces seem to be operating in your life, it is really pointless to try to change at all.

In the very next chapter, I will present a number of Procrastination Bypass Techniques which will help you to avoid coming in contact with, and being effected by, those negative magnetic forces which are standing between you and what you have to do or have chosen to do. One or more of these bypass techniques will lead to an immediate change in the way you approach certain tasks. The techniques will help you get going; right away, without delay! They will help you get out of your rut and energise yourself. You can even turn to Chapter 4 right now and start making some positive inroads to your procrastination without knowing anything further about the real reasons you procrastinate.

This book also provides a summary of some of the main techniques for helping you modify the underlying causes of your procrastination. Tackling these causes will help you eliminate opposing magnetic forces from your life and insure a smoother, direct passage in getting important things done.

What follows is a further description of the 10 main reasons for procrastination. Checklists are included which will enable you to judge and compare your main reasons for procrastinating. You may want to complete the checklist which appears at the beginning of each section to find out more about the real causes of your procrastination. After each checklist you will be able to compare your total score with the average score of people in the general population.

You'll also see the average scores of members of the Born Procrastinators' Club. These are people who readily acknowledge that they frequently procrastinate. You'll notice that, for all of the 10 checklists which assess the extent to which particular reasons explain your procrastination, born procrastinators score much higher. The directions for completing each checklist of the 'real' reasons for procrastination are as follows.

Directions: A number of statements that people have used to describe themselves are given below. Read each statement and then circle the answer to indicate how you generally think, feel and behave. There are no right or wrong answers. Do not spend too much time on any one statement but give the answer which seems to describe how you are generally.

Circle 1 for Almost Never

Circle 2 for Sometimes

Circle 3 for Often

Circle 4 for Almost Always

Real Reason Number 1: Anxiety

	Almost Never	Some-Times	Often	Almost Always
1. I seem to worry a lot as I get ready to do something I should be doing.	1	(2)	3	4
2. I lack confidence in being able to get things done.	(1)	2	3	4
3. I feel nervous and restless when I think about doing things I should be doing.	1	(2)	3	4
4. I worry much too much about things which are not all that important.	1	(2)	3	4
5. I feel insecure.	1	2	(3)	4

Total Score ___10___

Average total score for general population: 8.5

Average total score for members of the Born Procrastinators' Club: 13

I can state with a great deal of assurance that the more anxious you are, the more likely it is that you will procrastinate. (It is also quite common to procrastinate for other reasons besides anxiety). If you are a person who readily accepts that you are by nature a worrier, you'll be in a good position to do something about the causes of anxiety I discuss in Chapter 5. If you are defensive in admitting to being anxious, then it will be harder for you to address your anxiety.

Anxiety serves as an opposing magnetic force which surrounds certain tasks you wish to accomplish and certain people with whom you may wish to interact. Highly anxious people tend to put off activities such as applying for promotion, public speaking, asserting themselves with colleagues, friends and significant others, meeting new people, asking questions in class and asking for help. What makes anxiety a particularly strong cause of procrastination is that it also seems to contribute to other causes of procrastination such as lack of assertion, getting started on boring or hard tasks, giving up before finishing, and stress and fatigue.

There is another way in which anxiety has a negative impact on your follow-through on decisions. High anxiety increases the discomfort you experience in connection with performing certain activites like public speaking. If you have Low Discomfort Tolerance (Reason Number 4), you will be much likely to avoid the situations and people who activate the anxiety. And avoidance equals procrastination.

Real Reason Number 2: Self-Depreciation

	Almost Never	Some- Times	Often	Almost Always
6. I think I'm totally hopeless when I see myself putting off things I should be doing.	1	(2)	3	4
7. When I compare myself with what others have accomplished and what I haven't, I think I'm a real 'loser'.	(1)	2	3	4
8. I really give myself a hard time when I waste time on unimportant things.	1	(2)	(3)	4
9. I get down on myself for not doing the important things I want to get done.	1	(2)	(3)	4
10. I think I'm a born procrastinator.	1	2	(3)	4

Total Score __17__

Average total score for general population: 8.5

Average total score for members of the Born Procrastinators' Club: 13

You might be suprised to learn that over 25 percent of people have an over-developed tendency to put themselves down when things go wrong. If, when someone forgets your name or you make a mistake, you are likely to conclude that you are a total loser, a failure and hopeless then you are probably a 'self-depreciator'. Rather than just focusing on the one bad thing which might have happened and concluding that it was bad and that, hopefully, (especially with some re-newed effort on your part or a different approach) it won't happen again, in your own mind you over-generalise and think, because one bad thing occurred, it is totally your fault and, therefore, you are totally bad. You throw all the other good qualities out the window.

As I've suggested in Chapter 2, chronic procrastinators who are prone to rationalisations have a distinct tendency to de-value themselves when they observe themselves procrastinating.

Over the years, this tendency to de-value yourself, takes its toll. As a 'self-depreciator', you may well have developed relatively low opinions of yourself as well as having experienced frequent periods of low self-esteem and depression. As a consequence, you may find it hard to imagine yourself performing at a level within your capabilities. Your confidence tends to be shakey. Moreover, by getting angry with yourself for not being better than you are, you develop an attitude that you do not really deserve the good life. You condemn yourself to 'louse-hood'; this is all that a louse really deserves.

So it is quite common to find self-depreciation as a cause of different types of procrastination. 'Self-depreciators' put off applying for higher paying, better jobs, they avoid meeting interesting and exciting people ("Why would anyone be interested in a 'no-hoper' like me"), getting started and finishing work which requires extended intellectual effort such as studying for exams, as well as spending time reviewing and up-dating important information. And, most critically, 'self-depreciators' tend to perpetuate their own procrastination!

Real Reason Number 3: Low Discomfort Tolerance

	Almost Never	Some-Times	Often	Almost Always
11. I can't be bothered doing boring and tedious work.	(1)	2	3	4
12. I get extremely tense and frustrated by certain tasks I have to do at work.	(1)	2	3	4
13. I have a hard time putting up with hassles.	(1)	2	3	4
14. I find it too hard to make the effort to do the things I should be doing.	1	(2)	3	4
15. I find myself giving up too easily.	1	(2)	3	4

Total Score ___7___

Average total score for the general population is: 9

Average total score for members of the Born Procrastinators' Club: 13

If your total score is above 13, it is likely that you delay doing certain tasks because of the discomfort that you experience in doing them and as you think about doing them. If you score above the average on this scale, you may tend to put off tasks which you find anxiety provoking such as returning important phone calls, asserting yourself with negative or difficult people at work, attending family gatherings, resolving conflicts with friends and relatives, asserting yourself in your significant relationship and studying for exams.

High discomfort intolerance may also manifest itself in you putting off tasks you find boring, hard or frustrating such as work you take home to do, daily chores around the house and studying material you find deathly dull.

Real Reason Number 4: Pleasure-Seeking

	Almost Never	Some-Times	Often	Almost Always
16. I can't seem to make the sacrifices in the short-term to get what I want in the long-term.	(1)	(2)	3	4
17. I get too distracted by the enjoyable things around me.	(1)	2	3	4
18. I seem to be someone who needs to be comfortable.	1	2	(3)	4
19. I find it pretty disagreeable when I have to give up my relaxation and freedom in order to get something 'more important' done.	(1)	2	3	4
20. My life should be fun and exciting. *peaceful*	1	(2)	(3)	(4)

Total Score _8_ 9 10 13 12 11

Average total score for the general population: 9

Average total score for members of the Born Procrastinators' Club: 13

If you are high in pleasure-seeking, you will be someone who has a strong desire for immediate pleasure to enjoy yourself, have fun, play and seeks out excitement and pleasure while having poor impulse control. That is, you may feel almost driven towards pleasurable activities without being able to do anything about it. As you face having to do some boring, mundane and routine task as well as more demanding tasks, you almost seem to search around for something more enjoyable to do.

By being a pleasure seeker, you tend not to sacrifice the pleasures of the moment. That is, you put off until tomorrow the less exciting, but important tasks in order to enjoy yourself at the moment. You are a psychological spender rather than saver.

My research into pleasure seekers shows that they are more likely to procrastinate at tasks at home such as showing up at 'boring' family get togethers and making the effort to meet new people. The area of their life where short-term hedonists really come un-stuck is study. Despite their best intentions, our pleasure-seekers tend to avoid reviewing and revising notes, getting started and finishing work they find either boring or hard, asking for extra help and studying for exams.

For some pleasure seekers, there is an interesting connection between pleasure seeking and another real reason for procrastination; namely, hostility with others. It appears that for some people, the two work closely together. The more angry you get with someone, the more you can justify your tendency to play ("It's unfair that you are asking me to do this. No one else has to. Everyone else is doing interesting work and enjoying themselves. I deserve as much fun as the next person."). And by playing rather than working, you are more likely to attract criticism and possible 'unfair' treatment by others which, in turn, is likely to give rise to your anger and a rationalisation to play even more ("I'll show them!").

Real Reason Number 5: Time Disorganisation

	Almost Never	Some-Times	Often	Almost Always
21. I always seem to be running late.	1	(2)	3	4
22. I have a hard time setting priorities.	1	(2)	3	4
23. I seem to waste a lot of time.	1	2	(3)	4
24. Things seem to take a lot longer to get done than I think they will.	1	2	(3)	4
25. I have a hard time setting goals.	1	2	3	(4)

Total Score ___14___

Average total score for general population: 9.5

Average total score for members of the Born Procrastinators' Club: 13

It might appear to others that the reason you don't get things done is that you're lazy. And while there may or may not be an element of truth in their explanation, it might well be the case that you don't get around to doing things because you are not skilled in managing your time. For example, one of the skills necessary for good time management is accurately predicting how long something will take. We know that some people, especially when they are under pressure to get things done, under-estimate how long things will take and so run out of time. Other aspects of poor time organisation include not being good at deciding what is important to do today and what is less important (priority setting). Everything seems as though it is equally important so you have a hard time deciding what to schedule first.

Some people by nature are good time planners. They seem to carry around with them time schedules when everything has to be done - and they stick to them. Others are not so fortunate. Their heads are filled with more important and, quite often creative, ideas and they lack the type of mind which would enable them to plan and organise their time more efficiently.

Over the years I have run many workshops on the topic of procrastination. And when I ask to see a show of hands as to the number of people who are poor time managers, I am always greeted with a sea of hands.

If you suffer from Time Disorganisation, it is likely that it will show up at work and in study. You probably have a poor track record in tidying your office, finding time to do your long-term planning, getting around to your paper work, prospecting for new business and finding the time to do the work you've taken home. If you are a student, you are likely to be so disorganised that you don't get around to studying, miss a number of classes because of everything you have to do in your life, and even avoid taking notes in class.

Reason Number 6: Environmental Disorganisation

	Almost Never	Some-Times	Often	Almost Always
26. There seems to be too many distractions for me to get things done.	(1)	2	3	4
27. The area where I work is generally a mess.	(1)	2	3	4
28. I seem to be missing important materials, tools or ingredients to get my work done.	1	(2)	3	4
29. I never seem to have any privacy or quiet.	(1)	2	(3)	4
30. I find I am very disorganised in the way I keep track of and file my past, present and future work.	(1)	2	3	4

Total Score ___16.9___

Average total score for general population: 9

Average total score for members of the Born Procrastinators' Club: 11.5

This particular reason for your procrastination can be seen to be lodged more outside you than within you although the fact that your environment is disorgainised may partly be your fault. Environmental Disorganisation takes many forms and can include distractions such as telephone or people interruptions, lack of privacy and a work area which is over-run with papers or equipment that haven't been properly filed or put away. Environmental Disorganisation may also mean that when you actually sit down to work, you haven't organised the right material or equipment that you will need to perform the work.

If your home or work environment is very disorganised then, of course, it will be more difficult for you to concentrate on the task at hand. Many of the tasks we have to do, or choose to do, require the full application of our intellect; that is, they are not that easy to do. When we have many distractions around us, our ability to tune out the outside world becomes almost impossible and the frequent result is that we give up in extreme frustration before even beginning to work. As well, frequent distractions will divert our attention on to something else and will make it less likely that we will get back to the original task we've set out to do, but may not feel like doing.

If you have a disorganised environment at work, you will be more likely to have trouble achieving a variety of tasks including returning phone calls, keeping up with paperwork and long-term planning. Chaotic environments are also somewhat stress-creating. As a result you may find it difficult to maintain a proper diet and modify the bad habits of smoking and drinking. My research also suggests that you might be more likely to avoid seeing a medical or health specialist.

Real Reason Number 7: Poor Task Approach

	Almost Never	Some- Times	Often	Almost Always
31. I have a hard time knowing how to get started at doing new tasks or activities.	1	2	③	4
32. I find it hard to find the right words when I want to discuss something with a negative or difficult person.	1	2	③	4
33. I need to know everything about how to go about doing something before I can get started.	1	2	3	4
34. I find myself overwhelmed by the size of certain tasks.	1	②	3	4
35. I have a hard time breaking down a task into manageable bits.	1	②	3	4

Total Score _13_

Average total score for general public: 9

Average total score for members of the Born Procrastinators' Club: 13

If you tend to be a bit of a worrier, get easily frustrated by boring or difficult tasks, like short-term pleasures a little too much, have difficulty managing your time, or experience a fair amount of stress, it is likely that your initial approach to whatever you have set out to do might put you off doing the rest of the task. A main reason for your procrastination at certain tasks might well be Poor Task Approach.

I recently worked with a student who appeared very unmotivated to do his work even though he knew that if he didn't study he wouldn't pass his final year at his university. One of the major causes of his predicament was that when he settled down to study, within a few minutes he would give up. He had a classic case of low discomfort tolerance and pleasure-seeking. And what increased his frustration with his work was that he had a hard time 'getting into' his work. He had a Poor Task Approach. He seemed easily overwhelmed by the length of the papers demanded of him and by some of his practical work. He seemed very unsure of what part of the different pieces of work he should be attacking. As well, being a 'perfectionist', he found it almost impossible to write down anything where he might make a mistake. He constantly worried whether he had done enough research to start a paper and, at times, would start to write and then run back to the library to do a little more background reading. For a smart fellow, he had some major problems.

No matter what the causes, having a Poor Task Approach can definitely contribute to you putting off work to be done. I have found that people with a Poor Task Approach are just as likely to put off boring tasks (paperwork, updating reports) as they are to put off highly demanding and stressful activities (applying for a job promotion, studying for important exams). A Poor Task Approach is most likely to contribute to your procrastination over study tasks.

Real Reason Number 8: Lack of Assertion

	Almost Never	Some-Times	Often	Almost Always
36. I think people should know what I want without me having to ask or tell them.	1	2	3	4
37. I have a hard time saying "no" when asked to do something.	1	2	3	4
38. I have a hard time sticking up for what I think or want.	1	2	3	4
39. I avoid saying things or asking questions for fear of appearing stupid.	1	2	3	4
40. I really find it very hard to ask someone to do something for me.	1	2	3	4

Total Score _____

Average total score for the general population: 9

Average total score for members of the Born Procrastinators' Club: 11.5

Lack of assertion means that you are someone who has trouble sticking up for your rights and this may result in an inability to make reasonable requests of others for better treatment and having difficulty saying "no" to unreasonable requests from others. I'll describe in more detail characteristic ways people think, feel and look when they are being unassertive.

To be assertive requires that you have particular conversational skills and non-verbal, body language (e.g., good eye contact, firmness of voice) so that you can get your point of view across. As well, it requires that you do not experience high amounts of anxiety in the face of having to assert yourself. High anxiety will kill off your desire to assert yourself and will result in you having to bear whatever is happening.

Lack of assertion contributes to two types of procrastination. It can cause you to put off being assertive in situations where you would want to be, such as when you are unfairly treated by someone at work or at home. It will also make it harder for you to speak up to resolve interpersonal difficulties.

A lack of assertion contributes indirectly to your procrastination by making it harder for you to say "no" to requests people make of you which take up your time. The request may be as simple as giving them a lift home or attending a meeting after work. If these requests are unreasonable and you still say "yes", then you will have less time to accomplish other, possibly more important, things you've set out to do, leading to procrastination.

Real Reason Number 9: Hostility With Others

	Almost Never	Some- Times	Often	Almost Always
41. I get extremely angry when a person gives me something unfair to do.	(1)	2	3	4
42. I find myself getting back at people who are un-supportive and critical of me.	(1)	2	3	4
43. I feel like hitting out when I am not given recognition for doing good work.	(1)	(2)	3	4
44. I can go on a work slow down when I find people looking after their own interests and forgetting about mine.	(1)	(2)	3	4
45. I feel furious when I've done a good job and get critical comments.	(1)	(2)	(3)	4

Total Score ___

Average total score for general population: 8.5

Average total score for members of Born Procrastinators' Club: 11

Anger with the world in general, or with a specific person, for the way you have been treated can leave a bad taste in your mouth. By bad taste I mean ongoing resentment and hostility which can lead you to develop an attitude towards resisting what others are asking of you. "I'll show them," you think, "If that's the way they are doing to treat me, the hell with them, those S.O.B.'s, I'll fix their wagons by doing what I want to do, not what they want me to do."

This attitude is frequently observed in certain adolescents who seem to collect injustices and punish the world accordingly. They refuse to do their homework if a teacher has been critical of them. And if they are not allowed to stay out until 3 am, they retaliate by going on a deliberate work slowdown at home.

Unfortunately, this attitude towards authority can maintain itself into adulthood. I say unfortunately, because in procrastinating over certain tasks as a way of punishing someone else, you attract negative consequences for yourself. For example, if your boss gives you something to do which you consider especially demanding and he fails to provide you with any support, you might decide that your boss is an ass and that you'll deliberately perform the task slowly as a way of punishing him for his inconsiderate behaviour. However, the 'bottom line' for you is that when your boss notices you procrastinating at the task he assigned you, his opinion of you lowers and, down the line, others at work will be given the better opportunities.

Real Reason Number 10: Stress And Fatigue

	Almost Never	Some-Times	Often	Almost Always
46. I am under a great deal of stress.	1	2	3	(4)
47. I seem to tire very quickly in the day.	1	(2)	3	4
48. I feel emotionally drained.	1	2	3	(4)
49. I find myself not caring.	1	2	3	(4)
50. I lose patience easily.	1	(2)	3	4

Total Score ___16___

Average total score for general population: 8.5

Average total score for members of the Born Procrastinators' Club: 11

One of the more obvious causes of procrastination is stress and fatigue. Carrying out decisions you've made requires effort and energy. This is especially true of tasks you don't feel like doing. Moreover, at the end of the day, or week, when you've already done your fair share of work, if you feel very stressed and tired, it will be much harder for you to rise to the occasion.

In Chapter 9, I'll suggest some of the causes of stress and fatigue and ways to manage your stress. Stress can be understood to be a product of the number and intensity of the negative demands on your life in combination with your lifestyle, coping skills and your attitudes towards the demands. The more demands and the poorer your attitudes, coping skills and lifestyle, the higher your stress.

If you experience a great deal of stress, you are very likely to delay self-development tasks such as spending time on hobbies and recreational activities. Moreover, you are more likely than others who are not as stressed to delay demanding tasks such as applying for promotion and studying for exams.

Summary Profile of Your Check-up from Your Neck Up

You may find it useful to compare which of the real reasons for procrastination are most characteristic of you, and, therefore, require your attention and work. Opposite you will find a blank chart which will enable you to graph your results. Enter your Total Score for each of the 10 reasons in the space provided. Then make a dot next to the number above each reason. Once you've done that, connect the dots.

By way of example, I have included the 'Summary Profile' of the reasons that Bill and his wife, Denise, procrastinate.

Summary Profiles of the Real Reasons Bill and Denise Procrastinate

Bill's Total Scores ▬   Denise's Total Scores ▬ ▬ ▬

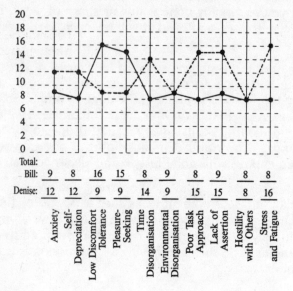

	Anxiety	Self-Depreciation	Low Discomfort Tolerance	Pleasure-Seeking	Time Disorganisation	Environmental Disorganisation	Poor Task Approach	Lack of Assertion	Hostility with Others	Stress and Fatigue
Bill:	9	8	16	15	8	9	8	9	8	8
Denise:	12	12	9	9	14	9	15	15	8	16

Summary Profile of the Real Reasons You Procrastinate

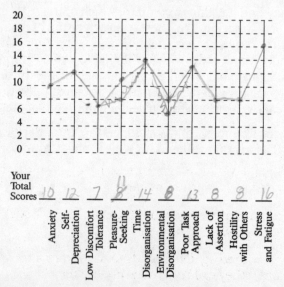

Your Total Scores	10	12	7	11/8	14	8	13	8	8	16

Now that you have a better sense of the real reasons you procrastinate, you can go to one or more of Chapters 5 through 9 for specific information on how to modify these causes. The following table will help you locate these details.

Reasons	Information on Management
Anxiety, Self-Depreciation	Chapter 5
Low Discomfort Tolerance, Pleasure-Seeking	Chapter 6
Time Disorganisation, Environmental Disorganisation, Poor Task Approach	Chapter 7
Lack of Assertion, Hostility with Others	Chapter 8
Stress and Fatigue	Chapter 9

Larry, Helen, and even Denise couldn't stop laughing. Bill was hunched over with cramps.

"Okay Larry, you win. I gotta go now but it's a win by forfeit. A weak victory." shouted Bill as he ran off to get some relief from all the apples he'd been eating.

Larry put his arm around Helen which sent shivers up her spine. They'd been dating for awhile but this was the first time he'd actually been close to her in public.

"I thought you said that you'd have to study this weekend with your exams coming up."

Helen turned visibly red. "I know. It's just such a beautiful day."

Larry laughed again. "Sounds to me you're a bit of a - what do they call it - a pleasure-seeker."

Helen turned even redder and threw his arm off her shoulders.

"You should talk. Weren't you the one going to hire someone to help you at work? Now who's Mr Procrastinator?"

"But, I've had more important things to do ... Like spending time with you." winked Larry.

Denise couldn't resist jumping in. "Larry, that sounds to me to be a bit of a rationalisation. What about all those times when Helen was studying. You could have done it then."

"Hey, what's this, Get Larry Week. I'm going to see what's happened to Bill. Hope he hasn't wrecked the plumbing."

Actions Speak Louder Than Words

Once again focus on a particular important task or activity you've been putting off. See if you can use the list of 'real' reasons to explain why you have been delaying unecessarily.

So that you see how these reasons actually block you from doing what you have to or want to do, use the following illustration to visualise the reasons more concretely. On one end of the illustration is you and opposite from you is what you want to do. Once again, imagine you are a magnet attracted to the task, represented by a magnet at the top of the drawing. Place a tick next to each of the reasons which describe the different forces which are standing in your way of doing what you want to do.

The Magnetic Theory of Procrastination

TASK YOU WANT
TO ACCOMPLISH

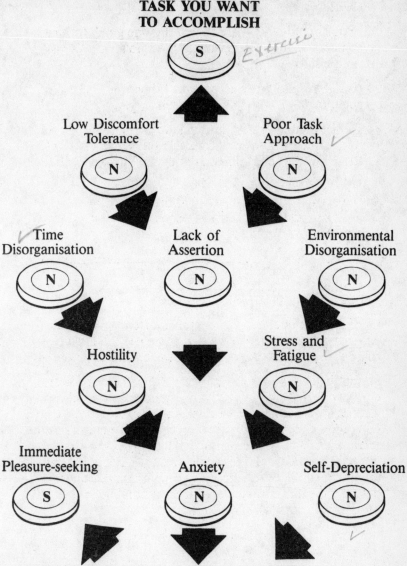

Low Discomfort
Tolerance

Poor Task
Approach

Time
Disorganisation

Lack of
Assertion

Environmental
Disorganisation

Hostility

Stress and
Fatigue

Immediate
Pleasure-seeking

Anxiety

Self-Depreciation

YOU

4

25 of the 'Best' Procrastination Bypass Techniques

"If it were done when 'tis done, then 'twere well it were done quickly."

Willam Shakespeare

Have you heard the expression, "paralysis through analysis"? Sure you have. It means that the more you think about something and try to figure it out, the more likely you are to put off doing it or not do it well. Take the example of wanting to talk to someone who interests you. The more you think about doing it, the less likely you are to do it. You'd be more likely to rationalise your way out of it.

Sometimes the best way to do something you don't feel like doing is to do it without thinking about it too much; do it right away! The more you think, the more likely it is that your anxiety will go up, your frustration or discomfort level will increase, other more appealing activities will occur to you and you will find yourself being diverted.

This chapter presents 25 proven techniques which will help you to procrastinate later. Many appear relatively simple. This is a good thing. Many of them do not require much thought. This is also a good thing because they will help bypass many of the obstacles you may have which make it easier for you to procrastinate. The chapter concludes with a more elaborate "Self-Control Strategy" which can help you procrastinate later.

The techniques described need to be tested. What works for many may not work for you. And, while I will say which

Bypass Techniques work for me, these may not work for you.

Another point to note is that specific Bypass Techniques are appropriate for doing certain things, but not for others. For example, the "Bits and Pieces Approach" helps you to get moving on very large tasks like filling out your tax return or refurbishing a boat. It is not very useful if you wish to assert yourself more with a significant other.

It is, therefore, vital for you to have clearly in mind what it is you wish to start doing. Make sure what you want to achieve is not a 'wandering generality' such as "I want to be more effective at work". By saying effective, you might be referring to different tasks which require different methods. You might mean applying for a promotion, motivating your staff or writing monthly reports. So before continuing, please be sure you have a list of 'meaningful specifics' which you wish to accomplishe more effectively.

Bypass Technique Number 1: The Knock-Out Technique

The harder and more distasteful a task is, the better it is to do it immediately.

This technique is especially useful for doing specific tasks and activities which can be accomplished in one hit and which you tend to put off. Suppose you dilly-dally around in deciding whether to accept invitations. "Should I go or shouldn't I. Will it be okay or a drag?". If deep down you really want more social contact, then rather than spending time analysing the pros and cons and agonising whether you will or won't, as soon as you get asked say "Yes" (or "No") and stick to it.

I find this technique has helped me become more efficient in attending to some small things I used to always delay doing, like paying traffic fines and answering telephone messages. I now do these things immediately and get them out of the way.

The Knock-Out Technique can also be used to get closer to people. I've worked with a number of people who, on the one hand would like to develop their relationships, but who seem to get diverted from doing anything on their own because of their anxiety. They are very unsure of themselves and how their overtures will be received. If this is your situation, when an opportunity presents itself, take a responsible risk and act immediately on your impulse. (You may also want to read the section in Chapter 8 on handling rejection - just in case!).

Bypass Technique Number 2: Worst-first Approach

Identify the most difficult part of the task and do it first.

Sometimes the thing that increases the time it takes to complete a task is getting around to that aspect which you find most difficult to confront. For example, it might take you twice as long to complete a form because you keep avoiding the mathematics required in one of the sections.

So if an activity has different parts to it, find the most difficult part and do it first. If you hate doing overheads for a talk you have to give, do them first and then finish preparing the talk. If you have a number of phonecalls to make, do the hardest one first. Then the others will be a breeze. (If you think that doing the easier ones gets you in the mood for the harder ones, then you wouldn't be putting the harder ones off).

Bypass Technique Number 3: Remember-Forgetting Technique

Whenever you remember forgetting to do a task you've been procrastinating at, do it - at least some of it - immediately.

Let's suppose you've been forgetting to return a call to a friend and you never seem to get around to it. You remember to do it at odd times like when you are driving to work or bathing the kids.

The Remember-Forgetting technique helps to stop the flow of whatever activity you're involved in and gets you started on the task. In the case of the forgotten phone call, whenever you remember to do it, you need to stop what you're doing and make the call. So whether you remember while watching a favourite show on television, showering or making passionate love, yes, stop and make the call!

Bypass Technique Number 4: Bits and Pieces Approach

Do anything in connection with the task you want to accomplish. Gradually do more and more until the task itself doesn't seem so impossible to do.

This approach is good for getting started on tasks or activities which are quite large and overwhelming or a bit stressful. The approach helps you to break the ice and get going. So looking up a phone number may help you to make the phone call. Sharpening a pencil can lead to sitting down and writing. Purchasing new jogging gear may spur you on to actually jog.

Now, the trick to using this approach successfully, is that you can't get hung up on whether you are doing it the right way. You have to take more of a 'trial and error' approach to the activity. If you are a bit uncertain about how to actually attack getting to know and use your new computer, do anything. Read the introduction to the manual. Make a list of important vocabulary you'll need to know. If there is a 'tour' for beginners contained on a disk, try to see, through reading and trial and error, whether you can get it on your screen.

Bypass Technique Number 5: Salami Technique

List all the different steps you have to take to complete a job. Concentrate on taking the first step, then the next, until you complete the full journey.

The philosophy upon which this technique is based is summarised in the maxim: "A problem well stated is a problem half solved". The technique itself appears to have been coined by Edwin Bliss, author of <u>Doing It Now</u>, who compares the contemplation of an overwhelming task with looking at a large uncut salami:

"...It's a huge, crusty, greasy, unappetizing chunk; you don't feel you can get your teeth into it. But when you cut it into thin slices, you transform it into something quite different. Those thin slices are inviting; they make your mouth water, and after you've sampled one slice you tend to reach for another."

Now you don't have to be an afficianado of salami to appreciate the sense of the technique. By breaking down a large task into smaller segments and focusing your attention on one of the segments, the task doesn't seem as awesome and the individual segements have more appeal.

So, if you are facing a task which seems too large and unwieldy, take a few minutes and break it down in to smaller segments. Suppose that, even though you are not known for your green thumb, you want to spruce up your garden - especially the area around the front door. Being an inexperienced gardner, you might put off the task because you're not quite sure where to start. The last time you tried, by simply pulling out the old flowers beds and planting some new flowering shrubs, everything died. Rather than investing your money in acquiring seedlings and new plants and ending up with nothing, you sit around wondering what to do.

The above scenario pretty well describes what I was doing and not doing this past spring. I was starting to procrastinate at planting a new garden area because the task of doing it well, so that things survived, seemed beyond me. The Salami Technique rescued me and at the moment, my garden looks beautiful with flowers in full bloom. To overcome my procrastination, I broke down the task into smaller bits. (I spoke to an expert at my local nursery who helped me analyse my task into various steps). The steps for planting successfully included:

1.   ask an expert for assistance in knowing what to do

2.   prepare the area to be planted with nutrients appropriate for what I was planting. In my case, I was planting rhododendrons so I purchased a bag of gypsum

3.   water in nutrients

4.   after several days, turn the soil over (with fallen leaves) and water in some more nutrients

5.   make sure that the location has the appropriate amount of sunlight and shade

6.   dig holes deep enough so that the top soil of the plant sits just below the surface of the ground. This will ensure the root system will receive enough water

7.   to transplant, remove the plant from its container and carefully untangle roots which might have knitted together

8.   place plant into ground and pack loose dirt around plant firmly

9.   To insure the roots take well, when first watering, add some plant food to the water.

While you may not agree with all these steps, they certainly helped me get off my butt and produce a desired result.

Bypass Technique Number 6: Five-Minute Plan

Take a task you've been procrastinating at and work on it a minimum of five minutes a day. Once you've finished five minutes, then you can set yourself another five minutes and then another.

The Five Minute Plan is a good way of getting started on those activities which are going to take a bit of time. Let's take cleaning the house.

The key to cleaning is overcoming the inertia of getting started. So, whether you are still in your pajamas or decked out in your best leisure gear, get started on cleaning some part of your home for five minutes. (Don't worry about how you are dressed. The thought of having to change into your old cleaning clothes can delay cleaning until the day that you somehow, mysteriously, find yourself already in your cleaning gear).

Now the reason the Five Minute Plan is a good one is that once you get into a job you've been putting off, you will be more motivated to continue either because the task no longer presents itself as being so unpleasant or you are eager to finish. With cleaning, after becoming covered in dirt and dust, you'll often commit yourself to making the area cleaner than ever before and making sure it never gets that way again. (Nothing wrong with a little bit of wishful thinking).

The Five Minute Plan is also useful for those more taxing projects you've been avoiding such as doing some strategic planning at work, writing a chapter for your thesis or book or studying for an exam. Getting yourself going is frequently the key.

Bypass Technique Number 7: Switching

This technique helps you to use the momentum you gain from working on one activity and switch over to another less attractive task you've been procrastinating over.

Switching is based on the maxim which says: "If you want something done, give it to a busy person". Suppose you've just finished doing something enjoyable such as playing a game of squash or working on a tree house for your children. Rather than rest, use the energy you still have to switch over to a more onerous task such as paying bills or cleaning up.

Bypass Technique Number 8: Referenting

Make a list of all the goods things which will happen if you stop procrastinating at important tasks and of all the miserable results of your procrastination.

It's very human to think about the disadvantages of doing something immediately (frustration, discomfort) and the advantages of delaying (immediate pleasure, absence of misery). This tendency makes it especially hard for you to break long-standing bad habits as it destroys any motivation you will need to get going.

Take 'dieting' a subject close to my stomach. To be quite truthful, I used to be a very poor eater in that I over-indulged and found that every six months or so I had to diet. I found it extremely easy to procrastinate at both more sensible eating and going on diets. It used to be that it was only when I couldn't look at myself in the mirror and my wife couldn't get her arms around me that I was motivated to temporarily change my eating habits.

Referenting has helped me put a break on my short-term hedonistic impulses in the area of food consumption. I regularly review the following list of the disadvantages of over-eating and the advantages of sensible eating:

Advantages of sensible eating:

1.   look good

2.   feel good in the morning

3.   more energy

4.   people hold me in higher regard

5.   I don't have to go on crash diets

6.   better health

7.   clothes fit better.

Disadvantages of over-eating:

1.   My wife finds me less appealing

2.   less energy for recreational activities

3.   spend money on second wardrobe

4.   am not practicing what I'm preaching

5.   health suffers.

Referenting is effective if you want to gain control over some strongly ingrained habit such as drinking, smoking, over-eating or excessive partying.

Bypass Technique Number 9: Premack Principle

The Premack Principle is a way of understanding what motivates people to do things they don't enjoy doing. The Premack Principles states that people are more likely to engage in low probability behaviour (say, hanging up clothes when arriving home) if what immediately follows the low probability behaviour is high probability behaviour (something which they enjoy and engage in often, such as having a snack).

The Premack Principle is often used to modify someone elses' inappropriate behaviour. For example, you might have an adolescent who comes home from school, dumps his book bag just inside the door and leaves a trail of his school clothes through the house to his bedroom. Your child may then get into some more comfortable clothes and head straight for the refrigerator. To motivate your child to be neater and to put things away, you can have a rule that they are not allowed to have any snacks until after they have put things away. If you wanted to get even tougher, you could hide their favourite footwear (e.g., Reeboks) and inform them that they can have them back only after they've put things away.

Now you can apply the Premack Principle to motivate yourself to stop procrastinating. To do this, you have to identify the job you tend to put off as well as some type of reinforcer you enjoy. Do not allow yourself the chosen enjoyable reinforcer until after you've done the job. So, for example, you could withhold your favourite book from yourself until after you've done your exercise.

Bypass Technique Number 10: Getting a Round Tuit

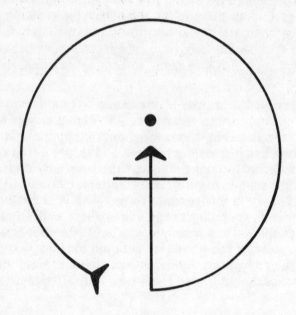

a "round tuit"

"I'll get a round to it" you say and promptly do something else. Getting a 'round tuit' can be the hardest thing in the world for some people. If it is for you, here is a 'round tuit'. Now get on with what you've said you'll do.

Bypass Technique Number 11: Face the Music

Procrastination can be self-perpetuating when you find it hard to admit to yourself and to others that you have been delaying something which you said you'd do. However, when you do eventually face the music, the criticism and pain that you predict will actually be less than more.

A page out of my own book - so to speak. A while ago I had committed myself to delivering a book to my publisher by a certain date. As the days wore on and the deadline passed, I had not written much and could see that my manuscript was going to be very overdue. For several months I avoided facing the music by not telling my publisher. I think I imagined that somehow the book would be written over-night and that I would deliver it. As time wore on I began to feel ashamed and guilty. I knew then it was time to face the music. I telephoned my publisher to make an appointment. When we met he thought the reason I wanted to have the meeting was to back out of the book altogether. When he learned that I just wanted an extension he was greatly relieved and happy to extend my deadline. He was pleased with me being upfront and so was I.

Bypass Technique Number 12: Swap Out Technique

This technique was recommended to me by a lawyer who was attending one of my recent workshops on procrastination. He said that his firm had a policy that, if one of its members was working on something and was, after some time, getting stuck, rather than procrastinating about doing it they could ask someone else at the firm, who had the time, to give them a hand to break their mental log jam. So that the arrangement wasn't perceived to be one-sided, the person who provided some help could, the next time he or she was stuck, approach the other person for help. He reported that the Swap Out Technique improved his firm's efficiency.

Bypass Technique Number 13: Peak Performance Time

Schedule the task or activity you've been putting off at a time when you are most alert, rested and energised.

Charles Kozoll has written about a condition which busy people suffer from called the "battered mind syndrome". It describes people who, because of having many thoughts at one time and worrying about what has to be done, lose their concentration on their task at hand and thereby, waste time. Not only does this syndrome result in you taking much longer to finish a task because you use less of your 'brain power'; the end result is often quite ordinary.

Kozoll offers the following six-step process for enhancing your concentration and, thereby, overcoming your tendency to procrastinate.

1.   Select a task, time and place where your energy is high and there is less chance of interruption.

2.   Write down and rehearse a simple message to yourself which clarifies the importance of centering on the task such as: "Now concentrate, what do I have to do?"

3.   Relax for a moment by taking a few slow, deep breaths or relaxing your muscles.

4.   Develop a mental picture of what the final product will look like.

5.   Take a few deep breaths which will help you 'lock in' to the task just as athletes do before a competitive event.

6.   In order to establish persistence towards task completion, you should say a motivational message to yourself such as: "I'm going to finish this task, now!".

Controlling your concentration will result in heightened intensity and arousal which will enhance your ability to complete the task in as short a time as possible.

Bypass Technique Number 14: Do It, Delegate It, Ditch It

In discussing this technique for managing paperwork, Edward Bliss provides the observation that "if you leave two pieces of paper on a desk at the end of the day, in the morning there will be four. The little rascals breed overnight!".

The idea behind this technique is that you will procrastinate less often if you leave as few loose ends as possible from one day to the next. This idea should apply not only at work, but also at home. Instead of getting in the habit of leaving things until you get a "round tuit" or putting things away temporarily, it is a good policy to deal with things immediately.

On my desk at work, I receive quite a few memos and letters which request me to take some form of action, and professional journals and articles to be read. I have recently developed into the habit of making sure I have a clean desk every evening before I go home. I have four plastic file compartments stacked on top of each other sitting on the right hand front corner of my desk. The top one is labelled "Today's Work", the second "For Filing", the third "Tomorrow's Work" and the fourth is the all-important "Out Basket". I also have a folder located on the shelf behind my desk where I keep material I should read. As soon as I collect my mail, I sort through it, placing things where they belong, passing on those things which others should be acting on and trashing the trivial.

This technique has not only made me more organised in dealing with my mail, it's also freed me to get on to other pressing activities. And the best outcome of all is arriving the next morning to begin work on a clean desk.

Bypass Technique Number 15: Establish Priorities

I think it a fair comment to say that if you consider all the different activities you are supposed to do every day there is simply not enough time to do everything. The result is a type of procrastination that is literally beyond your control because of the lack of enough hours in the day. So it is important for you to have a clear idea which are the most important things to get done and which are the less important. Knowing the important ones will enable you to concentrate your efforts and procrastinate at the less important tasks.

Charles Kozoll in his book <u>Time Management for Educators</u> offers an organising routine which I think everyone can find useful.

1. Identify all the work to be done and sort it into three groups: A-highest priority, B-important, C-routine or trivial.

2. Take the B items and divide them, putting about 20% in the A group and the remainder in the C group.

3. Now take the larger C group and divide it into two groups, perhaps 30% to 40% in C1 and the remainder in C2.

4. Take the C2 items and put them away.

5. Place all C1 items in a folder; when a folder becomes too thick, work on some of them.

6. Review the C1 folder one or two times each day to be sure items with a deadline are finished on schedule.

Kozoll's priority setting routine helps you to accomplish your highest priority activities first and ensures that, if you are to procrastinate, the tasks you'll put off (Folder C2) will result in the least negative consequences for you.

Bypass Technique Number 16: Establishing a Set Time

Scheduling a fixed time to begin your work may be of more help in getting started than organising your work according to priorities. Sometimes you can spend heaps of time setting out your goals, describing activities to achieve the goals and prioritising these activities and still find that you are procrastinating. If this is the case with you, you might find that allocating a specific time to a job will be more productive. Once you have committed yourself to a time, if you also use the Worst-First or Bits and Pieces approaches, you might find that you get into a routine of acting rather than procrastinating.

Bypass Technique Number 17: Change Your Environment

Sometimes the time of day and your location can seem to trigger bad habits. Your mind and body get used to acting a certain way in certain situations, circumstances and with particular people and that way may be procrastination. For example, 5.30pm at home might automatically signal to you 'snack time' even though you have decided to curb between-meal snacks. Or, perhaps, sitting at your desk primes you to do what's in front of you, including answering the telephone, rather than doing strategic planning.

Sometimes, making simple changes in your environment can help you give up bad habits. You might decide to make sure that at 5.30pm you are out jogging or at the library, well away from the cues at home which signal food and eating. At work, you might decide to do certain types of work at your desk and other types in a conference room. Clearing your desk of everything save the bare essentials and having the secretary hold your calls might also interrupt the automatic chain of behaviours which block you from your higher priority activities.

Bypass Technique Number 18: Isolation

This procedure I have found extremely effective in helping me to get started and finish tasks which require sustained periods of effort lasting over days and weeks. Take notice. It is a very hard procedure to implement. Hard on you, hard on others.

I have found that I am more likely to procrastinate when their are sources of enjoyment and pleasure freely available. And for me, these sources tend to be my family. I am much more likely to 'close down shop' if I know that waiting for me at home are my family to play with and talk to and a nice meal. One of my main causes of procrastination is pleasure-seeking, I admit and I am drawn away from high priority activities towards the more pleasurable ones.

I use Isolation at times when I have a lot of important work to get done which, for me, tends to be finishing writing a chapter or book or outlining a workshop I have to give. When I find myself behind the proverbial eight-ball, I ask my family to go on a holiday to visit friends or family. I find that by isolating myself from distractions, my efficiency is dramatically increased. I can also spend longer periods of time on what I have to do without interruption.

So if you can isolate yourself by inviting your significant others to go away, timing yourself out from others at work, or identifying a room at home or at work where you can isolate yourself, then you might be able to make inroads into tasks you've been putting off doing.

Of course, given that most of us are social animals with attendant responsibilities, it will take the good-will of others to enable you to take a holiday from your usual responsibilities. Isolation requires a supportive environment and good negotiation skills on your part.

Bypass Technique Number 19: Visible Reminders

Another technique for modifying your environment, so that you will be more likely to work at particular tasks, is to display a small or large sign at work or home which contains words which remind you there is a job to be done. The use of visible reminders make it harder for the "out of sight, out of mind" principle to operate. The following mottos or sayings have been used to motivate people to procrastinate later.

* "Do, don't stew."

* "Doing gets it done."

* "Do it now."

* "Do the worst first."

* "He who rests, rots."

- "Is it not often your biggest problem and obstacle: To Get Started?"

- "From this day, expect great things and work enthusiastically on it."

- "Problems can form a mountain that blocks the light. Cut it to little pieces and light will come through."

- "Success is not giving up. Failure is giving up too quickly."

- "Our main business is not to see what lies dimly at a distance, but to do what clearly lies at hand."

Bypass Technique Number 20: Monitoring

Richard Nelson Bolles in his popular book on job-hunting What Color is Your Parachute, describes how confiding in and seeking support from someone else can help you better tolerate the frustration and unpleasantness associated with finding jobs.

"Decide whom you know (spouse, roomate, friend, etc.) that you can take into your confidence about this. Tell them what you need to do, the hours it will take, and how much you need them to keep you at this task. Then put down in your appointment book a regular weekly date when they will guarantee to meet with you, check you out on what you've done already, and be very stern with you if you've done little or nothing since your previous week's meeting. The more a taskmaster this confidant is, the better."

Monitoring can be a useful support. If you view your monitor's contribution as being supportive of your efforts and not as someone either to provide you with answers or to do the work for you, then it would seem to be that by taking someone who you greatly respect into your confidence you will be more likely to work at winning their approval and hence, procrastinate later.

Bypass Technique Number 21: Guided Imagery

For some people, visualising getting a task done can actually lead to its successful completion. This is especially the case for activities where you might lack confidence or experience anxiety.

The key to using visualisation successfully is to form very vivid and real pictures of you completing a task using as many of your senses as possible. Visualise every aspect of the activity.

Suppose you've been putting off asking your boss for a promotion. You can never seem to find the right time and there is always something you believe you can still do to improve your chances of getting the promotion. You could use guided imagery to help program your mind to achieve what you want to be able to say and do. Start off by lying or sitting in a comfortable position with your eyes closed. Relax as much as you can breathing slowly and deeply through your nose. When you feel relaxed, picture yourself as if you were actually getting ready to enter your bosses office. See his secretary behind her desk and hear her invite you to go in. See yourself in the clothes you think will create a good impression and feel yourself getting up and walking into his office and taking a seat. Look around his office taking in all prominent features including the carpet, pictures on the wall and equipment on his desk. Imagine and feel what the room temperature would be. Feel you hands confidently grasp the arms of the chair you are sitting in. When asked what's on your mind, feel yourself being relaxed and confident. Look your boss directly in the eye and in a firm, controlled voice, state each of the reasons why you think you deserve your particular promotion. See your boss listening to your explanation as he leans back in his chair. (You can choose to visualise different outcomes of your request from him enthusiastically agreeing with your proposal, to asking for time to consider your request and even having your proposal rejected outright!).

Guided Imagery works best if you use it every day. It can be used for any task which you have difficulty completing. Sometimes it takes several tries before you can vividly form pictures of the activity you would like to complete.

Bypass Technique Number 22: Rational-Emotive Imagery

This technique, popularised by Maxie Maultsby and Albert Ellis, is designed to help you remove the discomfort that is blocking you from initiating some action. With practice, rational-emotive imagery (REI) can give you greater power over your discomfort levels thereby increasing the chances that you'll stop procrastinating.

I'll describe how REI can be used to help you stop avoiding public speaking. As I'll indicate, REI consists of you forming two seperate images. Here are the directions:

"I want you to imagine that you are going to give a talk to your colleagues on some of your work and that you are sitting at the head of the table just before you begin. I want you to imagine that you are extremely nervous and uptight, as uptight as you can be about having to give the talk. Take a minute and see if you can get in touch with these uncomfortable feelings ...

"Now this time, I want you to imagine the same scene. Once again you are sitting down at the head of the conference table before having to give the talk but this time I want you not to feel as nervous and tense. Make yourself feel less uptight, calmer, concerned about how you'll be received, but not off the wall. Take as much time as you need to change your feelings. You can do it ...

"Now that you have been able to change your feelings so that you were not so worried, think about how you were able to achieve this."

In REI, people spontaneously come up with a variety of ways they can gain control over their feelings. Some report that they just relaxed themselves while others report that they changed the way they were thinking about the task and, for example, stopped blowing it out of proportion. You can use REI to reduce a variety of procrastination-creating negative feelings such as anxiety, extreme frustration about having to do the task, and even guilt about having delayed the task.

Bypass Technique Number 23: The Catastrophe Scale

This popular technique is designed to help you keep things in perspective. When you delay doing something, you frequently blow the unpleasantness and frustration of doing the activity or task out of proportion. When you think about having to clean up, do the ironing, assert yourself with an un-cooperative colleague, you can blow the 'badness' of having to do the event out of proportion. Rather than just thinking to yourself: "I really don't like doing this. It's a pain in the bum but it's not the worst thing I could be doing", instead you tell yourself "I can't stand doing this. This is terrible and awful to do - the worst thing in the world."

To use this technique, think about a time when you are procrastinating at something. Be specific as to what you're putting off. At the time you are putting it off, how bad is it for you to have to do the task on a scale of 1 to 100 where 100 is the worst thing in the world and one is the most favoured. Think of a number between 1 and 100.

Now look at the scale of catastrophes below. Where on the scale would you put having to do the task you've been putting off?

Catastrophe Scale

100	World war; death of a loved one; life-threatening illness; permanent paralysis
90	You have a serious car accident; house burns down; family member very ill; you are fired from job; you break your leg; house burgled
50	You break an antique vase; you have a fight with a friend
10	You have a flat tyre
0	

When most people apply the Catastrophe Scale to their procrastination, they can see that they have been blowing the unpleasantness of having to do the task or activity way out of proportion. At the same time, they put having to do some activity at the top of the Catastrophe Scale. Then, when they've had a chance to view things in perspective, they place their procrastinating task somewhere lower down the Scale. They see that while having to do some activity like give a talk or assert ones self - or do the ironing for that matter - may be hard, it is not a catastrophe.

Bypass Technique Number 24: Paradoxical Intention

Paradoxical Intention is recommended if you strongly believe that there is nothing you can do about your procrastination. That is, the cause of your procrastination is beyond your control and, therefore, there is nothing you can do. If you believe that you are powerless to do anything to improve your procrastination, let me suggest the following activities:

1.   Procrastinate to the best of your ability for a week. Continue to put off as many important and unimportant jobs and activities as you can.

2.   Observe your procrastination for a week. Keep track of how often and for how long you procrastinate at different tasks. Keep careful recording of what you procrastinate at, where and for how long.

These two activities will hopefully provide you with evidence that you have some direct influence over your procrastination. You may find, for example, that you are able to procrastinate more by encouraging yourself to, which demonstrates that you do have power over it. Or you might find that by having to observe your procrastination, you actually procrastinate less, once again proving you can exercise control over yourself if you so choose.

Paradoxical Intention can also involve exaggeration and humour to prove that you can change if you so choose. In his book, <u>Do It Now</u>, Bill Knaus provides a dialogue you can carry out with yourself to shed some light on the real causes of your procrastination:

"You poor soul, you really can't handle discomfort. You really have a good reason to doubt yourself because in truth you are helpless to fight your urges. These urges are too big and strong for you to give in to them and keep giving in to them. Feel good for the moment. Your living in the moment is all that matters now. Don't look to the next moment. You won't be able to handle that one any better than you are handling this moment. So why bother trying?".

Bypass Technique Number 25: Behavioural Self-Control

If you are interested in a more systematic strategy to tackle your procrastination, then Behavioural Self-Control might be the answer. My review of the research in the area of procrastination reveals that, not only is Behavioural Self-Control one of the most widely researched techniques, it is also one of the most effective.

Before you can use the technique, you have to define very concretely and precisely what task, activity, job or behaviour you would like to improve; that is, what have you been putting off. Once you have a task identified, then you can apply the four stages of this widely used strategy.

1.   **Goal Setting.** Set a specific goal for yourself in terms of how much change you would like to observe in your behaviour. Make your initial goals realistic. Set goals at minimum levels (e.g., <u>at least</u> two hours a night studying). The goals change over time after you achieve your initial goal.

2.   **Environmental Control.** Make whatever changes to your environment you think necessary to improve your working conditions (see Bypass Techniques 17-19).

3.   **Self-Observation.** Keep track of how often you engage in the desired behaviour. The data you record

can vary from the amount of time you spend on the job to how often you engage in the activity.

4.   **Self-Rewards/Self-Penalties**. Self-Rewards involve giving yourself something you enjoy after you have achieved your goal. Self-Penalties are not permitting yourself something you enjoy if you haven't achieved your goal.

An example of a Behavioural Self-Control program in the area of studying more would be as follows (Week 1).

1.   **Goal-Setting.** I want to study at least two hours each night.

2.   **Environmental Control.** I will make my study area as organised and free from distractions as possible. I'll make sure I have all the important study materials, notes and resources.

3.   **Self-Observation.** Record the actual amount of time I spend studying.

4.   **Self-Reward/Self-Penalty.** Reward myself with watching a special news show on television each day I study more than two hours. On those days I study less than two hours, I will not allow myself to read from my favourite book.

Behavioural Self-Control can also be used if you want to stop engaging in a bad habit. Here is an example of a Behavioural Self-Control program designed to help someone stop procrastinating at giving up smoking (Week 1).

1.   **Goal Setting.** I want to smoke 10 cigarettes less each day than I currently do for a whole week (70 cigarettes down from 80).

2.   **Environmental Control.** I will spend less time in situations where I and others generally smoke.

3.   **Self-Observation.** Number of cigarettes smoked daily.

4.   **Self-Reward/Self-Penalty.** For each day that I
      smoke 70 or less, I will reward myself with
      putting $2 into a jar which I will use just for
      myself when I go on holiday. For each day that
      I smoke more than 70 cigarettes, I will force
      myself to clean the toilet.

Bill was startled by the alarm clock. He pried his eyes
open and saw it was 6 am. He took a swipe at the off
nob and only succeeded in knocking over his glass of
water on his bed side table. He finally managed to pull
the clock's cord out of the electrical socket. "Who the
Hell put the bleeping alarm on?", snarled Bill.

Denise stirred from her sleep. "You did, darling.
Remember, your jogging routine. Your idea. Now let
me go back to sleep."

Bill cursed himself under his breath. "Bloody fool. So
I am a bit overweight. What do you expect. I'll be 40
in 6 weeks. Everyone puts on a bit of weight in their
middle age." Bill turned over to go back to asleep but
was interrupted by another little voice inside his head.

"C'mon Billie Boy. You haven't put on 'a bit' of
weight. You're a FAT SLOB, a VERY BIG FAT
SLOB!! And if you want to look good for your 40th
birthday party next month, you've got a bit of work to
do, pal."

"You're no pal of mine", thought Bill.

Bill did, however, agree with the voice of reason. He
was well over the top and couldn't get into clothes he
could fit into only last year. Drastic measures were
needed if he was to look at all presentable for his 40th.
But the pain of it all!

Bill looked over at his wife sleeping. "How come she
hasn't put on any weight. She's as attractive and slim
as the day I married her. All I want to do is to snuggle
up to her. Not get out of bed."

This was a pretty typical conflict for Bill. On the one hand, wanting to look attractive and be fit, but on the other, loving to eat.

Denise, being the ever supportive wife, sensed her husband's predicament. "Darling, sweet heart, if you don't get your backside out of bed now, you're not getting 'any' for a week".

"Any 'what'?", Bill asked, full knowing what she had in mind.

"Any of my sweet body, that's what, now hop to it!". Denise almost laughed out loud. She could be real tough if she wanted to be.

"Hey, that's dirty pool," whined Bill.

"It's literally up to you. I'm going back to sleep."

Bill grabbed for his watch which read 6.14am. "Hm, still have enough time to do it if I want to", thought Bill. "And I now clearly see the disadvantages of staying in bed and the advantages in going jogging. Look, the worst thing about doing this is getting out of bed. C'mon, Big Bill, shake it now!".

Actions Speak Louder Than Words

Now is the time to stop stewing and start doing. Using the Knock-Out Technique, knock over at least one of those tasks you've been procrastinating at.

Over the next week, study your mental and physical energy levels to determine your peak performance time. Also notice the conditions around you to determine whether your peak performance time is sabatoged by environmental distractions.

Finally, the 25 Bypass Procrastination Techniques can be grouped into sub-categories which help you attack your procrastination in different ways.

Category 1. Bypass Techniques to Help You Get Started:
>   1, 2, 3, 4, 5, 6, 7, 10, 12

Category 2. Bypass Techniques to Help You Use Time Better:
>   13, 14, 15, 16

Category 3. Bypass Techniques to Help You Get Motivated:
>   8, 9, 21, 24, 25

Category 4. Bypass Techniques to Help You Deal with Discomfort:
>   11, 22, 23

Category 5. Bypass Techniques to Help Improve Your Environment:
>   17, 18, 19, 20

From each of these categories, select one Bypass Technique which sounds like it might work for you. Try to put each of them into action.

5

Managing Your Anxiety and Self-Depreciation

That job I had in the White House, it wasn't so very different from other jobs, I didn't let it worry me. Worrying never does any good. So I've never worried about things much. The only thing I've worried about is to be sure that where I'm responsible that the job is properly done. I've always tried my best and to some extent have succeeded in doing the job as well as it's been done before me.

Harry S. Truman, 33rd President of the United States

One of the foremost causes of procrastination is anxiety. The reason for this is quite simple. Anxiety contains elements of fear and discomfort and, given that human beings have an aversion to both, they will tend to remove themselves from the proximity of tasks, activities and people which lead to such feelings. The more anxiety, the more you are likely to be diverted away from the task which you associate with anxiety.

Now the cause of your anxiety is both biological and psychological. You were born with a constitutional make-up which leads you to experience anxiety in a particular way when you are confronted with negative demands and threats. The amount of anxiety you experience and how long it lasts partly depends on your constitutional make-up. Your anxiety response to an event will often be different from another person's response because of each of your biological-proneness to anxiety. However, we now know that anxiety is also strongly influenced by thoughts and attitudes and that people bring with them to their world certain attitudes and beliefs which make it more likely that they will experience high anxiety and, as a consequence, avoid certain tasks. This is especially the case if they have low discomfort tolerance.

This chapter is designed to give you more power over your anxiety and, therefore, more power over that type of procrastination which is caused by your anxiety. Your increased power will come from greater understanding as to why you experience anxiety and from learning techniques for reducing your anxiety.

The final part of this chapter will discuss the cause of, and cures for, self-depreciation. Self-depreciation leads people to believe they are inferior and unworthy, conditions which maximize the likelihood of procrastination. You'll have a chance to examine whether you are a self-depreciator and learn new ways of thinking about yourself.

The ABC's of Anxiety and Its Management

People are not disturbed by events but by the view they have of events.

Epictetus, Roman Philosopher, 2nd Century A.D.

Let's imagine that two young men are preparing to go to the same party to which they've been invited. Ryan and Ian are both 24 years old and are employed as engineers; Ryan at the state's electricity commission and Ian at his city's board of works department. Both are of similar intelligence, come from families where they are the second child each having an older sister and both have similar education and religious backgrounds. Both Ryan and Ian are eligible bachelors and each would like to meet someone and form a relationship. Let's listen in on what they are thinking as they prepare to go to that night's party.

Ryan: "I really don't like parties where I don't know many people. The first hour can be a real drag until I meet someone to talk to. I hope there'll be some interesting females there who I can talk to. I'll just go and see how I get involved and have a good time." With these thoughts, Ryan would be most likely to experience some nervousness about the party - and possibly some curiosity as well. He'd probably walk into the party with butterflies in his stomach which would, after a while, settle down.

Ian: "I really don't like parties where I don't know many people. I always get so uptight. I hate standing around feeling nervous and uptight. If I do see someone who looks interesting I'll get so nervous I'll go hide or, if I try to say something, I'll just sound stupid. She'd probably just laugh at me and think I was a nerd. What's the point of even going? Rather than putting myself through all of that, I'll just stay home and watch MTV." With these thoughts, Ian would feel extremely nervous. He would be nervous not only about being rejected, but also about being nervous.

The common conception that people have is that their emotions are caused by events or circumstances. This relationship is really a misconception.

MISCONCEPTION

Events ⟶ Emotions

If this were true, then both Ryan and Ian would feel exactly the same about going to a party, about their anxiety, and about the possibility of being rejected. But, as the above example clearly shows, they don't and the reason is that they have different attitudes towards the party and what might happen at the party.

REALITY

Events ⟷ Attitudes ⟶ Emotions

And why am I talking about emotions? Because you tend to avoid situations when you feel high anxiety and discomfort. And this type of avoidance is synonomous with procrastination.

PROCRASTINATION

Threatening/ Frustrating Events	Stressful Attitudes	High Anxiety Extreme Discomfort	Avoidance and Procrastination
⟷	⟶	⟶	

If you want to procrastinate later at tasks you've been putting off because of the anxiety you experience when you think about doing them, then modify the different attitudes which increase your anxiety in the first place.

I place a great deal of emphasis on attitudes because they are the things which give rise to negative thinking which create high anxiety and discomfort. The thoughts that Ian has about going to the party are strongly influenced by 'approval-seeking attitudes' such as "No one will want to speak to me. If I start to talk to someone they'll think I'm a geek and that would be awful." These thoughts lead to high anxiety and procrastination.

Getting In Touch With Your Anxiety: Self-Awareness

The first and most important step in managing stress and its harmful effects is recognizing that it exists and the individual is fully capable of managing it.

Sheldon Greenberg, <u>Stress and The Teaching</u>
<u>Profession</u>, 1984

What needs to be said about anxiety is that some people are better at knowing when they are anxious than others. They are aware of their muscle tenseness, shallow breathing, rapid heart beating, flushing etcetera. However, for many different reasons, you can fail to detect anxiety even when it is there. Other people may see anxiety in your face, the sound of your voice and your posture. Sometimes, even others are not aware of your anxiety.

There are people who show definite physiological signs of anxiety and arousal which do not register in their conscious mind. This may be because they are into their heads a great deal and are not sensitive to cues that they are anxious.

You might be wondering why, if so much of anxiety is caused by people's attitudes and thoughts, that they are not aware of their anxiety-creating thinking. This is a good question. The answer has to do with the fact that much of our thinking is subconscious; that is, we are not immediately aware of what we are thinking. Our thinking tends to be fairly automatic. And unless someone invites us to pay particular attention to our thoughts, we don't as a rule do so. And becoming aware of your thinking is a skill which can take quite a while to acquire.

The point I want to make is that for you to be able to change attitudes which are causing you unecessary anxiety and procrastination, you must first become aware of your signs of anxiety. You will also need to practice becoming more aware of your thinking as you become anxious in certain situations. Without self-awareness, it will be almost impossible for these procedures to reduce your anxiety.

One other point about detecting your anxiety surrounding having to perform certain tasks. You can sometimes divert yourself so quickly from confronting a potentially anxiety-provoking activity that you may have little time to experience anxiety. In thinking about confronting a negative colleague, the rationalisation "It's not really that important to say anything. It doesn't really matter." will divert you away from the anxiety you may well experience in asserting yourself. When asked to report on your anxiety, you'll report little. The *mañana* principle can also block you from feeling any anxiety about doing something important such as introducing yourself to someone or sending back a steak that has been poorly prepared at a restaurant. "I'll do it later. I'll do it next time."

Below is a list of physical symptoms which may suggest you are experiencing anxiety and possibly don't know it. I've organised the list of symptoms into different physiological systems. Look over the list and see if you can identify your typical physical symptoms when you are under stress.

Cardiovascular

- heart pounding
- high blood pressure
- erratic heart beat
- dizziness
- cold, sweaty hands
- heart racing
- headaches (throbbing pain)
- palpitations

Respiratory

- rapid, erratic or shallow breathing
- shortness of breath
- difficulty in breathing because of poor breath control
- asthma

Gastrointestinal

- upset stomach
- sharp abdominal pains
- diarrhea
- nausea, vomiting, cramps
- constipation

Muscular

- headaches) (steady pain
- arthritis
- nervous ticks
- stuttering
- jaw pain
- neck, back, shoulder, chest pains
- muscular tremors, hand shaking
- frowning
- grinding, clenching teeth
- finger or foot tapping

Skin

- acne
- dandruff
- perspiration
- excessive dryness skin/hair

Immunity

- allergy flare up
- catching the flu
- skin rash
- hives
- catching colds
- general, lowered immunity
- low grade infection

Metabolic

- increased appetite
- feeling of increased nervousness
- increased craving for tobacco or sweets

Sometimes, your anxiety surrounding performing a particular activity and your consequent procrastination may be more evident to you from your psychological symptoms which can be seen in both emotional and cognitive reactions.

Emotional Symptoms

— not feeling in control

— extreme panic lasting more than a few days

— feeling not able to cope

— feelings of doubt, poor confidence and insecurity

— feeling desperate

— feeling tired, listless and emotionally drained

Cognitive Symptoms

— poor concentration

— poor memory and forgetfullness

— indecisiveness

— poor problem solving ability

— mental confusion

— irrational thinking

— poor self-image

— racing thoughts

— difficulty falling and staying asleep

So when you think about the task your procrastinating at, consider whether it is one where other people are likely to make judgements; such as giving a public talk, asserting yourself with a colleague or relative or studying for exams. Then, ask yourself whether there is any evidence that you are putting off the task because of your avoidance of the anxiety you feel when you think about doing it. If you are putting off any task for reasons of anxiety, then the following discussion of the different types of anxiety will help you gain further insight into yourself and ways of modifying your anxiety.

Fear of Failure and Perfectionism

Those who have conquered doubt and fears have conquered failure.

James Allen, U.S. novelist

One of the most basic of human desires is to be achieving and successful in one or more areas of one's life. And this is a very sensible desire for, when you are being successful in using your talents and abilities, you will usually experience significant amounts of intrinsic pleasure, satisfaction and happiness. This is, afterall, the basic motivation to achieve.

It is, therefore, extremely self-defeating for a person to procrastinate at tasks which, if they mastered, would bring with them significant satisfaction. And yet, significant numbers of people avoid attempting such tasks. You might be someone who finds it very difficult to take on new responsibilities at work and procrastinates at making important decisions.

Several years ago, I worked with an extremely talented graphic designer and illustrator who had won several major awards for her illustrations of stamps. As she became quite successful in her field, she expressed the desire to branch out and start to paint and work on a larger scale than her normal work demanded. She believed quite rightly that she had a rare talent for humour and colour and wished to know whether she was good enough to be successful in the art world. When I first met Roberta, she expressed a number of concerns about where her life was going, including the fact that she had not followed through with her ambitions and was delaying starting to make the transition to working with a larger medium. Roberta explained her procrastination as being caused by the ever-increasing demand of her graphic design work and that she simply did not have the time.

While it was partly true that Roberta had less time available to devote to painting because of increased popularity, her good fortune became for Roberta a convenient rationalisation for procrastinating at doing what she really desired to do, which was to paint. In trying to give Roberta insight into the 'real' reasons for her procrastination, I helped her get in touch with the anxiety she experienced as she thought about making time for her painting. She described sensations of discomfort including tenseness and shallow breathing as she imagined painting. I asked her: "So when you think about starting to paint, you get anxious because ...?".

Roberta thought for awhile and then said: "Because maybe it wouldn't be very good. Maybe my skills wouldn't be as good as they could be?" "And if they were not?", I asked. "That would be terrible. I couldn't stand it!" replied Roberta. "Because?" I gently probed. "Because my work must be good and if it isn't, that would show I'm really a no-hoper."

What became apparent to Roberta was that she was being diverted from her painting because of her anxiety and the thing that was driving her anxiety upwards was her 'need' to be successful in her work. Roberta also experienced low discomfort tolerance which led her to avoid tasks where she had to endure high amounts of discomfort and frustration. More on this in the next chapter.

Recently, I worked with Barry, the owner of a very successful restaurant, who was complaining that over the past few years he had missed out on business opportunities because he was overly cautious in committing his money. "I had the money to spend and if I had, I'd have made a packet and been able to move on to new and more exciting projects. Instead, I waited until I was totally sure of getting my money back and by that time, it was too late."

Indecisiveness is a type of procrastination which is motivated out of a fear of failure. In discussing this relationship with Barry, he became aware that, for as long as he could remember, he was very conservative when it came to making business decisions and the thing he feared the most when faced with a decision was not the actual loss of money but rather that he would make a mistake. Fear of mistake-making can disrupt your natural journey towards trying out and accomplishing more difficult and challenging tasks which, when achieved, would bring you instrinsic satisfaction. The fear of making mistakes acts as a negative

force diverting you from things you know deep within
yourself you would be best to take on.

So why do people like Roberta and Barry fear failure? The
reason has to do with their attitude and thoughts about
completing the task. There are three particular ones which
lead to high anxiety. Let's deal with them one at a time.

**"I must be successful all the time in everything important
that I do."**

Now on the face of it, this idea seems reasonable. Aren't
you supposed to strive hard for success? Yes, indeed! The
trap in the above idea is in the word 'must.' It is, for the
reasons discussed above, quite sensible to desire and
strongly prefer success. However, when you take that rational strong desire and convert it into an irational demand
of having to be successful all the time, then you are setting
yourself up for high levels of anxiety. What the above
attitude often does is to place too much pressure on yourself
to be successful. As well, the notion that you must be
successful all the time further increases your anxiety because you know from past experience that it is only a matter
of time before you make a mistake (all humans are mistake-
makers some of the time).

So the above attitude starts to generate high anxiety and
can result in you (as it did for Roberta and Barry) avoiding
'worrying' tasks. If you endorse such a tyrannical belief, ask
yourself the question: "Where is it written that I **must** be
successful all the time? Is there a law of the Universe which
says that I have to always be successful and never make a
mistake?" Of course, when you look at it rationally, there
is plenty of evidence of people encouraging us to be successful, but no one really assumes that it is possible for
anyone to be always successful.

"It is terrible to not be achieving and make mistakes."

The more you believe that making mistakes at things you
set out to do is horrible and terrible, some kind of real
catastrophe, the more likely you will be to experience high
anxiety and, therefore, either perform the task poorly or
procrastinate at getting around to doing the task. In the
above scenarios, Roberta and Barry literally create their

own anxiety by telling themselves how totally bad it would be for them to make a mistake or not be successful.

To help people like Roberta and Barry modify their 'awfulising' about not doing well or making mistakes, I ask: "Compared to becoming permanently paralysed, having a heart attack, having someone in your immediate family suffering an incurable disease, your house burning down, getting fired or going bankrupt, how bad is making a mistake in this particular situation?". I further point out that the words terrible and awful mean 100 percent bad or worse and ask whether that's how they would evaluate making a mistake.

"To make a mistake or fail would make me a failure."

I'll have a great deal to say about this anxiety-creating attitude shortly. Briefly, in equating your total self-worth with your performance, you are putting your ego on the line every time you set out to achieve something and by so doing, you imbue the task with unhealthy anxiety. And given the belief that you **must** do well, and that if you don't you're no good, it is better to procrastinate and do nothing than to risk the possibility of failure and finding out that you are worthless. Learning to accept yourself with your imperfections is a key attitude to overcoming procrastination.

In case you would like to know the extent to which you have a high need for achievement relative to others in the general population, you can complete the following Need for Achievement Scale. After answering the questions, you can compare your score with the average score of members of the population in general.

The directions to complete the scale are as follows:

Here are a set of statements which describe what some people think and believe. Read each statement carefully and decide how much you agree or disagree with it.

If you **strongly agree** with the statement, circle 5

If you **agree** circle 4

If you are **neutral** circle 3

If you **disagree** circle 2

If you **strongly disagree** circle 1

Need For Achievement Scale

	Strongly Disagree	Dis- Agree	Neutral	Strongly Agree	Agree
1. It's unbearable to fail at important things and I can't stand not succeeding at them.	1	2	3	4	5
2. If you do not perform well at things that are important, it will be a catastrophe.	1	2	3	4	5
3. I must do well at important things, and I will not accept it if I do not do well.	1	2	3	4	5
4. It's awful to do poorly at some important things, and I think it is a catastrophe if I do poorly.	1	2	3	4	5
5. I can't stand not doing well at tasks which are important to me.	1	2	3	4	5
6. It's essential to well at essential jobs; so I must do well at these things.	1	2	3	4	5
7. I cannot tolerate not doing well at important tasks and it is unbearable to fail.	1	2	3	4	5
8. If I do not perform well at things which are important, it will be a catastrophe.	1	2	3	4	5
9. I must be successful at things that I believe are important, and I will ot accept anything less than success.	1	2	3	4	5

Total Score _____

The average score for members of the general population is 23. If your Total Score is higher than 29, it is likely that you experience moderate to high amounts of anxiety surrounding your achievements at work.

If the anxiety becomes quite high and if you have a low tolerance for anxiety, you may well find yourself procrastinating at important activities or jobs.

There is one other dimension of anxiety which I'd like to discuss in this section on fear of failure. When people get very anxious in preparation for some activity, they often over-estimate the likelihood of them not doing well or failing, and under-estimate the likelihood of them having the personal resources to enable them to cope with a bad result. In spite of having pretty good track records, the Robertas and Barrys of the world think "I'll probably not do very well at this". To make matters worse, they reduce their confidence by telling themselves "I couldn't handle it if I goofed up".

In conquering performance anxiety, have more faith in yourself that you will succeed. Maybe not at first but eventually. And even if you do not succeed at first - or make mistakes - it's not the end of the world nor you; only a stepping stone, not a stopping stone, on the road to where you want to go.

Perfectionism

Now 'perfectionism' is an extreme form of fear of failure. Not only must you be successful in what you set out to do, you must do it perfectly. There is nothing wrong with striving to be perfect although I'm not convinced that setting an unrealistic goal for yourself is going to bring out the best in you. (Why unrealistic? Because no matter how smart and talented you are, there will be times and areas of your work in which you will not achieve perfectly). However, the factor which leads to your anxiety and task avoidance is that you **demand** that you perform perfectly.

It is not easy to give up your perfectionism. You have grown up and got to where you are today believing that 'perfectionistic' attitudes towards your work helps you achieve what you want and brings out the best in you. When you were younger, perfectionism probably was a good psychological insurance policy in that it helped you, up to a point, perform well and possibly feel secure within yourself. The question you could ask yourself is whether perfectionism is still getting you what you want. Does insisting on doing tasks perfectly help you achieve what you want? Do you have excessive anxiety which interferes with your performance because of your need to be perfect? And does high anxiety ever lead you to delay doing or finishing things which are not perfect?

If you are a perfectionist, try to see clearly that it is sometimes good to perform less than perfectly. On certain occasions, by finishing tasks which are less than perfect - but good enough to get by - you will find more time to concentrate on other tasks. Moreover, performing less than perfectly will help you discover what you can and cannot do, thus enabling you to focus your attention on your areas of strength. Much important learning and self-discovery takes place through "trial-and-error" learning. To not permit yourself to err, is to deny yourself vital information about yourself.

Let me suggest the following general steps to combat the type of perfectionism which leads to high anxiety and, at certain times, procrastination.

1.   Acknowledge your anxiety. Don't try to deny it.

2.   Accept that anxiety is part of the human condition.

3.   Accept responsibility for making yourself anxious. Don't blame your environment or your parents. After all, as I've shown, it is your own attitudes which largely determine your degree of anxiety.

4.   Recognize that although anxiety is bad because its uncomfortable, it is not terrible and can be tolerated.

5.   Work hard at accepting yourself even with your anxiety and convince yourself that while anxiety is bad, you are not bad (see section in this chapter on rational self-acceptance).

6. Dispute with yourself the belief you have that you must perform perfectly all the time. Give up totally unrealistic standards you may have for yourself as well as your demands that your standards must always be achieved.

Fear of Disapproval

The two most common fears are the fear of rejection and the fear of failure. These two fears are possessed by millions of persons at least some of the time and a good many have them almost all the time. The fear of rejection is probably more prevalent than the fear of failure. People are often afraid to fail for the very reason that they might be rejected if they do.

Paul A. Hauck Overcoming Fear and Worry 1975

Another type of anxiety which can lead to procrastination is the fear of what others might think of you. Fear of disapproval is probably the main cause of lack of assertion. You decide that you should talk to your mate about his rudeness to your friends but you avoid actually saying anything because of your disapproval anxiety. "What will he think of me if I say something to him?" You may needlessly delay handing in a report to your superiors because you are afraid of how they might evaluate your work and, therefore, you. The Need for Approval Scale which follows will enable you to judge your own attitudes towards disapproval. Once again, indicate how strongly you disagree or agree with the following ideas.

Need for Approval Scale

	Strongly Disagree	Dis-Agree	Neutral	Strongly Agree	Agree
1. I can't stand being disliked by people who are important to me and it is unbearable if they dislike me.	1	2	3	4	5
2. It's awful to be disliked by people who are important to me and it is a catastrophe if they don't like me.	1	2	3	4	5
3. I must be liked by important people, and I will not accept not being liked by them.	1	2	3	4	5
4. I can't stand being disliked by certain people and I can't bear the possibility of their disliking me.	1	2	3	4	5
5. It's essential to be liked by important people and I will not accept their not liking me.	1	2	3	4	5
6. I must be liked and accepted by people I want to like me and I will not accept their not liking me.	1	2	3	4	5
7. When people who I want to like me disapprove of me or reject me, I can't bear their disliking me.	1	2	3	4	5

Total Score _____

The average total score for the general population is 14.5. If you score higher than 19, then it is likely that your need for approval causes you unnecessary anxiety and may lead you to procrastinate at activities where you and your work are being evaluated by others.

It is quite normal to want to be liked by people you work with and for, as well as by friends and family members including your significant other. Being liked satisfies your desire to be affiliated with others and can, by providing evidence that you are likable, lead you to feel good about yourself and be happy.

However, many believe that because it feels good when people like them that, therefore, they **need** approval from people. People with a high need for approval depend too heavily on what others think of them. If they are getting good feedback, they feel good about themselves; but when the feedback is negative, they feel lousy about themselves. Why some people are like this and others not has to do with biological make-up and the way their parents related to them while growing up.

The important point, however, is that you might be someone who brings with you to your relationships at home and work a high need for other people's approval. And the problem with this "approval-seeking" attitude is that you will tend to be overly focused on other people's opinions of you and you will go out of your way not only to please others, but also to avoid doing things which might invite their displeasure and criticism. Not only will you have a hard time saying "No" to unreasonable requests others might make of you, but you may also find it difficult to make reasonable requests of others. And, most importantly, you will have a tendency to procrastinate at activities which you have decided to do for your own good, including sticking up for your 'right' because of your fear of what others will think.

Not too long ago I worked with a university student who had fallen behind in his work. He was reasonably bright and capable of doing a good job providing that he knuckled down and put in the effort. Being a pleasure seeker, however, he tended to take whatever opportunities presented themselves for play and, by mid-semester, had not spent enough hours on his assignments. This problem was particularly acute in one of his seminar classes which required him to hand in a written report every second week. And, even as the deadlines for handing reports in came and want, this student continued to procrastinate.

Once again, it was not immediately obvious to him why he was needlessly and harmfully delaying getting in the work. Because he had not been keeping up with his background reading for the reports, I was fairly certain that even if he had started to submit reports, they would only be of an 'average' standard. "What would your professor think if you handed in a piece of work and it was only fair?", I asked. "He'd think I was dumb, not good enough to pass," he replied. "And how does that make you feel?" I further inquired. "Very uptight and down," he answered. "And would it be a fair comment to say that you put off handing in your work because you are afraid of what he will think of you? By not handing something in, he might form the impression of you that you are not interested or lazy, but, at least, not dumb. By procrastinating, you are actually protecting yourself from his negative opinion of your intelligence which in your book seems worse than actually flunking the course!" He pleaded guilty.

If you would like to be more assertive in situations and to stop procrastinating at volunteering for new assignments and handing in reports on time, you will need to ask yourself whether you are anxious in these situations and whether this anxiety has to do with being afraid of what others really think of you. If your procrastination is caused by fear of disapproval, then you will need to work on increasing your tolerance for other people's negative opinions of you.

To conquer your fear of disapproval, you can start by asking yourself whether your really need people's approval or just strongly prefer it. After all, need means necessity and the only real necessities in life are air, food and shelter. It does not logically follow that because you enjoy people liking you that, therefore, they must like you and that you need their approval all the time.

As well, it will be important to tackle the common idea which drives disapproval anxiety; that it would be terrible to have someone think badly of you and that you really couldn't stand it. Once again, ask yourself whether someone thinking you're stupid, or an ass, is as bad as serious illness or bankruptcy. That is, try to keep the unpleasantness of someone else's negative opinion of you in perspective.

Again, ask yourself "Where is the evidence that I can't stand criticism or rejection?" When I asked our procrastinating student for evidence that he couldn't tolerate being thought badly of by his professor, I asked him: "Does your hair fall out. Will it kill you? I know you don't like it, but you can stand it."

You will also need to work on detaching your own rating of your self-worth from someone elses' rating of you. No matter how hard you try to please people and create a good impression, some people will, from time-to-time, think negatively about you. And the important question here is; how does someone elses' opinion of you, with regard to your interaction together, make that opinion valid?

Another technique you can bring to bear here, is <u>referenting</u> which I described in Chapter 4. Rather than think of the advantages of putting off the task and the disadvantages of doing it, make a list of all the advantages of getting the job done or asserting yourself despite the effect it might have on other people's opinions of you, and the disadvantages to you in delaying.

Fear of Success

...Consider someone who is putting off taking a boat trip down a river. Any of the above strategies (getting started, setting intermediate goals, just plain making oneself work), which would ordinarily succeed in getting the person to start the trip and continue on it, will fail if the person believes there is a dangerous waterfall somewhere down the river, because anything which tends to get the person on the river tends to

*simultaneously to get the person closer to (and therefore raise
the person's fear of) going over the waterfall.*

Leonard G. Rorer, <u>Essay on Procrastination</u>, 1983

You may be someone who puts off certain tasks not because
you fear you will fail or be rejected, but rather because you
are afraid you will be successful or accepted! Let me illustrate with two scenarios.

Richard, a 32 year old successful architect, avoids dating
women because he fears what will happen after they accept.
He has had plenty of successful encounters to know that he
is attractive to women not only because of his looks, but
because of his sensitivities. However, his fears begin to
abound after he imagines a women accepting his invitation
to go out. "Perhaps we'll have nothing much in common. I
won't know whether to take the relationship further. What
if I ask her to bed and she doesn't want to? What if I don't
and she does? Suppose, she thinks I'm an unexciting lover.
Suppose I don't want her to spend the whole night. Suppose
I do and she wants to leave". In Richard's case, it will be
more important for him to work on his fear of the consequences of success than on his fear of failure or rejection.

Marilyn, a 39 year old managing director of a motivational
magazine for entrepreneurs, is procrastinating at putting in
the time on strategic planning which she needs to do in
order for her company to keep ahead, and grow, over the
next decade. Aside from being a poor time manager and,
as a result, finding she never has any private time to do the
concentrated work required in developing a strategic plan,
Marilyn also procrastinates because of anxiety. As with
Richard, her anxiety is not motivated out of the fear of not
being able to complete her plan successfully or from how
she thinks the plan will be received by her staff. She knows
she can complete a detailed analysis of her company's
resources, the strength and weaknesses of her competition
and the changing needs of the market, to come up with an
excellent plan for the future. Rather, the negative force
which diverts her from doing the plan is her fear of what a
successful plan might mean for her and her company in
years to come. "Maybe I won't be up to the task of running

a bigger company and expanding into new markets with a different product line. It's possible I might fail. Then what would people think of me. I'll also have to work a lot harder for the next few years and I'm not sure I really want to." So for Marilyn to procrastinate later at strategic planning, it will be vital for her to focus away from her immediate fears of failure which do not surround the task she's putting off, and to concentrate on reducing her fears and frustrations surrounding events beyond the immediate task of strategic planning.

If your procrastination is motivated out of fear of success rather than failure, then it will be important for you to have clearly in mind the consequences of success for you. Are you imagining that success increases the possibility of failure? If it does, then do the potential benefits of the long-term success warrant the risk of failure? This analysis will be made much easier if you can face the decision without fearing failure because you believe you always need to be successful or cannot tolerate failing in the eyes of others.

Your previous experience may lead you to predict that beyond the initial success, punishment lies in wait. In the case of Richard, he may have had a number of experiences with women which have taught him that the pain in relationships far outweigh the pleasures. If this is the case, than his avoidance of relationships may be motivated out of the fear of getting into a relationship which requires him to suffer pain as he has in the past. In this case, Richard would need thorough convincing that the past is not always a good predictor of the future and that his potential relationships hold the promise of greater enjoyment rather than pain.

The fear of success may also stem from your fear of having to face particularly stressful events which will follow on from your success. I know of one student who has been working on his doctorate day and night for the past five years. He always appears very busy and might be mistaken for a perfectionist in that he always finds parts of his thesis which could be improved. However, what really scares this fellow is having to face up to life's responsibilities which will follow immediately upon finishing his degree. While in school, he has successfully dodged forming intimate relationships using his dissertation as an excuse. Once completed, unless he finds other distractions, he will he forced to confront his fears of intimacy. So, in helping him to finish his dissertation, rather than working on his perfectionism and fear of failure, I concentrated more on the procrastination which was already occurring in his personal relationships.

Putting an End to Self-Depreciation

Suppose I said to a Martian, "I'm talking to this intelligent Earthling and he's devoutly believing 'One of my behaviours stinks and, therefore, I am a stinker'" Let's suppose the Martian is intelligent, perceptive and rational. What would he think about this Earthling? Probably, 'How can he be so nutty? His behaviour stinks, but he has millions of behaviours and they are all different and all tend to change. How can he, therefore, rate his self, his totality?' The Martian would be right.

Albert Ellis, Founder of Rational-Emotive Therapy

Let's be clear about what I mean by self-depreciation. It is the tendency to think, when something bad happens to you such as making a mistake or being criticized, that you are a total flop. A simple example is when someone who you know reasonably well forgets your name. Now there are two ways to go in response to this event. A rational attitude would have you thinking: "Gee, I thought she knew me better. I guess I haven't made as much an impression on her as I thought. Or maybe she's just stressed out and short-circuiting. It happens to me sometimes." These rational thoughts would lead you to feeling somewhat upset, but not off the planet. The other irrational way to interpret the same event would have you thinking: "This is awful, she has forgotton my name. I must be a real dud." Such thinking would lead you to feel exceptionally hurt and depressed. As well, it might create within you so much emotional discomfort that you might decide to put off meeting up with this person again.

Now, over the years I have developed ways of measuring this type of thinking in different people. I have developed a scale to measure self-depreciation in children and adolescents, teachers, parents and for people in general. I have noticed it occurring in children younger than seven and people over 70. Some people have a stronger tendency to put themselves down, when the slightest bad thing occurs, than others. And in all groups, I have found that self-depreciators experience greater amounts of anxiety and anger than non self-depreciators. Now anxiety and anger are two of the main reasons people procrastinate. Additionally, as self-depreciation leads to a poor self-image and as a poor self-image is at the core of someone who chronically procrastinates, it is important to spend time on discussing ways of eliminating self-depreciation.

Once again, you may wish to take a few minutes to assess your degree of self-depreciation by answering the following questions.

Self-Depreciation Scale

	Strongly Disagree	Dis-Agree	Neutral	Strongly Agree	Agree
1. I believe I would be a worthless person if I did not do well at things which are important to me.	1	2	3	4	5
2. When I feel tense, nervous or uncomfortable, I think it just goes to show what a bad, worthless person I am.	1	2	3	4	5
3. If important people dislike me, it is because I am an unlikable person.	1	2	3	4	5
4. If I do not perform well at tasks that are so important to me, it is because I am a worthless, bad person.	1	2	3	4	5
5. When people I like reject me or dislike me, it is because I am a bad or worthless person.	1	2	3	4	5
6. If important people dislike me, it goes to show what a worthless person I am.	1	2	3	4	5
7. I would not be a worthwhile person if I kept failing at work, school, or other activities that are important to me.	1	2	3	4	5
8. When I experience hassles and my life is unpleasant, I believe I am a worthless person because I have hassles or an unpleasant life.	1	2	3	4	5

Total Score _____

The average total score for the general population is 16.5. If you score higher than 22, it is likely that your tendency towards self-depreciation is causing you excessive anxiety, anger and low self-esteem. Your procrastination may partly be a result of a long history of negative self-appraisals.

Self-depreciation can have a very destructive influence on achieving what you set out to do. As a self-depreciator, you may well see yourself as someone who not only doesn't perform adequately in a given area (work, socially), but also as never being able to perform adequately. As a consequence of focusing on your negative deficiencies in a number of different areas, you come to see yourself (self-image) as someone who doesn't deserve success or acceptance by others and who will never really be happy in life. With this as a standard, is it any wonder that you give up before you ever really get going? After all, what would you expect of someone as lousy as you?

As I've said in discussing the fears of failure and rejection, people who have high needs for success and approval tend to put themselves down in the face of failure or rejection. Rather than telling themselves, "I goofed up, let me see what I can do better the next time around", they seem to interpret the failure or rejection as meaning they are totally hopeless, bad or a failure. Rather than telling themselves "I'm not very good in forming relationships", they over-generalize and conclude "I must be a real failure". Over the years, this way of thinking serves to de-energise people and leads to a sense of not being capable enough to take control of events which are troublesome or which require sustained effort to achieve. I think you'll clearly see the connection between self-depreciation and procrastination.

The Remedy

There is a two step process in learning to minimise self-depreciation. The process involves you resolving not to use external signs such as success/failure and approval/rejection as the measuring stick for rating your self-worth. The use of external signs gives the power over your emotional life to others and outside events. This appears to be a risky way of arriving at good self-esteem, given other people's tendency to occasionally be negative and critical and your own fallibility which prevents you from being totally successful. The two steps you can take to enable yourself to put a brake on self-depreciation involve establishing a clear and objective picture of your self-concept combined with an attitude of rational self-acceptance.

Self-concept is the picture you have of yourself. Self-depreciators' self-concepts are focused on the negative with the positive being taken for granted. So, to begin the process of reformulating your sense of self-worth, you need to take an inventory of your assets and liabilities. What are the things about you that you do well - including talents and abilities - and aspects of your personality, including the ability to relate to people? If you work, start your inventory with how you see yourself at work. Concentrate on being objective and make a list of your good and not-so-good characteristics. Then move on to describing things about yourself in other areas of your life: home, friendships, recreational, community life, spiritual world. This inventory should result in you having a clear picture of your strengths and weaknesses. These are your characteristics which don't change from one moment to the next. They are your essences and you have many.

Now don't worry if you seem to have more negatives than positives. The important thing is to know what strengths you have so you can build on them. If you find this impossible, talk to someone who you can trust, who likes you and who can help you fill in your picture of yourself.

Now the second step involves you ridding yourself of the "I'm hopeless" attitude towards yourself and substituting instead what Albert Ellis, the world famous psychologist and philosopher calls "rational self-acceptance". Rational self-acceptance involves you refusing to measure your intrinsic worth by your achievements or by what others think of you. Instead, you choose to accept yourself unconditionally and avoid rating yourself when something good or bad happens. Ellis argues that healthy people are usually glad to be alive and accept themselves just because they are alive and have some capacity to enjoy themselves.

In practice rational self-acceptance works as follows. When
something goes bad for you - say you get yelled at and put
down for a mistake you made, rather than thinking "I must
be a real idiot" and becoming depressed, you remind yourself that even though you may have goofed up in one
situation or been thought badly of by someone important,
these events do not take away all your good qualities (you
know, the one's your included in your inventory of assets).
By learning to accept yourself and disliking your mistakes,
you will be in a far better position to change yourself. If you
put yourself down, you'll be more likely to get defensive and
shut down. And importantly, you'll start to procrastinate
later.

Self-Talk to Reduce Anxiety and Self-Depreciation

When you are sitting around muttering to yourself about
whether you are going to do a task and, possibly, making
some pretty negative forecasts about what will probably
happen in the future and what things will be said about you,
we call these mutterings self-talk. Self-talk can be irrational
or rational, pessimistic or optimistic, discouraging or
motivating. Below is a list of examples of self-talk I have
put together over the years which can help you gain control
over your anxiety and feelings of low self-esteem and self-
depreciation. See which of the statements feel right for you.

- "Just because things are not succeeding today does not
  mean I'm a 'no-hoper' or that I will not succeed tomorrow."

- "While it is very desirable to achieve well and be recog-
  nised by others, I do not need constant achievement and
  recognition to survive or be happy."

- "Mistakes and rejections are inevitable. I will work hard
  at accepting myself while disliking my mistakes and
  knockbacks."

- "My performance at work - imperfect or otherwise -
  does not determine my worth as a person."

- "Things are rarely as bad, awful or catastrophic as I
  imagine them to be."

- "I accept who I am."

- "There are many things about me that I like and do well."

- "It's definitely nice to have the approval of people I work with but even without it, I can still accept and enjoy myself."

- "Doing things well at work is satisfying - but it's human to make mistakes."

- "I am confident that everything will turn out okay given that I have my goals, know what to do and work hard."

If you are faced with tasks which you associate with anxiety and self-depreciation, in as strong and passionate way as possible, say to yourself one or more of the above sayings which you think will help you be more resolute in approaching and following through on activities.

It was Saturday night and Larry had cooked a special meal for Helen. They'd been dating for almost six weeks now and it was the first time they decided not to eat out. Larry was beginning to really like Helen. She was the first woman he felt at all strongly about since his divorce from Jane officially came through eight months ago. He was still unsure of his feelings and their age difference of 10 years was a bit of a worry. As well, the fact that Helen was Bill's graduate student was a little too close for comfort, although he wouldn't have met her had it not been for Bill. "It's probably a good idea to still play it cool," thought Larry as he stirred his pasta sauce.

Had Helen known how Larry was feeling she would have died. She really was taken by him the first time they met. His initial coolness seemed to be evaporating, although he was still a hard one to read. He seemed to create a few too many barriers for her liking. But dinner at his house; now things were 'cooking'.

For some time now Helen had wanted to get closer to Larry but she'd always been afraid. "What if he doesn't really like me? What if he knocks me back? I couldn't handle a rejection from him." She could feel her anxiety whenever she thought of doing anything like touching him or even bringing up the subject. "But tonight, tonight I'm going to take matters in my own hands - so to speak. What's the worst that could happen? I'm not going to die if he is uninterested. I'll pick the right time and do something so he gets my message. I wonder what it'll be?"

Larry greeted Helen at the door with a sheepish smile. "I hope you like spaghetti bolognese. It's the speciality of the house."

"That's great, I'm starved. Tennis really gives be an appetite."

"For what?" Larry asked cheekily.

"For something besides nouvelle cuisine," retorted Helen, not taking the bait. She was determined to keep some control over the way things were going.

"Oh, right. It'll be ready in ... six minutes. How about a glass of wine?"

"Well, maybe just one. I've really got to be firing in the morning. I've got all this studying to catch up with!."

"No problem. One glass and an early night."

After a scrumptuous dinner and two and a half glasses, Helen looked at her watch and decided that in five minutes she'd have to get going. "It's now or never," thought Helen, "I'll just relax. He'll probably be flattered. And if he isn't, that's his bad luck."

"Well, " said Larry, "Any way I can help you get your work done?"

"Disappear for four weeks so I can concentrate on my work," thought Helen. "I think it should be okay. I'm actually working on a plan that Bill showed me. It's called Behavioural Self-Control."

"Behavioural Self-Control?"

"Yeah. I've set a goal of a minimum three hours of study. Then I time myself and see how long I actually work. If I achieve my goals, then I reward myself with something special and if I don't, then I have to penalize myself. And this afternoon I studied almost three and a half hours!"

"That's fantastic. What's your reward?"

Helen thought for awhile and then smiled. "I haven't been able to come up with one ... until now." She stood up, picked up her bag and walking over to Larry suprised him with a kiss on the lips. "This is my reward. Call me Monday."

"Hey, wait a minute," gasped an overwhelmed Larry, but it was too late. Helen was out the door.

Actions Speak Louder Than Words

If, from the above discussion, you believe your need for approval is holding you back from doing and saying things you really want to, deliberately go out of your way to do or say something which will lead to other people either disapproving of you or thinking you're a bit weird. This activity, called 'shame attacking' helps you eradicate the cause of shame and disapproval anxiety by showing you that nothing all that bad happens when someone forms a negative impression of you and that you can tolerate others' disapproval. The key to 'shame attacking exercises' being effective is for you to select something in advance to do, the thought of which fills you with anxiety. It might be walking down the street backwards, wearing your pajamas when you go to the store to buy milk or singing out the stops on the bus. (Make sure you don't do anything to get arrested).

My favourite example of a successful 'shame attack' was done by a middle-aged women who had spent many years pleasing others but felt that life was passing her by. She wanted to try new things but was too self-conscious about other people's opinions of her. To combat her need for approval from others, this was what she did. She walked over to her neighbours house whom she had known for some time, banged on the door, and yelled at the top of her voice "Hurry up, I'm hungry and horny." When the be-wildered neighbour opened the door, she marched down to her neighbour's kitchen, opened the refrigerator, grabbed some brocolli and said: "Right, now where's the bedroom?"

If you are a perfectionist and find yourself becoming very anxious about doing things which might not be perfect and avoiding completing tasks which you do not consider having been done perfectly, you may wish to try a 'risk-taking exercise'. Designed to prove to you that you don't need to do everything perfectly and that you can survive doing things imperfectly, deliberately select a task and force your-self to do it imperfectly. Even if you don't know totally how to do something, do it anyway and take the chance that you might even fail!

6

Discomfort Tolerance: The Vital Key

The act of accepting discomfort has a profound effect upon the intensity of the discomfort - it becomes bearable and less threatening.

Abraham Low, <u>Mental Health Through</u>
<u>Will Training</u>, 1950

Imagine that close friends have invited you over to their house to celebrate your birthday. Both of them are great cooks and know very well how to prepare your favourite meal. Imagine that they have told you what they are going to serve for each course, including dessert, and that they have selected those dishes which you simply adore. Suppose they have invited you over on Saturday night.

Now, during Saturday, what would you be feeling inside about the prospect of having your favourite meal that evening? No doubt you would feel excitement and pleasure in anticipation. You would be eagerly awaiting the night ahead of you. These positive anticipatory feelings of what lies ahead would help to motivate you to arrive on time as well as insuring that there would be no reason for you to make up an excuse for not attending.

Imagine that you are half-way through your first course and are enjoying yourself immensely. Your stomach is in seventh heaven and you are feeling fantastic. What is the likelihood that you'll give up half way through the first course and go home? How likely is it that you would procrastinate at eating the rest of the meal?

This example is a relatively simple one but it does illustrate two important points. You are not likely to procrastinate at tasks which you anticipate to be pleasant and which do not provoke high anxiety. This is because when you anticipate good times and feel pleasantly aroused when you think about performing the task there is no discomfort to divert you. You are also more likely to apply yourself to starting and completing activities which are easy and fun to do. This is because while you are engaged in the task, you are feeling good inside - relaxed or positively aroused as the case may be.

Once again, imagine being invited over to a friends' house for dinner but this time your friends are terrible cooks and are more than likely to have a variety of courses and dishes which you hate. In this case, as you remember their last meal and start to get worried and uptight about having to eat what's served or decline one or more dishes, possibly hurting their feelings, would you not be inclined to procrastinate at showing up for dinner as long as possible making up as many convincing rationalisations as your creativity allowed? And suppose you failed to avoid the dinner and found yourself mid-way through a revolting dish. How motivated would you be to continue eating the rest of the meal knowing the effort and discomfort already expended in eating the first dish?

This second scenario, hopefully, clearly illustrates the main principles of procrastination I have already discussed in Chapter 2. You are more likely to put off activities and tasks which lead to or involve you in experiencing large amounts of anxiety and discomfort. In the second scenario, you would be inclined to procrastinate at attending dinner because of knowing that you'd have to eat food you dislike as well as having to cope with the anxiety of putting up with your friends' disappointment or disapproval when you do not eat everything. As well, this scenario demonstrates another of the general rules of procrastination; namely, when you are confronted with doing things which you find highly frustrating and which prevent you from doing other preferred things, you will also tend to procrastinate.

Finally, imagine once again being invited over by those friends who can't cook. This time, however, you decide ahead of time you want to encourage the friendship and, by accepting their invitation and eating some of their food, you would help to accomplish this. Even though their food remains the same and the situation is as unpleasant as before, a different attitude on your part will prevent you from procrastinating. You will accept the invitation and eat the meal regardless of how you feel, because you have an important longer-term objective in sight. This is a vital lesson to learn in managing discomfort which leads to procrastination.

Sometimes your anxiety and frustration, which serves to divert you from doing certain tasks, is not immediately obvious to you. You do not see clearly that it is your discomfort and tension which you experience when thinking about or doing jobs or meeting with people which leads to your procrastination. By becoming more aware of your discomfort you can start to develop strategies for coping with it or reducing it.

Sensation Sensitivity

If your body says 'I don't feel like doing this', don't trust your body. Do it anyway!

Dr Robert Dawson, Australian Psychologist

People experience frustration differently. Some people, when faced with having to do work that is boring or hard, appear to get bombarded and over-whelmed by unpleasant physiological sensations such as pounding temples, rushes or surges of energy as well as a sense of wanting to explode. Other people, when faced with the same hassles, do not react as strongly physiologically. The same internal systems seem to be turned on, but not as strongly. Those people whose systems seem to activate strongly and quickly when they experience frustration can be called 'sensation sensitive'. Because they experience so much inner physiological turmoil, they find it very hard to persevere. Their 'inner sensations' are overriding their will to get the job done.

In a similar way, certain people when faced with anxiety-provoking circumstances such as public gatherings, asserting themselves or preparing an important report, experience heightened and painful 'internal sensations'. They experience a variety of highly discomforting physiological sensations such as rapid heart beat, muscle pains in chest, head and shoulders, extreme nausea, dramatic flushing and shortness or shallowness of breath. And, as a consequence of their sensitivity to these extremely powerful and unpleasant sensations, they tend to avoid entering situations which give rise to their inner pain. You may or may not be someone who gets quickly 'turned on' by painful sensations when you think about or experience stressful situations.

Sensation sensitivity is a strong factor in determining whether you procrastinate at doing certain tasks. The more sensation sensitive you are, the more prone you are to avoid the situations which provoke the painful sensations and, hence, procrastinate.

What actually determines your sensation senitivity thresh-hold? This partly depends on your native biological equipment. Some people have a biological system which readily registers high amounts of discomfort and are very prone to being sensation sensitive and experiencing low discomfort tolerance. As well, your attitude towards your discomfort has a large bearing. If you have a high need for comfort (which you will tend to have if you are biologically pre-disposed to sensation sensitivity), you will be less able to cope with your high level of physiological arousal. You will be able to assess your attitude to discomfort using the Need for Comfort scale, to be presented shortly.

If you are someone who is sensation sensitive, help is at hand. Human beings have a great capacity to override their biological instinct and all of the techniques offered later in this chapter such as relaxation and stress-inoculation are tools you can use to take control and manage your 'sensation sensitivity' so that you can motivate yourself to hang in and do things which you may not feel like doing.

Low Frustration Tolerance and Discomfort Anxiety

The longer I live, the more importance I attach to a man's ability to manage and discipline himself...The man with the capacity for self-discipline can tell himself to do the truly important things first ... Here is the most interesting thing about the capacity for self-discipline. He who wants it may have it! ... The one ingredient we most want for success is ours for the asking, for the wanting, if we only want it enough. "

Ray Kroc, Chairman of the Board, MacDonalds

This chapter will discuss two types of discomfort and the main reasons you tend to avoid one, or the other, or both. The first is the discomfort you experience while working on boring, difficult and time-consuming tasks. This discomfort we usually call frustration as it results from situations where you have to do what you don't want to do, as well as being deprived of things you would prefer to do. For example; having to study is frequently frustrating for, not only do you have to put up with sometimes difficult, boring and time-consuming activities, you also have to do without enjoyable and pleasurable activities. You may also experience frustration when you have to confront people who are blocking you from achieving what you want or when confronted with the cumbersome and miserable ways organisations can operate which thwart you from getting what you want. Frustration is, therefore, a natural and frequent part of life. It's when you become overly frustrated, tense and angry about life's hassles that you are likely to procrastinate. This is called 'low frustration tolerance' or LFT.

Let me try to make the different aspects of LFT as clear as I can. To begin with, you are faced with situations, events, tasks or people which block you from getting what you want in the short-term. Studying blocks you from doing more pleasurable activities. Doing background research on a project takes you away from the excitement of the creative process involved in production. Your mate's sloppiness in not hanging up his clothes can make your life harder - if it is your responsibility for house care - as well as taking you away from things you would prefer to be doing.

Your attitude towards these boring, time consuming tasks and hassles in addition to the tasks themselves will determine the amount of frustration you experience and how long it lasts. A rational attitude involves you accepting though not liking what you have to do (and do without). Such an attitude would enable you to keep your initial level of frustration low and find it easier to tolerate. If, however, you irrationally believe that because you would prefer your life to be easier, therefore, you must always have what you want and that conditions in your life should be arranged so that you never have to do anything boring or hard and never have to put up with hassles, then you'll experience an extreme amount of frustration, tension and anger which you'll find harder to put up with.

At this stage, the thing that determines whether you hang in there or give up and procrastinate is how well you cope with feeling tense and frustrated. If you believe you shouldn't have to put up with frustration and that you can't stand being tense, you will be less likely to be able to handle high amounts of frustration and anger towards tasks, people or organisations. Rather than facing up to the task or situation, you avoid it because of your LFT.

An example? One night my daughter, who has just turned three and thinks she's 33, refused to come and have a bath with her brother before bedtime. The more I lightly, politely but firmly asked her to come, the more she refused until she threw herself on the floor. At that point, I became extremely frustrated and angry. If I let her have her way, my frustration would have evaporated and I could have gone in and read the paper. That would be an example of me procrastinating at teaching her that she cannot always have what she wants. As well, I would be teaching her the lesson that, if she screams long enough, she'll actually get what she wants. So I decided not to procrastinate. In order for me to put up with the hassle of the moment and to postpone my own pleasurable activity of newspaper reading I had to manage my own level of high frustration, tenseness and anger. I did this by reminding myself I could still stay in control and manage the situation even though I was uptight, that it wasn't all that awful if I couldn't relax after my hard day, and I helped relax myself a little with some deep breathing. Once I got on top of my frustration, I decided the best course of action was to take my wind out of her sails, so I turned my attention to my son who was already in the bath wondering what daddy was going to do and I shut the door. After a few minutes of me ignoring her screams, I heard a little knock on the door and there was my daughter wanting to play her favourite bath game.

The second type of discomfort is often closely linked to the anxiety and discomfort you feel in certain ego-threatening situations where you or what you're doing is being rated by yourself or others. When you are faced with having to perform certain tasks where you might not succeed and where people might judge you badly, you will experience anxiety and associated unpleasant sensations in your gut. And the degree to which you can tolerate the discomfort you experience in anticipation of stressful tasks will determine the likelihood of you putting off the task until a later time. The tendency to avoid the discomfort you feel when you worry about what others will think of you if you do badly as well as when you worry excessively about whether you will make a mistake at some important task or even fail, is what can be called 'discomfort anxiety'. 'Discomfort anxiety' refers to being afraid of how it feels to be anxious, worried ("I can't stand it!") and a tendency to avoid situations which give rise to your anxiety.

As I described in the previous chapter, your needs for achievement and approval as well as your self-depreciating attitudes can dramatically increase your anxiety which will be much harder for you to tolerate. The strategies I've outlined in Chapter 5 will help you to reduce both performance and disapproval anxiety. However, some people find it hard to put up with any discomfort and nervousness due to their pre-disposing need for comfort. They escalate any emotional tension into panic from which they escape because they indoctrinate themselves into believing "It's awful to feel uncomfortable, I can't bear it, I really need to feel comfortable all the time."

Some forms of 'discomfort anxiety' can stem from your need to feel in control and to avoid general feelings of unease which you experience in mildly threatening circumstances, such as entering elevators, going outside for a walk or being in a car where you don't have control. In extreme forms, this type of 'discomfort anxiety' is a clinical condition called 'agoraphobia'. This conditions requires the expert treatment of a properly trained psychologist or psychiatrist and will not be discussed here.

'Low frustration tolerance' and 'discomfort anxiety' are related in certain ways. Their main similarity is that they are triggered off by unpleasant sensations from within. Extreme frustration and anxiety are, however, experienced differently. Extreme frustration and anger is often experienced as a 'heady' sensation with accompanying sensations of wanting to lash out and explode. High anxiety is often experienced as 'shallowness' in the gut, tightness in the chest and an overall sense of weakness. For this reason, not all people experience LFT and 'discomfort anxiety' equally. Some people have a hard time putting up with high frustration while others seem to be extremely sensitive to and intolerant of the sensations which go along with anxiety. If you have high needs for achievement and approval and worry a lot about these issues as well as being a chronic self-depreciator, my experience has been that you are more likely to experience "discomfort anxiety" because you are more likely to experience high anxiety in the first place. The higher your anxiety, the more likely you will be to procrastinate than someone who is less pre-occupied with proving themselves to others or through their work. Similarly, if you are someone who believes you **must** always have what you want and that conditions in your life **should** be organised so that your demands are met, the more likely you are to experience high frustration and the higher your frustration, the more likely you will be to have LFT.

A summary of LFT and 'discomfort anxiety' is provided below.

Steps to low frustration tolerance:

1.   Demands for ease, rapid solutions to problems; the demands for fairness and consideration; the need for immediate gratification

2.   facing tasks which are hard, take a long time to solve, boring, hassles with people, organisational blunders

3.   frustration and accompanying unpleasant sensations of tenseness, explosiveness, headiness

4.   high need for comfort; low tolerance for feelings of frustration

5.   extreme frustration and anger.

6.   procrastination in the form of aggression and giving up.

Steps to discomfort anxiety:

1.   High needs for achievement and approval

2.   facing the possibility of failure, rejection or criticism

3.   anxiety and accompanying sensations of discomfort, tenseness, shallowness and weakness

4.   high need for comfort; low tolerance for feelings of anxiety

5.   anxiety about anxiety, panic

6.   procrastination in the form of withdrawal, running away, avoidance.

The items on the following 'Need for Comfort' Scale will, perhaps, make the idea of 'discomfort intolerance' even clearer. A high score on this scale will indicate a tendency towards low frustration tolerance, discomfort anxiety or both.

Need for Comfort Scale

	Strongly Disagree	Dis-Agree	Neutral	Strongly Agree	Agree
1. It's unbearable being uncomfortable, tense or nervous, and I can't stand it when I am.	1	2	3	4	5
2. I can't stand being tense or nervous and I think tension is unbearable.	1	2	3	4	5
3. Sometimes I think the hassles and frustrations of everyday life are awful and the worst part of my life.	1	2	3	4	5
4. I must have a pleasant, comfortable life most of the time, and I can't accept when life is a hassle.	1	2	3	4	5
5. I must have a pleasant life and I will not accept hassles when I don't want them.	1	2	3	4	5
6. It's awful to have hassles in one's life and it's a catastrophe to be hassled.	1	2	3	4	5
7. I think it's awful and terrible to experience tension, nervousness or frustration, and having such feelings is the worst thing that can happen to me.	1	2	3	4	5
8. I can't stand hassles in my life.	1	2	3	4	5
9. I must not feel tense, nervous or uncomfortable and I believe that I cannot accept feeling bad.	1	2	3	4	5

Total Score _____

The average total score for the general population is 22. If your total score is higher than 28, then it is more than likely that your need for comfort leads you to avoid anxiety-provoking situations, frustration-creating tasks and hassles.

There are a variety of solutions for increasing your tolerance for discomfort. Some of them have to do with learning to go with the discomfort rather than to fight it. Adopting a philosophy of long-term hedonism as discussed below will inevitably lead you to becoming more prepared to put up with short-term discomforts. Relaxation is a wonderful skill which can help take the edge off your tension. In addition, learning more rational things to tell yourself in anticipation of stressful situations will increase your toleranace level. Let me describe some basic strategies which you can use to develop high discomfort tolerance.

The 'Lining Up' Technique

To kick a field goal in American football, the "center" passes the ball back through his legs to the "holder" who places the ball on the ground readying the ball for the field goal kicker who takes a few steps and then kicks the ball off the ground through the goal posts - hopefully. In order for the field goal kicker to be successful, it is very important that his 'holder' lines the ball up tilting it at the right angle so that it's maximally aligned to fly through the uprights.

One very effective way to overcome procrastination is to 'line up' the discomfort which is diverting you from the task or activity you wish to accomplish. The problem with discomfort is that it frequently is not something which you immediately recognise as blocking you from your goal. You are vaguely aware of its existence, but you haven't really seen it as the main reason you are putting something off.

Let's take another page from my recent life history - literally. In writing this book, there are times I've had 'writer's block'. I sit down at my computer, log in to where I finished off the previous day, and then after sitting around for a few minutes feeling dazed, I can, on a bad day, start to find other things to do in my office and end up procrastinating at my writing. Indeed, after four or five days of intensive writing, it is very easy for me to find other 'important' activities to distract myself with rather than keeping to my schedule. Being on a tight writing deadline, I cannot afford to procrastinate very much. I have to get the work done. I frequently use the 'lining up' technique to get me back on task. Here's how it works.

As I find myself putting off writing, I ask myself what is the cause of the procrastination. When the answer is simply that I don't feel like doing it, I place the discomfort clearly between me and what I've set out to do. I then ask myself whether the discomfort I feel in getting on with my work is so great that it justifies me failing to keep to my deadline and bearing the negative consequences which would follow (having to work at nights, on the weekend, publisher's aggravation about my not keeping to deadline). "What's more important," I ask myself, "dodging the discomfort of the moment or getting my work done?"

By lining up the frustration so that I can clearly see it as the main reason for my procrastination, I can exercise much more control over myself then if I just had a vague sense of feeling like I don't really want to do the job.

This technique is also very useful for overcoming 'discomfort anxiety.' When you are putting off some activity such as public speaking; bringing up a 'difficult' subject with an important person or dating, and believe that one of the main reasons for your procrastination is the avoidance of the discomfort you feel in these situations, recognise that your discomfort is the real reason for opting out. Then, mentally place the discomfort between you and the task which deep down you really want to accomplish and ask yourself whether the short-term pain of putting up with your discomfort is worth the longer-term gain.

The Lining Up Technique involves the referenting technique described in Chapter 4. Once you line up the discomfort between you and your goal, in order to tolerate the discomfort you, review your list of the disadvantages of avoiding the discomfort and the advantages for you in achieving your goal. In the case of work, the advantages of getting the job finished and on time, as well as giving the public talk or applying for a better job, need to be very clear to you. As well, the advantages of accomplishing certain tasks you've been putting off in your personal relationships, in home maintenance and in the area of your own self-development need to be crystal clear. Unless you have a strong sense of the benefits to you in becoming more intimate, fixing the gutters or taking a course, it will be harder for you to justify to yourself having to put up with the discomfort associated with accomplishing particular tasks.

Long-Term Hedonism and Delay of Gratification

Life wasn't meant to be easy.

    Malcom Fraser, Former Prime Minister of Australia

In the previous chapter, I illustrated how, by disputing and changing your attitudes towards your need for achievement, approval and self-depreciation, you can bring about a dramatic change in the way you approach, not only certain tasks, but also yourself. You can also increase your discomfort tolerance by adopting more rational attitudes towards frustration and gratification.

When you are faced with a situation where you are not getting what you want and start to feel frustrated, your frustration will stem from you rationally telling yourself something like: "I really don't want to work right now. It's such a beautiful day. Oh well, how can I make the best of this bad situation?" However, the extreme frustration which often leads to the avoidance of work stems from an irrational attitude towards the same circumstance: "This is really terrible that I have to deprive myself. Not only is this work boring, it's too boring. It's so unfair. I shouldn't have to work so hard." You can see once again that irrational attitudes can escalate your frustration levels to the point of no return.

You might wonder why certain people have low frustration tolerances and needs for immediate gratification. In the 1950s, Abraham Low wrote of an increasing societal trend for people to deify "comfort" as the ultimate to aim for in life style. Low believed that this "comfort cult" stemmed from the popular mass psychology of his times which elevated pleasure seeking and fun while rejecting the notion of self-sacrifice. No long-term sacrifice became too great in the interests of short-term pleasure. I believe that today, in our westernised culture which celebrates and over-emphasise ostentatious wealth, it is even easier to become seduced into a value system which embraces compulsive short-term pleasure seeking. Irrational beliefs which surround this life style can be seen in a number of pleasure-seeking, discomfort-reducing ideas: "I need constant stimulation and excitement"; "My life should be comfortable"; "I shouldn't have to do what I don't feel like doing."

The origins of low frustration tolerance can be traced to your early childhood temperament and your parents' child rearing practices. As I wrote in Chapter 1, all children are born without the ability to tolerate frustation, and with maturity and parents expecting, teaching and reinforcing them, they gradually develop the ability to delay gratification and tolerate frustration. Some people, however, due to an especially 'difficult' temperament and/or inconsistent or permissive parenting practices, never really learn self management skills and attitudes to help them cope with inevitable life frustrations.

Regardless of its origins, it is important for you to fully recognise that your demand for immediate gratification and for always getting what you want comfortably, quickly and easily increases greatly the likelihood of you putting off important things which will hold you back from living life to its fullest, and developing your full potential. To change the attitudes which drive discomfort intolerance, ask yourself "Where is it written that my life must be easy and that I always must have what I want?" If you answer the question honestly and admit that the only place it may be written is in your head, then you are in a sound position to adopt a more sensible attitude towards frustration, pleasure-seeking and discomfort avoidance.

In recent times - and for the past 35 years - Albert Ellis has argued that a moderation of short-term and long-term gratifications is the best recipe for individual happiness. Rather than only living for tomorrow or living for today,

Ellis counsels to have as much fun as you can today as long as in so doing you do not prevent yourself from making the sacrifices involved in hard work which will gain pleasure for you in the future. As you probably know a fair amount about having pleasure in the short-run, listen to what Ellis has to say about long-term hedonism (from A. Ellis & W. Knaus, Overcoming Procrastination, 1977).

"Long-range hedonism recognises that some inconveniences in the present increase chances for a happier and more productive life in the future. If you desire pizza and ice cream, as a long-range hedonist, you allow yourself to experience the discomfort of not having what you would like to eat today in order for you to have the physique you would like tomorrow. A sanely hedonistic student forces himself to study the night before the examination, even though he might have a more pleasurable time on the date. A person interested in obtaining a Ph.D. degree gracefully accepts the 'unfair' preliminary exams that seem irrelevant to future goals ... .

"You can, of course, foolishly continue to sacrifice the present for the future. However, you can also recognize that priorities such as losing weight have more importance than eating pizza. Long-range hedonism does not exclude going to parties, watching a favorite television show, going on a vacation, or reading interesting novels. It merely means at times you choose to deprive yourself of some immediate pleasures by viewing them as minor, in comparison to attaining more desirable goals."

The following three strategies can help you gain control over and reduce your discomfort which you can experience when thinking about, performing or procrastinating at certain tasks.

Relaxation

By using our own physiological ways of breathing we can steady the system, stop panic from mounting, or deal with a very difficult situation in which our blood pressure is likely to rise and make us hot, tense and uptight. By using the breathing related to the system 'at peace', you can count on reducing the pressure and remaining cool and clear headed.

Dr. Audrey Livingston Booth, Director of the Stress Foundation (U.K.), author of <u>Stressmanship</u>, 1985.

"...The body registers stress long before the conscious mind does. Muscular tension is your body's way of letting you know you are under stress."

Martha Davis, Elizabeth Eshelman & Matthew McKay, <u>The Relaxation and Stress Reduction Book</u> 1982

When you start to feel very frustrated, tense, nervous and uncomfortable inside, your body's involuntary reflex will be to divert away from the task, situation or person which seems to be occasioning the negative internal sensations. This was okay when your internal sensations were signals for fear and the outside stimulus was a pre-historic animal getting ready to attack. However, when you dodge away from stimuli which are merely frustrating or threatening to your ego, then you have evidence that your body's innate programming which worked thousands of years ago has outlived its usefulness. There are many times when it does you more harm than good to be diverted away from doing things. To override your programming you can, as I've indicated, work hard at changing your attitudes to modern-day dinosaurs so that you experience less discomfort and, are therefore less inclined to put off whatever it is you've set out to do.

Another important way to increase your tolerance for discomfort is through learning to relax at those times when you are becoming tense, nervous, uptight and uncomfortable. The methods which I will now describe can be used to help you tolerate both anxiety and frustration. The controlled breathing relaxation techniques I initially describe are good for use in the heat of the moment when your discomfort is the highest in either anticipating having do do something you find stressful or while confronting a frustrating task or interpersonal hassle. The Progressive Muscle Relaxation technique, which I also present in some detail, can be used as a way of reducing the overall tension and arousal in your body and mind which have accrued in response to the variety of demands and stress in your life. Done ahead of time, progressive relaxation will make it easier for you to endure discomfort associated with performing a particular task.

The quieting response

The quieting response was developed by Dr Charles F. Stroebel and his colleagues as an instant response to stress. It takes approximately 6 seconds to perform and therefore is suitable for use on the spot. Here is how to use it.

When you notice your stress level increasing (e.g., muscle tension, changes in breathing, headache, anxiety):

1.   Imagine yourself smiling inwardly especially with your eyes

2.   think to yourself "Alert mind, calm body"

3.   take a slow, deep breath of air

4.   while exhaling, relax your muscles beginning with your face, shoulders, and then feel the relaxation spreading downward to your toes.

Dr. Stroebel recommends regular practice of the quieting response as then it has a good chance of becoming an automatic reflex which is triggered by increases in your stress level.

The squeeze technique

The squeeze technique is an abbreviated deep breathing relaxation technique designed to reduce physical agitation as well provide a burst of added energy.

Take a slow deep breath filling your lungs as much as possible. Now stiffen your stomach muscles as if someone is about to hit you and hold your breath for a count of three. Now exhale forcefully.

If you use this technique several times in succession you can bring down your anxiety and tension levels before having to perform some stressful task.

Calm breathing

This technique will introduce you to a very easy form of controlled breathing. The aim of the activity is for you to begin to use more of your lung capacity especially in your upper chest cavity.

Sit in a comfortable chair allowing your shoulders to drop down naturally by your sides for full lung expansion. Sit up straight in order to expand your lungs upwards. Looking straight ahead take five slow deep breaths. You are now ready to begin calm breathing.

Breath in easily counting to yourself 1-2-3 and then breath out just as easily to the count of 1-2-3. Rather than trying for deep breathing allow your chest to gently expand outwards.

Because your relaxed breathing is not noticeable to others, you can use it in public places such as just before saying something to someone at work or, preventatively, such as when you are in the car.

The 5-3-5 technique

This controlled, deep breathing technique can be used either when sitting or lying down. Use the following instructions:

To begin with, rapidly exhale all the air from your lungs. Next, slowly to a count of five, inhale ... one ... two ... three ... four ... five .... Hold your breath of air for a slow count of three, one ... two ... three .... Now, slowly exhale the air to a slow count of five, one ... two ... three ... four ... five ... . You have just completed one repetition. To continue to relax, breathe in slowly again to a count of five, hold for a count of three and exhale to a slow count of five.

Progressive relaxation

Progressive relaxation is a muscle relaxation technique developed in the 1920's by a Chicago physician, Dr. Edmund Jacobson, to help people take the anxiety out of their lives, which he attributed to the increased competitive pressures of the times. His research revealed that when people were simply instructed to "relax", most people still showed significant electrical activity in their muscle fibres indicating that they were not fully relaxed. He discovered that by tensing a muscle before relaxing it, the muscle would return to a more deeply relaxed state than it would by simply relaxing it. By teaching people to tense and relax major muscle groups, he was able to teach people how to more fully relax. His technique is based on the simple principle that it is impossible to be physically tense if you are relaxed.

Progressive relaxation has you focused on the eventual removal of tension from four major muscle groups:

1.   Hands, forearms and biceps

2.   head, face, throat and shoulders including forehead, cheeks, eyes, nose, jaw, lips, tongue and neck

3.   chest, stomach and back

4.   thighs, buttocks, calves and feet.

By becoming aware of the difference between how a muscle feels when it is tense and when it is relaxed, you will become more attuned to detecting and removing muscular tension from different parts of your body.

In learning this procedure, it is recommended that you practice at the same time each day for at least 15 minutes and that you do not schedule practice within one hour of eating. Using this schedule, you will develop initial mastery of progressive relaxation within one week.

In learning this technique, you will initially have to follow a set of instructions concerning the order in which you progressively relax your muscles and the method of actually relaxing a muscle. There are a variety of commercially avaliable cassettes which provide such instructions which

you may wish to purchase. Other options include familiarising yourself with the instructions which I will shortly
provide, making your own cassette recording using these
instructions, or having a friend reading the instructions
aloud to you.

To begin progressive relaxation you need to find a very
quiet place where you will not be interrupted by the
telephone, kids, T.V., etcetera.

You may wish to hang a 'do not disturb' sign on your door
and take the telephone off the hook. You can learn this
technique lying on the floor or a comfortable bed, or sitting
in a chair. You should wear comfortable clothing, loosen
your belt, remove glasses/contact lenses, tie and shoes.

Instructions for progressive relaxation

In the instructions which follow, you will notice that you
begin with relaxing your head followed progressively by
your shoulders and arms, body and legs. In order to learn
how to relax, you will follow a four-step instructional se-
quence.

1.   Seperately tense your individual muscle groups

2.   hold the tension about five seconds

3.   slowly release the tension

4.   notice the difference between feeling tense and
      feeling relaxed.

Word by word relaxation

Head: Wrinkle up your forehead keeping the rest of your
body relaxed. Feel the tension. Your forehead is tight ...
now relax. Feel the difference between being tense and
relaxed .... Squint your eyes tight and feel the tension
around your eyes ... now, relax and let go .... Open your
mouth as wide as you can feeling the tension in your jaw
tense ... ; Now gently close your mouth ... notice the difference between tension and relaxation .... Close your
mouth and push your tongue against the roof of your mouth
... notice the tension ... relax and let go .... Keeping the rest

of your face and body relaxed, clench your jaws tightly ... feel the tension in your jaw muscles ... and relax ... let go ... notice the difference between tension and relaxation .... Think about your head, your forehead, eyes, jaws and cheeks ... notice your whole face becoming smooth and relaxed as tension slips away.

Shoulders and Arms: Shrug your shoulders up and try to touch your ears .... Feel the tension in your shoulders .... Now relax, notice the difference .... Stretch your arms out and make a fist with your hands .... Feel the tension in your hands and forearms .... Now relax, and let go .... Push your left hand down into what it is resting on .... Feel the tension in your arm and shoulder .... Now let go .... Push your right hand down into what it is resting on, hard ... feel the tension .... Now let go and relax ... Bend your elbows and tense your upper arms as if you wanted to show off your muscles ... feel the tension .... Now relax .... Feel the relaxation as it moves across your shoulders, your arms and hands .... Feel also the relaxation in your face and neck.

Body: Now take a deep breath that totally fills your lungs .... Notice the tension in your chest and around your ribs .... Slowly breathe out and notice the deepening relaxation as you continue to breath out .... Now arch your back up (or forward if you are sitting) paying attention to the tension, hold it tense .... Now relax ... notice the difference ... Tighten your stomach as if someone was going to hit you ... hold the tension ... and relax ... notice the tension filling your stomach .... tension out as relaxation comes in .... Now push your stomach out as far as it can go ... hold the tension ... and slowly relax your stomach muscles ... feel the waves of relaxation flow through your stomach ... your back ... your chest ... neck ... chin ... face ... head ... shoulders ... arms .. .hands.

You will learn that you can relax any part of your body by letting go of the tension ....

Legs: Tighten your hips and legs by pressing down the heels of your feet into the surface they are resting on ... press hard, tense ... relax and let go .... Notice the difference between tension and relaxation .... Curl your toes downward and try to touch the bottom of your feet with your toes ... feel the tension ... now relax and let go ... bend your toes as you let go of the tension ... feel the tension being replaced with relaxation .... Bend your toes back the other way towards your head ... feel the tension, tense and hold ... now, relax and feel yourself letting go of the tension ... relax and feel the difference .... Feel how good it is to be relaxed ... continue to feel more and more relaxed as you breathe in and out.

Once you have mastered the technique you will be able to gradually learn to focus on and relax specific muscle groups as you become aware of them during the day. With further practice, you can learn to let go of muscle tension without having to first tense the muscle. Your memory will have stored the sensation of how the muscle feels when it is relaxed and you can reinstate physical relaxation on your command using certain cue words such as "relax."

Stress Innoculation Training

How one responds to stress is, in large, part influenced by how one appraises the stressor ... and how he assesses his ability to cope.

Donald Meichenbaum, Cognitive Behaviour
Modification, 1977.

Donald Meichenbaum, a well-known psychologist, has popularised an approach to stress management which is particularly useful for people who wish to cope better with their level of discomfort. Meichenbaum offers an interesting insight into the nature of the internal arousal you experience when faced with frustrating or demanding tasks or people. He indicates that, rather than being in a state of no stress or full-on stress, you in fact experience a gradual build up of stress beginning when you are faced with the frustrating or demanding tasks or situation, to experiencing its impact, to, finally, reflecting on how well you dealt with the encounter.

As you'll see, Meichenbaum's stress innoculation training has you learning to say certain coping statements to yourself before, during and after you confront a person or situation.

If your rehearse them frequently over time, the coping
self-statements will help to over-ride your body's instinct to
become highly churned up and for you to avoid the situation.

In preparing for stressful situations where you experience
high anxiety and uncomfortable internal arousal, Meichenbaum recommends that you use the following set of coping
self-statements:

Preparing for a stressor

- What is it you have to do?

- You can develop a plan to deal with it.

- Just think what you can do about it. That's better than
  getting anxious.

- No negative self-statements; just think rationally.

- Don't worry; worry won't help anything.

- Maybe what you think is anxiety is eagerness to confront
  it.

Confronting and handling the stressor

- Just psyche yourself up; you can meet this challenge.

- One step at a time; you can handle the situation.

- Don't think about fear; just think about what you have
  to do.

- Stay relevant.

- This anxiety is what the doctor said you would feel.

- It's a reminder to use your coping exercises.

Coping with the feeling of being overwhelmed

- When fear comes, just pause.

- Keep the focus on the present. What is it you have to
  do?

- Label your fear from 0 to 10 and watch it change.

- You should expect your fear to rise.

- Don't try to eliminate fear totally; just keep it manageable.

- You can convince yourself to do it. You can reason your fear away.

- It will be over shortly.

- It's not the worst thing which can happen.

- Just think about something else.

- Do something which will prevent you from thinking about the fear.

- Describe what is around you. That way you won't think about worrying.

Reinforcing self-statements

- It worked; you did it.

- It wasn't as bad as you expected.

- You made more out of the fear than it was worth.

- Your damn ideas - that's the problem.

- When you control them, you control your fear.

- It's getting better each time you use the procedures.

- You can be pleased with the progress you're making.

- You did it!

While the above sets of self-statements can be used for dealing with threatening situations which can trigger off anxiety, a different set of self-statements can be employed when faced with frustrating tasks you don't really want to do, or hassles with people.

Preparing for a provocation

- What is it you have to do?

- You can work out a plan to handle this.

- You can work out an approach to get this job done.

- You can manage this situation. You know how to regulate your anger.

- If you find yourself getting upset, you'll know what to do.

- You can get this job done without getting too uptight.

- There won't be any need to get too angry.

- Time for a few deep breaths of relaxation.

- Feel comfortable, relaxed and at ease.

- This could be a testy situation, but you believe in yourself.

Confronting the provocation or task

- Stay calm. Just continue to relax.

- As long as you keep your cool, you're in control here.

- Don't put yourself down if it takes some time.

- Don't take it personally.

- Don't get bent out of shape; just think of what to do here.

- You don't have to prove yourself.

- There is no point in getting mad.

- You're not going to let this get to you.

- Don't assume the worst or jump to conclusions. Look for the positives.

- It's really a shame this person (or task) is so frustrating.

- If you start to get mad, you'll just be banging your head against the wall.

- You might as well just relax.

- There's no need to doubt yourself.

- You can handle this.

Coping with arousal and agitation

-   Your muscles are starting to feel tight.

-   Time to relax and slow things down.

-   Getting upset won't help.

-   It's just not worth it to get so angry.

-   You'll let him make a fool of himself.

-   It's reasonable to get annoyed, but let's keep the lid on.

-   Time to take a deep breath.

-   Your anger is a signal of what you need to do. Time to talk to

-   You're not going haywire either.

Self-reward

-   It worked!

-   That wasn't as hard as you thought.

-   You could have gotten more upset than it was worth.

-   Your ego can sure get you into trouble, but when you watch that ego stuff, you're better off.

-   You're doing better at this all the time.

-   You actually got through that without getting angry.

-   Guess you've been getting upset for too long when it wasn't even necessary.

Sometimes, it can be useful to write down some coping statements of your own which can help you to hang in there when you start to feel very frustrated or highly anxious. It is very important at those times to have things you can tell yourself to short-circuit your instinct to bail out, get furious or panic.

Attitudes to Increase Your Discomfort Tolerance

Gain through pain.

Popular Motivational Saying.

Developing high discomfort tolerance can be aided by acquiring rational attitudes towards frustration, discomfort and having to temporarily do without. Over the years, I have collected the following list of rational attitudes to help you increase your tolerance for discomfort.

- Things I do at work will often be hard, unpleasant and frustrating.

- Even though I don't like being frustrated, I can stand it.

- Why is it unfair that I have to work so hard, why must my life be easy?

- What makes this task too hard?

- No matter how onerous a task is to do, it is tough to do it now, but it is much tougher to do it later.

- While things I have to do may be difficult, unpleasant or boring, they are rarely too difficult, unpleasant or boring.

- Even though I don't like frustration, I can stand it.

- Yes, it is a pain to do this now, but I'd better because it's much harder and I get worse results if I do it later.

- I can cope with feeling stressed and strained.

- In order to obtain pleasant results, I often have to do unpleasant things.

- The more I keep at this, the better I'll get.

Denise was speaking to Helen on the telephone.

"C'mon, Helen, it's not like you slept with Larry. You only kissed him. No big deal!"

"Well why hasn't the bugger called me? I told him he should call me Monday and here it is, Monday, and nothing. Maybe I came on too strong? Maybe he thinks I'm silly? Maybe I should call him NOW?"

"Whoa, baby. Now don't go rushing off, otherwise he will think you're silly. He's probably just busy. Wasn't he going to be interviewing people for the new managerial position he advertised?" Denise could be very reassuring.

"Yeah, you're right. I'm surprised he did it at all. He kept putting it off, putting it off. Something's gotten into him. Got a bit more spunk in him. Only wish I could get some of his spunk!"

"Hey, don't talk dirty or they'll cut us off. Speaking of putting it off, Bill's away for a week next week and I can't seem to motivate myself to call a babysitter. Our regular babysitter is on holidays and I've got the name of someone who I know a bit. She's got a family of her own and volunteered to help out. I just don't think she really wants to do it. She'll think I'm pushy. I don't know. I just stare at the phone and then do something else."

"For example?" Helen was intrigued how Denise could put off something so simple as calling a babysitter.

"Well, I think what a dumbo I am: I'll be the one to lose out if I don't find one; I'll have to cook. Then I go in and make myself a gin and tonic."

"Even in the morning?" laughed Helen.

"No, in the morning I eat a doughnut. What's wrong with me?"

"Sounds like you just don't feel like doing it."

"Thanks, Anna Freud, some big help you are."

"No seriously, in fact your husband explained this to me when I was complaining about me not doing enough study. He said ..."

"I thought he said to you not to get involved with anyone until after your exams?" interrupted Denise.

"I'm not 'involved'. You're the one who even said I hadn't slept with him. No, shut up and listen. He made good sense."

"My Bill?"

"Yeah, he told me not to be down on myself just because I was procrastinating at my study and to remember my positive qualities. He also told me to concentrate on the advantages of getting my work done and the disadvantages of not studying. Then, believe it or not he said I should find out which part of me wanted to give up and make it feel ashamed for letting the rest of me down. And it's working!. Now I see my discomfort for what it is - a barrier to my achieving my goal of graduating this year and sleeping with Larry."

"Helen. You have a one track mind!"

"Never mind where my mind is. You're just a wimp. C'mon. All you have to do is remind yourself of the advantages of making the call. So what if she thinks you're a bit pushy. You ARE! Just kidding. Does it really matter all that much what she thinks? Either she'll do it or she won't. So stop putting yourself down. Bite the bullet. Are you going to let a little ol' discomfort block you from having a good night out? Now who's being silly?"

"Yeah, yeah. Points taken. I'd better hang up and do it now while I've still got the courage."

Actions Speak Louder Than Words

This week, when you start to feel 'uptight', anxious or frustrated, rather than dodging the feeling, allow yourself to experience as much discomfort as possible. By consciously deciding to 'go with the feeling', you are starting to exert some control over it.

When you start to feel very frustrated or anxious and feel like avoiding the situation or task which is provoking the feeling, scan your body to locate the greatest amount of discomfort. It may be in your head, shoulders, stomach, chest or elsewhere. Once you locate your physical zone of discomfort, ask yourself whether you are tough enough to put up with it. Pretend that you are talking to the zone and ask whether it wants to be the wimp responsible for you giving up and throwing in the towel (e.g., "Listen stomach, are you the weak link in my system? Are you going to let me down?").

7

Getting Organised, Getting Started

Good order is the foundation of all things.

Edmund Burke, Political Philosopher.

You may be someone who procrastinates because you never seem to have enough time to get things done or because you seem to waste a lot of time. You decide to answer a few letters which have been sitting around for a while yet, at the end of the day, you still haven't gotten to them. A related difficulty may be seen in the fact that you are simply too distracted by things going on around you and are too disorganised in the way you have prepared your work area and materials to have a clear run at what you've set out to do. The phone is always ringing, people are all the time at your door and you can't find all the material you need to start to tackle the job.

In addition to time and environmental distractions which divert you from directly attacking your work, you may have a hard time getting started because you are uncertain about the best way to begin. You are a bit like the reluctant swimmer. You've managed to get to the pool and remembered to bring your suit. Now you have spent five minutes walking around the pool wondering how cold the water will be, which end to get in, walked back to the locker for your towel, had a drink of water, put your toe in the water and still find yourself on dry land. You may have a cautious task approach which is inhibiting you from getting on with what you have to do.

In this chapter, I will address one of the main causes of chronic procrastination which is poor time management and offer suggestions which will help you to control your

use of time better so that the probability of doing what
you've set out to do improves considerably. I'll also tackle
how you can organise your work environment so that you
are not distracted by interruptions or diverted by not having
on-hand the materials and resources you need to start
work. Finally, I'll focus on ways to help you stop 'dilly-
dallying' around when you are getting ready to do the work
so that you get started sooner rather than later.

Time Disorganisation

*The one thing that people who know me best attribute to me
the most is an ability to manage my time efficiently....I begin
by viewing a week as 168 hours and I schedule time for
relaxation and rest as well as work. I force myself to have time
to relax whether it be to play tennis, read the morning paper,
take a nap in the office, or simply do nothing - to free my mind
from any sort of work-oriented thoughts or decisions. To make
sure I have this time I programme these non-work activities
into my schedule. If I know, for instance, that my first committment is at 7 a.m., I would rather get up at 5 a.m. and spend
an hour reading, relaxing and exercising than get up at 6 a.m.
and have to rush to my first appointment without having time
to myself. My schedule that day would therefore begin at 5
a.m.*

Mark H. McCormack, What They Don't Teach You At
Harvard Business School, 1984.

You may be someone who has an allergic reaction every
time they hear the words "time management". This is more
likely if you work for a large corporation which has had you
attend different "motivational" and "performance enhancement" workshops which have taken you through the basic
techniques of time management only to find when you get
back to the real world they don't work particularly well! The
main reason time management programs do not work is
that, as a rule, they fail to include the essential ingredient
of a person's attitudes towards their work and, in particular,
a person's ability to tolerate frustration and discomfort. No
time management program will be effective unless the
person who is learning the skills has high discomfort
tolerance.

You may also have an allergy to the notion of time control because of your philosophical leaning towards romanticism and approaching life and its opportunities from an intuitive rather than logical position. (An attitude which in my book often qualifies as a rationalisation is the belief that if something is meant to happen it will happen and there is no need to plan for it.)

However, the bitter pill to swallow is this. If you are a poor time manager and want to procrastinate less at what you do, then in certain areas of your life where self-improvement is needed, you will have to consider becoming more predictable and plan to get things done, rather than merely reacting and putting out bush-fires.

Time management is a vital skill if you find, because of your work and/or home committments, that you have too much to do and not enough time to do it. As this applies to just about everybody I know, I believe the techniques I introduce will have wide application.

Now I'm not going to propose that you compile a thorough inventory of the ways you use and abuse time nor will I invite you to conduct an analysis of your various roles in life specifying the different functions you are involved in. I will not be subjecting you to reading about how to do a cost-benefit analysis of how you spend your time relative to the priorities you have in carrying out the different functions of the variety of jobs you are involved in. This domain is the bread and butter of books and workshops on time management of which there are many good ones which you can avail yourself of if you so choose.

The author of the book you are now reading is not one of those people who rigidly sticks to a time management plan. Quite frankly, while it suits some of my colleagues, it doesn't suit my more laid back style of conducting my life. By laid back, I do not mean sloppy (I hope). It simply means that I do prefer to leave myself a fair amount of freedom to do what I feel like doing within the constraints of my day at work and home rather than planning what I will be doing Thursday afternoon the previous Sunday night. Now I am not knocking the power and importance of the 'time-managed' life style. Many of our top achievers use it because it either suits them or they require it so that they ensure everything gets done.

I seem to be someone who can manage my affairs so that I get just about everything I want done without depending on a time management program. A calendar and daily diary is sufficient for me to not only organise my future activities but also so that I get what needs to be done today, done.

However, there have been periods over the past few years where things have literally gotten on top of me so that my natural, simple approach to managing time has let me down. Generally, it is at those times when I have a bit too much on my plate that I need to plan what I am doing and budget and schedule my time. I know this time has arrived when I find myself procrastinating at finishing important jobs at work, when I find that I am not spending enough good time with my family or when I start to overlook my weight and feel worn out. At these times, I employ some of the following time management techniques to give me a lift and help me through the difficult times. A few of them are so powerful for me in helping me do what I want, that I have gradually incorporated them into my day-to-day lifestyle.

The logic of using time management procedures to overcome procrastination is two-fold. Firstly, by planning and scheduling your daily activities and by delegating activities to others at work and home, you will find yourself with more time available to do what you have been putting off because of time constraints. Secondly, by actually writing down the task you've been putting off, making it your number one priority, and scheduling a time to do it with a deadline clearly in mind, you will be more likely to do it.

The five techniques I will describe which can help you to find more time to get things done as well as to help you start doing certain tasks are: Weekly Planning, Daily Planning, Daily Scheduling, Priority Setting and Delegation.

Weekly Planning

Murphy's Laws
Nothing is as simple as it seems.

Everything takes longer than it should.

If anything can go wrong, it will.

When you have lots to do, it will sometimes help you to make better use of your time (and therefore procrastinate less) to write down everything you want to accomplish by the end of the week and exactly which activities you have to perform in order to achieve your objectives. A form such as the one which follows can be used for such purposes. Be sure to specify what it is you've been putting off and which you would like to accomplish by the end of the week.

Weekly Planner

Objectives (write down what you want to accomplish by the end of the week):

1._____

2._____

3._____

4._____

5._____

Activities (write down what you have to do to achieve your objectives, the priority of each activity; 1 = top, 2 = middle, 3 = low, the time you believe the activity will take and the day you will do it):

Activity	Priority	Time Needed	Day

You will notice that you are to indicate the priority of each activity. This ranking will make it easier for you to concentrate on accomplishing the more essential tasks when you are pressed for time.

An example of one of my own weekly planners is as follows (the task I want to make sure I get to is working on my procrastination book).

Objectives:

1. Work on procrastination book

2. Update correspondence

3. Prepare Semester 2 class

4. Prepare workshop

5. Spend special time with son

6. Exercise

Activities:	Priority	Time Needed	Day
1. Write ML, FG, TD, JH	2	60 mins	T
2. Write JW	1	30 mins	M
3. Finish reviewing research articles on causes of procrastination.	1	3 hrs	T
4. Finish writing Ch. 1	1	4 hrs	T
5. Read background material for Ch. 2	3	3 hrs	F
6. Write outline for Ch. 2	3	1 hr	F
7. Outline for Sem 2 class	1	2 hrs	M
8. Photocopy handouts	3	1 hr	F
9. Flyers for workshop	1	2 hrs	M
10. Write/place workshop advt. in newspaper	1	1 hr	M
11. Contact printers	2	30 mins	W
12. See movie with JD	2	4 hrs	Th
13. Jogging/calesthenics	1	60 mins	M/W/F

You can see from my own example that working on my book, which is a top priority, has to compete with other top priorities in my life. In terms of everything I had to do that week and their priority, it seemed as though book writing (finishing Chapter 1) would be best accomplished on Tuesday.

There are a few "rules of thumb" in completing a weekly planner. Make sure that the different activities lead to stated objectives. This requires that you have been reasonably careful in analysing all the different things you have to do to accomplish each objective.

Complete your weekly planner on the Saturday or Sunday before the beginning of the following week. Do not leave completion of the planner until Monday as doing so will interfere with those activities you have set out to accomplish.

Daily planning

Parkinson's Law

Work expands to fill the time available for its accomplishment.

I find that when I have many important things to accomplish on a day, a Daily Planner can help me get organised and make sure that I maximise the use of my time and that I do not forget the important things I have to do. During peak work times, before I go home from work I will complete a Daily Planner for the next day which includes all the important things I have to do the following day, their priority and how much time I predict the activity will take. Generally, when I use a daily planner in conjunction with a weekly planner, I first schedule those top priority activities I have not already accomplished during the week. I am just as likely to use a daily planner on its own without having first completed a weekly planner to speed things along. Once again, it is vital to write down the particular activities you have been putting off and hope to accomplish.

On the following form, first write down what you have to do on the day, its priority and how much time you estimate you will need. To use your daily planner to overcome procras-

tination in various areas of your life, indicate those important activities to be done during the day and after hours
associated with work, those activities centered on your
home, committments, activities focused on your self-
development, your personal and, if applicable, your study
committments.

Daily Activity Planner

Activity to be Done Today	Priority	Time Needed	Completed Yes/No

Daily activity schedule

The scheduling of different activities which will lead you to
accomplish what you've set out to do is really the goal of
time management. Rather than leaving it up to how you
feel and other activities which might intervene to divert you
away from your high priority activities, a schedule of daily
activities which you stick to religiously will get you on your
way.

By religiously, I mean that you strictly adhere to what
you've set out to do. If you are meant to start writing at
2.00pm and write for three hours, I put my answering
machine on and place a do not disturb sign on my office.
However, your Daily Activity Schedule also needs to be
flexible. If at the beginning of the day you schedule an
activity for a certain time but find out at lunch that there is

a vital meeting for you to attend at the same time, then you had better go to the meeting and make up your writing time at a later time or simply - if you can - modify your particular deadline.

Daily Activity Schedule

am		pm	
8.00	_____	2.00	_____
8.15	_____	2.15	_____
8.30	_____	2.30	_____
8.35	_____	2.35	_____
8.45	_____	2.45	_____
9.00	_____	3.00	_____
9.15	_____	3.15	_____
9.30	_____	3.30	_____
9.45	_____	3.45	_____
10.00	_____	4.00	_____
10.15	_____	4.15	_____
10.30	_____	4.30	_____
10.45	_____	4.45	_____
11.00	_____	5.00	_____
11.15	_____	5.15	_____
11.30	_____	5.30	_____
11.45	_____	5.45	_____
12.00pm	_____	6.00	_____
12.15	_____	6.15	_____
12.30	_____	6.30	_____
12.45	_____	6.45	_____
1.00	_____	7.00	_____
1.15	_____	7.15	_____
1.30	_____	7.30	_____
1.45	_____	7.45	_____

In scheduling your time for a day, do not schedule one activity right after another. Leave some time between blocks you have scheduled to allow for things which take longer than you expect and to deal with the unexpected.

Priority setting

If I do not do the activity, will the manner in which the person or organisation operates be significantly disadvantaged? If one is not significantly negatively effected, then the task becomes a low priority.

Professor Hedley Beare, Australian Educator.

Another key to making sure you get around to doing what you decide is important to do, is being able to determine the priority of different activities. While it might seem that it should be obvious as to what is important, it often isn't. Or if it is, many of us have a wonderful penchant for involving ourselves in the inessential. Oftentimes, spending time on lower priority activities is a way of diverting yourself from the discomfort of doing the hard stuff.

I recently worked with a 34 year old woman, Wendy, who had been teaching school for a decade and complained bitterly that she never had enough time to finish projects she started such as a cooking class and working on developing her considerable photographic talents. "As soon as I get started on what I want to do, I always think about all the other things that I am not doing and start to panic. I end up doing nothing very well and I'm getting pretty depressed about it!" In questioning her about all her other committments, I obtained a picture of someone who took on far too much for herself, largely because she had difficulty saying "No" to other people's requests. If someone at school asked Wendy to stay on for a meeting at work, she always obliged. She was always the one to volunteer to organise her school's fund-raising activities. The list was endless. And not only did she have too much to do in her own mind, everything she took on was a Number 1 priority. Why? The thought of not living up to her committments and what others expected of her was, for Wendy, too threatening. A further problem was her reluctance to ask other people for support. A high need for approval ruled this woman's life and made priority-setting a virtual impossibility. It was only after she was able to accept that she didn't always have to please everyone all the time that she was free to set priorities in her life. In Chapter 8, I will have more to say about the importance of assertion in refusing unreasonable requests and in asking for help.

The time management literature has identified the "tyranny of the urgent" as a main cause of not getting important things done. Rather than concentrating on one particular task at a time, this self-defeating work pattern has you working on jobs without regard to their importance simply because they are there to do. To overcome the "tyranny of the urgent", it will be useful for you to be able to assign what you have to do into the following categories:

1.   Urgent and important

2.   important not urgent

3.   urgent not important

4.   not important, not urgent.

Priority setting will, at times, involve you in deciding whether certain things simply do not get done when you initially thought and said they would get done. I think I am on safe ground when I say that if you wrote down everything you could be doing across all areas of your life that there is simply not enough time to get all the activities done. For example, if time permitted, Wendy could schedule meetings with each one of her students to discuss their projects in her subject and to revise her teaching program to suit the needs of each one of her students. Sounds nice doesn't it? Unfortunately, there are so many planned and unforeseen things which teachers have to do that some things like meeting with students get put off.

So when you find yourself starting to put off important things because you've got too much on your plate, it is a good idea to start to make judgments about the different priorities of the activities you perform. Priorities can be determined by how essential the activity is to the accomplishment of your objectives. And objectives themselves can vary in priority.

I invited Wendy to consider the following examples of sub-objectives and activities which go along with the achievement of each objective.

1) **Objective:** Familiarising myself with the latest curriculum programs in maths with an eye to modifying what I use next year.

    Activity: Locate and read McGraw-Hill's latest maths program.

2) **Objective:** Reduce the degree of student misbehaviour in my class.

    Activity: Meet with misbehaving students; supervise detentions.

Wendy was able to see that in terms of her goals as a teacher, the above objectives have different priorities and the enabling activities may also differ in their priority.

Another way to consider priorities is in terms of who it is that you are doing something for. The priority of finishing something requested by your mate or boss will be higher than that of an acquaintance. Higher priority activities performed for more important people will take precedence over activities you engage in for less important people.

The timing in which something has to be done is also important in judging priorities. If you are in charge of making a dinner reservation for a group of friends which are meeting to celebrate someone's birthday, then this activity is a higher and more immediate priority then organising the flowers for your parents 30th wedding anniversary which isn't for four months.

Delegation

A Parable

Once upon a time there was a Little Red Hen who owned a wheat field. "Who will help me harvest the wheat?" she asked.

"Not I," said the pig. "I don't know how."

"Not I," said the cow. "I'm too clumsy."

"Not I," said the dog. "I'm busy with some other things."

So the Little Red Hen did it herself.

"Who will help me grind the wheat into flour?" she asked.

"Not I," said the pig. "That is another vocation in which I'm untrained."

"Not I," said the cow. "You could do it much more efficiently."

"Not I," said the dog. "I'd love to, but I'm involved in some matters of greater urgency. Some other time, perhaps."

So she did it herself.

"Who will help me make some bread?" asked the Little Red Hen.

"Not I," said the pig. "Nobody ever taught me how."

"Not I," said the cow. "You're more experienced and could do it in half the time."

"Not I," said the dog. "I've made some plans for the afternoon. But I'll help you next time."

So she did it herself.

That evening, when guests arrived for her big dinner party, the Little Red Hen had nothing to serve them except bread. She had been so busy doing work that could have been done by others that she had forgotton to plan a main course, prepare a dessert, or even get out the silverware. The evening was a disaster, and she lived unhappily ever after.

Moral: A good leader will find a way to involve others to the extent of their ability. To do the job yourself is the chicken way out.

Edwin C. Bliss, <u>Getting Things Done</u>, 1976.

There are two main barriers to prevent you from using delegation to help you get more time for yourself so that you achieve more of what you want to do rather than what you have to do. If you are a perfectionist and believe that everything you have responsibility for must be done perfectly, then you'll be overly cautious in delegating tasks over which you have responsibility to others because you know that they won't do them as perfectly as you. And you need to be perfect, right? If you still see yourself as a perfectionist, you may want to re-read the material in Chapter 5 on combatting perfectionism. To delegate, you had better work on anti-perfectionism and for many tasks where it doesn't matter (like hanging up the washing or composing unimportant letters) use a "near enough is good enough" approach.

You will also be a poor delegator if you have a high need for approval and desperately want to prove yourself in the eyes of others. If this is the case, then you'll experience too much anxiety about what others think about you when you ask them to do things for you. This is especially the case if you suffer from the Super Woman or Super Man complex and believe you have to be judged by others (and yourself) as fully in control and capable of doing everything on your own. Unfortunately, this point of view inevitably results in less time for yourself and, ironically, more chances that you will end up procrastinating.

Delegation is especially important if you both work and have significant home responsibilities. Woman, especially, have to bear this cross and need to feel comfortable in asking and training others to do things. Delegation at home might involve assigning to children significant activities they are capable of doing, and not worrying too much whether they want to do them are not. They generally won't! Cooking, cleaning and shopping consist of a variety of tasks some of which others can do as well as you. You don't need a license to operate a vacumm cleaner or microwave oven. And cooking pasta with a simple sauce and salad is not all that hard.

At work, the principle which can help you become more efficient is "Do It, Delegate It, Ditch It". There is nothing more likely to lead to the procrastination of certain important tasks than having a desk littered with papers of vaying degrees of importance. The idea behind this principle is to deal with a piece of paper only once and if you respond to it immediately, do it, otherwise pass it on to someone else who you work with who can, or trash it.

The role of a secretary in delegation is vital. If you have a secretary, then it will be important to pass over to him or her those tasks which they are capable of performing without you. You need to pay particular attention to their secretarial and administistative talents as well as how much they have learned about your line of work so that you can hand over material which is suited to their knowledge and skills.

The same recommendations apply to people who work under you. You need to be able to pass on down the line things which you are reasonably confident others can accomplish independently of you. You need to be careful who you select. Picking someone who is not up to the job will only lead to more headaches for you than doing the job yourself in the first place. Or, if the person themself has a high need for approval, then you may also be plagued by them coming to you and making sure they are correct - once again, defeating the whole purpose of delegation. You need to communicate with what you say and do how much independence you expect of subordinates and, while you expect them to do it right without having to consult with you every minute, you do not harshly penalise them for their mistakes which would undermine your own desire to instill in them a sense of independence.

Environmental Disorganisation

Does the following routine sound at all familiar? Joe has been asked to check some personnel forms. As he starts the job, however, someone phones to ask about an overdue report. So he gets out the inventory file but stops to glance at the mail at the same time. A letter on top complaining about something in the machine shop catches his eye. He drops the inventory file, reads the letter, then starts to the machine shop to discuss it. On the way he passes the cafeteria and the coffee smells so good he decides to interrupt his busy morning and have a cup. His day's accomplishments so far: exactly nothing .... Many difficulties confront us in getting off and running. Joe appears to be drifting from one cue to another in a random fashion. The matters that he is allowing to distract him do not warrant the interruption .... If we judge what is important to people by what they do with their time, then we must conclude that Joe's priorities are in sad disarray. The aroma from a cup of coffee has taken precedence over everything else he has encountered. It is the only thing from which he has not gotten distracted.

R. Alec Mackenzie, <u>The Time Trap</u>, 1972.

Your environment can make it harder for you to stop procrastinating for two related reasons. First, procrastination seems to occur almost automatically in certain situations. You don't set out to procrastinate at report writing when you arrive at work, it's just that you seem to get diverted by what's happening around you. You don't set off home thinking today I'm going to go off my diet and eat a big chocolate bar, it's just something about being at home after dinner watching television which triggers off a pattern of behaviour you have been trying to avoid. The point here is that you get used to putting off doing things in certain environments - your bad habits seem to get triggered off because of what is or is not happening around you. It is almost like your mind has been programmed to put off doing things when you are in certain places and at certain times.

A second point is that there are specific things in your environment which are known to lead to procrastination, including too many distractions (phone calls, knocks on door), a messy work area, missing important materials and ingredients to get your work done and being disorganised in the way you have filed things. Noise, clutter and lack of privacy will virtually guarantee a high level of procrastination at tasks which require sustained concentration and effort.

With these two points clearly in mind, you'll clearly see the logic of the following recommendation:

If you want to stop procrastinating at a particular task or activity, make many changes in the environment in which your procrastination typically occurs.

This is something that is surprisingly easy to do and can lead to immediate benefits. By changing your environment, you are changing the particular 'cues' which start your procrastination. Change those 'cues' and you can change yourself.

At work there are a number of changes you can make to cut down on distractions and interruptions.

Telephone Calls. At certain times when you don't want to be interrupted, have your calls screened by your secretary or divert them to an answering machine.

Mail. As a fair amount of time can be consumed in dealing with daily mail, decide whether you want someone to screen your mail or when during the day you will deal with it.

Visitors. Have a strategy worked out for unwanted visitors. If someone arrives at an inopportune time, immediately get up out of your chair and tell them as you slowly escort them to the door that while you are happy to see them, you simply have to get a particular job done - or else.

The amount of change can vary depending on how urgently you desire to get started in doing what you've been putting off. Radical changes can bring dramatic results. If I have not been able to get to do something for some time, I use the Isolation Technique I described in Chapter 4. I remove myself (or have removed from me) my main sources of pleasure, distraction and lower priority activity. Usually, I ask my wife to volunteer to take the kids and herself away to visit her parents for a few days so that I can get a clear run at my work. Or I might come into work on a weekend where there is nothing or anyone around to distract me from what I wish to get done.

Changes can be less drastic than are involved in the Isolation Technique. You might decide, for example, to hang a Do Not Disturb sign on your office door. You could get up a half hour earlier or go to bed a little later. One of my former graduate students, a mother of three teenagers, got up at 4.30 am in order to have the peace and quiet of home in which to work.

Simple changes can have a big impact. If you study at home, make sure you only study at your desk and never on your bed. Further, you should only work at your desk rather than other more enjoyable activities such as reading, or working on a hobby. When you have worked for awhile and are ready for a break, get up out of the chair and only return to your desk when you are ready to work again. Over time, your mind-body will become programmed to work at your desk.

I recently had a phone call from the manager of one of the local branch real estate offices who had attended a procrastination workshop I offered several weeks before. During the workshop, his main complaint was that he never had time to do forward planning. He was also irritated that for the past six months a number of projects people in his office had been assigned had either not been done or in one case had actually been misplaced. His resolution at the end of the day was to re-design the general office area from an open plan to one where people had more privacy. He invested in portable and carpeted room dividers which he used to give people some separate space from each other. As well, he re-deployed the location of his desk in his office to face away from the door as well as acquiring bookcases and two new file cabinets. He also decided on one day a week, for awhile, to come in an hour later and work back in the evening of that day. The call was just to say how much things had improved not only for himself but that his staff seemed to appreciate the improvements as well. He reported that the noise level seemed lower and he wasn't suffering so much distraction.

A poor filing and record-keeping system can lead to unnecessary procrastination. Not only does an inefficient system result in needless clutter of material which requires to be acted upon and stored, it can also prevent finding of things you need to work on or complete.

At work, it is a good idea to have a system which enables you to keep track of, respond to and file memos and letters. Such a system will not only permit you to have a work environment which is free from visual distractions, but you will also be able to find what you want when you want it. I really need to work hard on this area as I find that with my involvement in many projects it is too easy to misplace

material including memos, letters, handouts and lecture
notes for different classes I teach, background articles and
accompanying notes for upcoming writing projects, etc.. I
have organised three file cabinets containing 12 drawers
around my different activities. As well, I have four different
plastic filing containers sitting on top of each other on my
desk labelled Today's Work, For Filing, Tomorrow's Work
and Out Basket which help me deal with material I am
currently receiving or working on. I also have a folder
labelled Important Reading which I use when I come across
important articles of interest.

Record-keeping at home is equally important in order to
free you from being overwhelmed by the accumulation of
records and other documents which come your way on a
daily basis. Donna Douglas, author of *Choice and Com-
promise: A Women's Guide to Balancing Family and Career*
(AMACON, 1980) offers some valuable advice on how to
get organised at home. Along with her suggestion of identifying a "work station" (desk, table top) where you can work
and do your planning, she describes a simple filing system
containing the following six categories of documents:

1. **Personal Documents:** These include key family
    records such as wills, birth, marriage and death
    certificates. Also included are passports and
    diplomas.

2. **Property Records:** Both real estate records (deeds,
    title papers, morgage documents and a record of
    capital improvements) and a household inventory
    should be filed.

3. **Financial Records:** Needing safekeeping are any
    stocks and bonds, records for pension and
    profit-sharing plans, bank account information and
    any retail and instalment loan contracts.

4. **Insurance Records:** The policies may range from life
    and accident to liability and car; keep any receipts.

5. **Health Records:** An up-to-date health record is an
    invaluable resource to have. This record should

include such items as health fund information and receipts, immunisation and infectious disease records and any other significant information relating to family illness.

6.   **Tax Records:** Not only should you keep copies of your tax return forms, you also need to file any relevant receipts plus any other verification of your tax return.

The above suggestions will, hopefully, be useful in showing you how to make your environment more conducive to getting things done. By changing where and when you do things, cutting down on distractions as well as organising your work space and filing system, you will find it much easier to devote your attention and energy to the task at hand.

Poor Task Approach

Go to work on a task as soon as you have everything you need to get started. The worst thing you can do is sit in the starting blocks and procrastinate. Forget about the contingencies that might occur. You can make adjustments as you go. If you find out later you've made a mistake, admit it and start over.

James R. Sherman, Ph.D., <u>Do It!</u>, 1988.

How you feel as well as your frame of mind right before you begin a task has a lot to do with whether you have a successful lift-off. If you lack confidence and feel restless and nervous about what you are doing you will find it much harder to get off the lauching pad. If you think you're hopeless because you procrastinate at important things - especially when you compare yourself to others - then your mood and spirit will be so heavy that, once again, you'll require extra thrust (motivation) to get moving. If you are someone who finds the effort of doing things you should be doing too hard, once again, forward propulsion will be questionable. If you are stressed out and fatigued, you will know how much harder it is to make things happen. As well, your motivation to do something for someone will be low if that person has failed to give you any recognition for good work you have previously done.

When you are feeling very anxious, down, frustrated, angry and emotionally drained, you will be much more tentative in your approach to all sorts of tasks. Because strong negative emotions make it much harder for you to think clearly and logically, you will have a hard time breaking down a task into manageable bits and be overwhelmed by the size of certain tasks. You'll find knowing where to begin a task much harder - especially if what you're embarking on is new and unfamiliar. For things you find boring or frustrating, you'll have little energy required to put up with the inevitable frustration of getting started. If the activity is anxiety-provoking where what it is you are about to do might fail or you might be crticised, you'll have little in the way of emotional reserves to call upon to help you put up with the discomfort and anxiety surrounding the activity.

There are definite indications from my research that being uncertain about what to do and how to get started and feeling like you need to know more about what you're doing, stems more from your feelings which surround doing the task than having much to do with your scholastic or intellectual ability. And even when you are attempting to work on a task requiring considerable mental application such as writing a dissertation or learning advanced computer programs, your anxiety and self-doubts which you may have, as well as your level of frustration tolerance, has a large bearing on the degree to which you persevere or give up.

So it would seem that the things which lead to you having a poor task approach and which often stop you from getting started have more to do with you than they do with the task itself.

I have already in Chapters 5 and 6 discussed ways in which you can control your anxiety and self-depreciation, and increase your discomfort tolerance level. In the two chapters which follow, I'll illustrate ways how to manage your anger and stress levels so that they no longer remain as negative forces diverting you from what you want to do. Let me offer a few summary ideas which might serve to improve your approach to your work, work relationships, your home and personal relationships and to areas of your own self-development and to your study.

1. Pay close attention to your level of discomfort when you think about doing, or are involved in doing, things. If you find yourself very anxious or frustrated, see if you can bring down your discomfort by relaxing it away. As well, talk sense to yourself about being able to handle and cope with your discomfort even though you don't like it. Remind yourself of the importance to you of following through and finishing what you've set out to do.

2. Don't be afraid to try something which might not work out. As Elbert Hubbard, the famous American philosopher wrote some time ago; "The greatest mistake you can make is to be afraid of making one." This idea is especially important in the early phases of what you are doing where it might seem that you are making a hopeless mess of that which you are attempting and that you are doomed to failure. If you get started in doing something even when you are very unsure about what to do or how it will turn out (e.g., meeting a new person; writing a short story), more often than not you will use your early mistakes as a basis to learn from and build upon so that you improve on your initial effort. Indeed, by not getting started and waiting around for the right moment or until you know everything about what to do, you prevent yourself from the vital learning which comes from your early mistakes.

3. Don't be afraid of hard work. This is especially important for work which calls upon the application of your brain power. When the work is hard, you will experience "brain strain" to master new concepts, principles and in solving problems. "Brain strain" and the frustration which goes with it will not kill you! In fact, the more you strain, the more you'll gain.

4.   Be confident in your ability to succeed. I don't mean
to be Pollyanna here. However, if you approach your
work replaying past experiences where you were not
successful and if your internal dialogue is filled with
negative stuff such as "I'll never be able to do this. I'm
hopeless at this. This is too hard, I shouldn't have to
do it. This is unbearable", what are your chances of
persevering when the going gets tough? No matter
what you are getting started on, writing a tough
chapter for your dissertation, learning to use the
computer or just cleaning up your house, believe in
yourself.

5.   Get in the habit of using positive self talk when you
are getting started on something you don't feel like
doing or when you feel like giving up. Here are some
examples:

Getting started

• I can do it!

• The harder I try, the easier it will be!

• Work now, play later!

• I can if I want to!

• Do it!

• It may be hard, but it's not impossible!

• It's not so bad!

Keeping your effort going

• Don't get discouraged!

• Keep concentrating!

• I am not hopeless if I make a mistake!

• This is not impossible, only hard!

• It's not the end of the world if I make a mistake or it
doesn't work out!

- The main thing is not to give up!
- Stick with it!
- Effort equals results!
- The harder the work, the more effort I have to put in!
- I am sure I can do it! I just have to keep trying different ways!
- Be confident!
- Think positively!

The following Procrastination Bypass Techniques which I've already described in Chapter 4 are especially good for overcoming a poor task approach. You may wish to refer back to them now.

The Knock Out Technique
Worst-First Approach
Bits and Pieces Approach
Salami Technique
Five Minute Plan
Switching
Referenting

The important point which each of these techniques make is to start doing 'it' NOW!

Larry looked at his watch. It was 5.55pm and everyone save himself had left for home. Larry was feeling pretty pleased with himself. The daily planning schedule he had set out for himself had worked well. He had gotten through the four interviews for his managerial position ahead of time. He still wasn't totally sure he needed to hire someone right at the moment but decided to take the risk anyway. He knew he wasn't going to lose any 'real' money by taking someone on and it would give him more time to concentrate on developing new opportunities and directions for his company. He got caught up on all his dictation and actually got work done on the proposal which was due at the end of the week. "None of this last minute stuff for me. I'm taking control of things now. Getting myself organised and planning my time. That's the key for me." He was also pleased because in five minutes, he was to meet with a management consultant to discuss with him the ins and outs of strategic planning and to get some advice about how best to deploy his current personnel in order to make more of their resources. He closed his eyes and leant back in his chair putting his feet on his desk to savour the moment. "Just a few relaxing breaths of air. Loose as a goose."

At that moment, Larry jolted himself so strongly in his chair that he toppled over backwards. "Helen. I forgot to call her. Damn. She'll probably think I don't care or was offended. Where's my time planner?....I forgot to write her in. I've got 60 seconds before my next appointment. I'll dial it now .... Busy!! It can't be busy. Redial .... Busy again!! I'll bet she's on the phone to Denise telling her what a jerk I am .... Too old. I'll call Denise .... Hell, her line's busy! I'll send Helen a FAX. That's it. 'Sorry, too busy to call.' No that's not right. Hell! She doesn't have a FAX at home. Idiot!! I'll send her a short telegram to be delivered by courier. With flowers and champagne. That's it! Now where's the number of the telegram office? Hell! My 6.00 appointment is here. I'll just have to call her when I finish. Quick!! Staighten the tie, get the jacket on and try to look the part!"

Actions Speak Louder Than Words

Break down a task you've been putting off, but would like to accomplish, into smaller activities. Be as specific as you can. Now, over the next week, schedule as many of these activities as you can. Try to schedule at least one. When you have accomplished that activity, reward yourself with something pleasurable. If you do not get around to doing it, withhold something you enjoy to do each day until you have done it.

Picture clearly in your mind where you are and the time of day in which you put off doing something you've decided to do. Before attempting it again, make a big change in your environment such as attempting to do it in another room or place or at another time.

Get started on doing something you've been putting off because you are not quite sure where to begin or how it will turn out. Try to reduce your discomfort before getting started or ignore it.

8

Managing Hostility and Lack of Assertion

You are what you are and where you are because of what has gone into your mind. You can change what you are and who you are by changing what goes into your mind.

Zig Ziglar, See You At The Top, 1983.

Helena had been married to Warren, a dentist, for three years and before marrying, had been dating him for some four years. Early in their relationship, Helena had worked for Warren as a dental technician although, since having married, was now staying at home on a full-time basis. Helena has a pleasant disposition, enjoys a good laugh and has plenty of friends. When I saw Helena last year, she was not happy and the cause of her unhappiness, in her opinion, was her husband. According to Helena, Warren would frequently get quite angry with her for no apparent reason and would pick on her for even the smallest of her picadillos such as when her shoes didn't exactly match her skirt or how she stored groceries. She was seeing me because of her anger with Warren for continuing his tirades with her. She had expected that after they got married he would feel more secure in their relationship and that she could, by staying home full-time, work at pleasing him by cooking his favourite meals and making him feel like the king of his castle. It hadn't worked and Helena found herself getting quite angry with Warren and depressed about their relationship.

In getting to know Helena, I found her to procrastinate in two areas of her relationship which as far as I could tell only added to her problems. One main area of her relationship that she shied away from was in being more assertive with Warren and expressing quite clearly to him what she felt about his tirades and how she wanted him to change. Whenever he got angry with her, Helena would retreat into her shell and wait until the storm had passed. Warren knew she was angry with him at times but clearly wasn't very motivated to change his behaviour towards her.

The other main area of procrastination for Helena was caused by her hostility towards Warren for being so unreasonable with her. Unable to express herself with him or get him to change very much, she would retaliate and rebel against his tantrums with her by deliberately putting off doing things around the house and for him. A clear example of this procrastination was when she didn't have time to iron the pants Warren wanted to wear to a party they were invited to. "I can't help myself. It's the only way I know to get back at the bastard," Helena admitted to me. Of course, by procrastinating at doing things which were important to her husband, Helena only invited more outbursts from Warren.

Helena's disturbed relationship with Warren reveals how different types of procrastination can really lead to damaging results. Helena's lack of assertion made it harder to communicate with Warren and the more she put off discussing her wishes with him, the worse he seemed to be getting. As well, her hostility towards Warren was the underlying cause as to why she procrastinated at doing certain things and, once again, her procrastination resulted in increased difficulties for her.

In this chapter, I want to examine two types of procrastination which can have very serious consequences for you. They are related in some ways although they sometimes do not co-exist in the same person. The two types are:

Procrastination due to your lack of assertion;

Procrastination due to your hostility towards others.

Dealing With Difficult People

The most common emotional stress reaction you have when confronted with a difficult person is anger. The more provocative, unfair and inconsiderate the difficult person's actions are, the more fury you are likely to experience. It is also not uncommon to feel put down and inferior in the face of unfair and negative treatment.

Michael E. Bernard, Taking the Stress
Out of Teaching, 1990.

It is unfortunate but true that from time to time you will come in contact with a person who acts in a very unfair, unkind, inconsiderate and negative way towards you. It might be someone at home such as Helena's husband, Warren, a parent who has been especially critical of you over the years, someone who you work with or for, or someone who is delivering a service to you such as your doctor, plumber or grocer.

There are a number of choices you have in responding to this person. You could - unless the person is likely to fire you or throw you out of the house - assertively stick up for your rights and request a change in the person's behaviour. If you are someone who gets nervous at the thought of freely speaking your mind, you might think about saying something, but procrastinate at actually doing anything. Or you could become so enraged with the treatment that you abuse the person. Or, once again, you might decide to do something but because you are not in the habit of confronting people who have done you in or because the consequences of direct confrontation would be negative for you, you decide, instead, to passively retaliate. You decide to refuse to cooperate with the person and to 'fix their wagon' by procrastinating at doing something they are expecting you to do.

How you actually respond to difficult people will depend on your attitude towards them and their unfair behaviour. Whether you procrastinate at being assertive will partly depend upon your need for their approval and your ability to tolerate how they react to you and how they think about you when you are being assertive. A high need for their approval and a low tolerance for their possible criticism of you will lead you to experience a high level of anxiety and to avoiding any confrontation.

Or if you get very angry with them because you believe they shouldn't act so unfairly and that anyone who acts so badly deserves to be punished, then you will be much more likely to respond directly to their behaviour with your own verbal or physical aggression or indirectly by procrastinating at doing things which they want you to do.

It may or may not be obvious to you that the "real" reason you put off asserting yourself has to do with your intolerance of the anxiety you experience when you think about asserting yourself with a difficult person. This issue I will address further in the final chapter of the book How to Get Others to Procrastinate Later. In order to motivate someone to be more efficient, you will need to be able to assert yourself and to do this you cannot be overly concerned with what they think of you.

It is even harder to realise that some of your procrastinating behaviour may be motivated out of anger you have towards others or the world. It might well be the case for you that this almost automatic and subconscious behaviour has its beginnings a long time ago. You may be someone who because of the way you perceived you were treated by your parents or school decided to rebel against many forms of authority. You may have gotten so angry about what they did or didn't do, that you decided to passively resist their directions as a way of getting back at them. If they wanted you to study, then you decided to procrastinate at your work and, therefore, obtain poorer grades as a way of retribution. If they wanted you to clean your room, you put off tidying for as long as you could. Today, the aftermath of your earlier days may have resulted in you becoming negative to other people's suggestions or requirements for what you should be doing. While you might lightly go along with your boss' suggestions on how to improve the quality of your work, deep down you think he's a bastard for criticising you and not giving you enough support. The result. You pay back by going on a work slow-down. You have become what can be called a passive-aggressive procrastinator!

In Chapter 5, the reasons why you experience anxiety when you are faced with certain threatening or demanding situations and people, have been explained in terms of your needs for approval, achievement and self-depreciation. As well, methods for modifying the attitudes which lead to high anxiety and low self-esteem have been elaborated. If you lack assertion, it may well be a good idea to review this material as well as the ideas on how to control your discomfort anxiety presented in Chapter 6. For you to become more assertive in your dealings with people, it will be very necessary and helpful for you to reduce the anxiety you experience when preparing to be assertive as well as to know how to cope with the physical discomfort you can feel while asserting yourself.

The next section addresses the other major emotion which can lead to passive-aggressive procrastination; namely, anger.

Managing Your Anger

You may at times show your anger in passive aggressive behavior that takes the form of procrastination. Instead of expressing your resentment to others directly, this kind of behavior enables you to do so indirectly.

Albert Ellis and William J. Knaus, <u>Overcoming Procrastination</u>, 1977.

One of the first questions you need to answer for yourself is twofold: first, does your high level of anger towards a person's poor behaviour help you get what you want; second, does putting off doing things as a type of retaliation help you achieve your goals. In answer to the first part of the question, it is almost always the case that when you get furious with someone (not just irritated) your aggressive behaviour towards them does not often bring about the change in their behaviour you would want. Your anger only brings with it more anger from them. And when you are furious, your ability to problem solve is greatly reduced and you tend to rely on previous methods which frequently haven't worked.

As far as the second part of the question is concerned, needlessly putting off doing things because of feeling angry generally results in negative consequences for you. When you put off doing things for others, not only do they form a lesser opinion of your work and you, you often find yourself unable to get to do what you really want to do because you have put off that very activity which needs to be accomplished before you can move forward.

So what I will argue is that a more appropriate emotional response to someone acting disagreeably towards you is not rage, but rather irritation, annoyance and displeasure. The reason that irritation is an appropriate albeit negative emotion is that even when you are extremely irritated, you are still in control. It is still possible for you to be assertive with someone when you are irritated and you are less likely to try to retaliate against someone's wishes by procrastinating.

While I am suggesting that extreme anger is bad, do not fall into the trap of thinking that because it's self-defeating and largely based on irrational attitudes you should therefore never be angry. This will lead to unhealthy suppression. It is better to acknowledge and express your anger if you can't modify it than it is to keep it all bottled up inside. After all, anger is a natural human emotion albeit extremely destructive. Recognise that even when you are harming others and yourself with it, you are not a failure or a bad person because you get angry. Your anger is like any other behaviour which you engage in that doesn't help you achieve your goal (e.g., smoking, over-eating); it is bad but it does not mean that you are a bad person. Once you can accept yourself with your anger, then you can go about working hard to modify it.

Anger-creating attitudes

Let me describe how you can literally make yourself overly angry about difficult people. Most people start off thinking quite rationally when they are faced with someone's unfair behaviour. Just about all people agree with the values of consideration, fairness, respect and kindness in our relationships with each other and that when someone acts contrary to these values it is bad and wrong. When someone acts out of line with these values, it is quite rational and desirable to think: "I would prefer that person to act more fairly and considerately. I really don't like it. I wonder how I can modify their behaviour." Such an attitude towards someone's difficult behaviour will lead you to feel irritated and, therefore, motivated to try to constructively change it. However, people who get furious with inconsideration take the rational preference for fairness and consideration and convert it into an irrational demand: "Because I prefer him to act nicely, he **must** act fairly. It's **awful** that he isn't. I **can't stand it** when he acts that way. He's a **no-good louse** who deserves to be punished." These irrational attitudes lead not only to you becoming furious and enraged, but also increase the likelihood of you acting aggressively and not achieving any positive change in the others' behaviour.

The general irrational attitude which turns annoyance into fury in the face of inconsiderate, unkind or unfair behaviour can be stated as follows:

"People must treat me considerately, respectfully and fairly; I can't stand it when they don't; if they don't act as they should, I consider them to be totally bad and deserving of my punishment."

You can hold this idea with respect to one person such as your mother, or child, or boss, or you can hold it about everyone. Here are some irrational thoughts which stem from this attitude:

"I can't stand it when my mother is unfairly critical of me."

"Children should be more considerate and respectful of their parents."

"It's really terrible to have to work for someone who is so negative and unsupportive towards me."

Let's examine the different parts of the anger-creating attitude to see why they are irrational. We can use Helena's thoughts about her husband for illustration.

When Helena tells herself that Warren shouldn't be the way he is, her belief flies in the face of the evidence that he is often that way because that's the way he is - at least some of the time. When you think about it logically, it doesn't make any sense for Helena to say to herself: "Warren shouldn't lose his temper so often. How can he be so insensitive?" The facts are that that's the way her husband is. An intelligent man who is off his head some of the time. That's bad, but that's the way he is. And he can do it easily.

Indeed, there are a significant number of people in life who are what are called DC's; Difficult Customers. Because of their personality and family background, they happen to be disagreeable a lot of the time. If you come into contact with a DC, it makes even less sense to insist that they should be pleasant and considerate towards you. That's not the way they are. It's reasonable to prefer that they change, but it makes no sense to expect that they should be what they are not.

When Helena tells herself that her husband's temper tantrums are "awful and horrible", she is taking something which is bad and making it worse than it is. The words "awful" and "horrible" mean "100% bad" and while there is no disagreement that his verbal attacks on Helena are very bad, things could be much worse. He could beat her! Or worse, she could have a serious, life threatening illness. By blowing the badness of Warren's behaviour out of proportion (it is very bad, but not a catastrophe), Helena is adding more emotional fuel to her fire.

When Helena tells herself that she really "can't stand" Warren throwing a tantrum, she is really telling herself a falsehood which is also escalating her anger. She needs to ask herself "Where is the evidence that I can't stand it?" and she would find that while there is plenty of evidence that she doesn't care much for it, she certainly can put up with it if she makes up her mind to. The expression "sticks and stones can break my bones but words can never hurt me" reinforces the reality of being able to stand things you do not like.

And finally, when she condemns her husband for being a total ass for his brutish behaviour, Helena is making an over-generalisation. While it is true that his behaviour is loutish and bad, there are many other characteristics of Warren that are good such as being bright, hard working and honest. Rating someone's total worth on the basis of one or more of their bad acts is not logical and leads to extreme rage. He is not totally bad even though his temper tantrums are. As well, Helena's desire to punish him for his bad acts is only back-firing. Procrastinating only makes matters worse.

In a nutshell, the key to effective anger management is to realise that people are fallible and that they will act in disagreeable ways towards you some of the time. That's bad, but that's the way life and people are. And when you encounter them acting fallibly, then it is best to accept, not like, what they are doing rather than blowing the significance or unpleasantness of their negative actions out of proportion. And with some people, you may actually be able to get them to change their behaviour for the better.

In the case of Helena and Warren, Helena eventually was able to calm herself down about Warren's behaviour to the point where she no longer retaliated passively by procrastinating. She accepted that her husband was simply the sort of person prone to getting easily frustrated and that it did her no good getting furious with him about his temper. She then started to become more active and assertive with him in terms of applying some pressure on him to try to modify himself. Today, after a full year of marriage counselling and two children, Helena and Warren are still married. And although Warren still loses his temper leading Helena to remain dissatisfied with elements of their realtionship, she reports that she has begun to enjoy the energy and stimulation Warren has to offer.

Rational attitudes to reduce anger

When you are faced with people and situations where you are likely to lose your temper, prepare yourself beforehand by thinking about and rehearsing to yourself one or more of the following rational attitudes:

"While it is preferable to be treated fairly, kindly and considerately, there is no law of the universe which says I must be."

"People who act unfairly, inconsiderately or unkindly may deserve to be penalised, but never to be totally condemned as rotten no-goodniks who deserve to be eternally damned and punished."

"Anger does not help in the long run, it is only temporarily effective at best."

"Anger towards others frequently prevents me from getting what I want."

"While it is undesirable to fail to get what I want, it is seldom awful or intolerable."

"I can cope successfully with unfair people though I strongly wish they would act better."

"I wish others would treat me better, but they never have to."

"I do not need other people to act well although I prefer it."

"People are the way they are because that's the way they are, tough."

"I can live and be happy - though not as happy - with his/her fallibility."

"My superior (mate, child, colleague, friend) is fallible and will often, not always, do the wrong thing; tough, that's the way fallible human beings work."

"I can put up with this negative and hostile person, though it would be better if he/she acted better."

Conflict-resolution skills

Conflict-resolution skills, when applied to a conflict between two people, have many things in common with anger management skills. They start with each person taking responsibility for their own anger without blaming the other, and either calming themselves down before their anger gets out of hand, or disengaging from the conflict surrounding a discussion and coming back to it when they have cooled down. If the other person is not prepared to take responsibility, it is even more important for you to follow this strategy.

When it becomes apparent that a discussion between you and someone else is going to lead to anger and conflict, take time out from the discussion and focus on the fact that anger is getting in the way of solving the problem and that before continuing, cooler heads need to prevail. Say something like: "Hold on a minute. I'm getting angry and I'd like to stop our discussion for a moment." Once you've stopped the action, you have a number of options:

1.   Continue the discussion making an effort to stay focused on the topics and remaining cool.

2.   Start the conversation again without letting either of you becoming sidetracked into other issues which can lead to conflict.

3.   Re-schedule the discussion to a later time and use the intervening time period to cool down and work out a plan to handle the issue more constructively when you meet again.

In summary, to effectively manage your anger:

1.   Think about the negative consequences for you when you get angry.

2.   Become aware of gradually becoming angry and tense.

3.   Use rational attitudes and self-talk to keep your anger in check.

4.   To manage the frustration, employ a relaxation skill (see Ch. 6).

5.   When you keep control of yourself, pay close attention to the positive consequences for you.

Your Assertive Option

If, then, your procrastination stems from a lack of assertiveness or from the fear of expressing your genuine displeasure with others' acts, you can sometimes assertively practice expressing yourself, thereby eliminating a prime reason for procrastinating.

Albert Ellis and William J. Knaus, <u>Overcoming Procrastination</u>, 1977.

If you lack the ability to assert yourself, you are likely to procrastinate at a variety of tasks. When confronted by someone acting disagreeably towards you such as talking too loud at the movies, not doing what they said they were going to do and you having to do it for them, or someone making an unreasonable request of you, you will delay having to stick up for yourself.

And as I have alluded to above, by not feeling comfortable about asserting yourself with someone who is making an unfair request of you or not giving you enough support to carry out a task, you will be more likely - especially if you are angry with that person - to deliberately delay doing things just to get back.

Lack of assertion frequently can be seen in you having difficulty saying "No" to unreasonable requests of your time as well as finding it difficult to make reasonable requests of others for help or support. The result of this type of lack of assertion is that you find yourself landed with too much to do and will, because of the lack of time, be forced to put off things you really want to do.

For these reasons, it will be useful to review the basic characteristics of assertive behaviour. By familiarising yourself with basic assertion skills, you will be better prepared to overcome your procrastination due to lack of assertion.

Assertiveness is a type of interpersonal style which involves you honestly and directly expressing your ideas, feelings and desires to others. Assertion is based on the belief that you have certain rights including the right to establish and protect your rights as long as insodoing, you do not violate the rights of others. Assertion involves among other things making reasonable requests of others and refusing unreasonable requests.

Besides assertion, there are two other interpersonal styles you can employ when someone behaves in ways which violate your rights. Aggression involves you standing up for your rights but doing so in a way which violates their rights and results in them feeling hurt, humiliated or embarrassed. Submission involves you not standing up for yourself, not expressing your own feelings and wishes, and agreeing to requests no matter how unreasonable.

Let's briefly examine these three different ways of communicating in situations where your rights might be at risk. Common situations are when people make unreasonable requests of you or when someone is being aggressive towards you. In recognising that around 60 percent of your message to another is conveyed by how you say it, it is useful to examine the differences in interpersonal styles by examining both the verbal and non-verbal differences among assertion, aggression and submission. As well, there are characteristic differences in the self-talk among the three styles.

Assertive interpersonal style

Verbal behaviour: You state clearly and directly what you are honestly feeling, thinking and wanting and what you would like to occur. You stick to the facts and make your own choices.

Non-Verbal Behaviour: You employ a confident, warm yet firm tone of voice. You have good eye contact reflecting openness. Your pose and expression is relaxed and you use your hands naturally.

Self-talk: "I would prefer that person not to act that way. If they continue that way, I'll never get the job done or get what I want. I'd better let them know, without being too critical and losing my cool, that I dislike what they're doing and that I would like them to change their behaviour. If I don't stand up for myself now, no one will."

Aggressive interpersonal style

Verbal Behaviour: You use emotionally-loaded accusatory words and statements and you demand you get what you want. Your statements convey your superiority and their inferiority. You blame and condemn them for what they have or haven't done. You threaten and make choices for others.

Non-Verbal Behaviour: You convey an air of superiority. Your tone of voice is sarcastic, tense, loud, icy and authoritarian. You eyes are narrowed and cold. You stand with you hands on your hips, chest extended, fists and jaw clenched and you appear tense.

Self-talk: "They shouldn't act so unfairly. I can't stand it. They should know better. I shouldn't have to put up with such inconsiderateness. What nerve! I'll show them. I'll get stuck into them so they'll know better next time."

Submissive interpersonal style

Verbal Behaviour: You never really say what you would like to say. You agree with what is being asked of you. You express yourself in a very rambling and disfluent style. You use apologetic words. Others make choices for you.

Non-Verbal Behaviour: You express yourself "faint-heartedly". Your voice is quiet and shaky. You do not look the other person in the eye. You look downward, lean forward and stand well apart from the person you are addressing.

Self-talk: "I don't like what she's done, but what can I do? I could say something, but she'd only get upset. Maybe it was my fault. Just thinking about saying anything gets me too uptight. I just couldn't cope. If I don't say anything, maybe she'll know I was upset and not do it again. Yes, that's what I'll do. Nothing."

The impact you have on other people will be greatly influenced by your interpersonal style. If you are assertive, others will feel more respected and valued by you and will be more willing to express themselves openly. Others will value you because they know where you stand. You often get what you want. You will feel confident and self-respecting.

If you tend to be aggressive, others will often give you what you want but they will not like or respect you. They will tend not to be loyal and will often feel inferior and hostile. Some people might try to get back at you. And you may feel uptight and anxious.

Submissive behaviour results in others feeling both superior and frustrated with you. People will lose respect for you and will continue to violate your rights. You will feel unhappy because you will not get what you want. You will never be able to fully please everyone and will feel inferior.

You might wonder why you or others fail to develop assertive interpersonal styles. I think our socialization has a lot to do with it. Some people from an early age have been conditioned to do things for others, but not themselves. Some people have been taught not to lose their temper, to put others first and be ever understanding. Others have been exposed to socialization patterns which have encouraged a more aggressive pattern of behaviour including being tough, putting themselves first, not showing or sharing feelings and never asking for help.

Whatever the origins of unassertiveness, we now know that it is very possible, through practice and encouragement from others, to become less submissive and aggressive, and to adopt a more assertive interpersonal style which can significantly improve the quality of our relationships.

Different Kinds of Assertion

Requesting a change in behaviour

1. *Describe the behaviour I see and/or hear in the other person. It is important that I use descriptive rather than attacking words.*

2. *Express the feelings I experience as a result of the other person's behaviour.*

3. *Ask for a specific change in behaviour.*

4. *Spell out the positive consequences for the person upon changing their behaviour and the negative consequences if they don't.*

> Recommendations from the Institute for
> Rational-Emotive Therapy, New York.

Depending on the nature of the offending behaviour which you wish to deal with as well as who the person is who is violating your rights, making unreasonable requests or whom you wish to request something of, a number of assertive behaviours are available.

1. **Basic Assertion.** This kind of assertion involves you confidently and, using a firm tone of voice, standing up for your rights. Examples of basic assertive statements include: "Excuse me, I haven't finished what I was saying." "Please don't smoke here." "I haven't any free time to join another committee."

2. **Empathic Assertion.** If you acknowledge someone elses' feelings or opinions while at the same time disagreeing with them, you are being "empathic." This is a more effective form of assertion because by you initially ackowledging them, they are more likely to respond to you. For example: "I can understand that you would like me to get this report to you by the end of the day. However, given that you have requested other tasks for me to complete by 5.00 pm today, I simply cannot get to this job today. Would tomorrow at lunch time be okay?"

3. **Escalating Assertion.** This type of assertion starts off with you making a simple request to someone else for a change in their behaviour. When the other fails to comply with your request and continues to violate your rights, you can escalate your assertion by becoming firmer and more forceful. For example: "This is the second and last time I am going to ask you to put your toys away." "I'm fed up with always being the one to have to organise refreshments."

4. **Confrontative Assertion.** This type of assertion is generally employed when someone has agreed to do something but has not followed through on the agreement. You confront them with the objective facts of what they said they would do, what they did (or didn't do) and point out the contradiction. You may also add a request for them to change their behaviour. For example: "You said you would leave the library in as good a shape as how your class found it. When I arrived this morning, the area of the library you used was a mess. I would appreciate it if you and your class could stop by and arrange the room as it was before you used it." "I was supposed to be invited to consult on the future location of my division. Yet, I noticed the final report already having been written. In future, I want to be consulted about any decision which effects my division."

5. **Levelling Statements.** Levelling statements involve you using "I-language" to express your negative emotions which are associated with someone elses behaviour. For example: "I get very angry when I see that you have put down my name to do certain tasks without consulting me. Next time, if you want my cooperation, I would like you to speak with me first."

6. **Persuasive Assertion.** This type of assertion is useful when you are in a group situation and you want to influence the position of the group without being aggressive. In using persuasive assertion, decide the issue which warrants an assertive stance. Then wait until about one-third of the group members have expressed their opinion before expressing yours. Finally, it is also recommended that you communicate your position tactfully by including something good which you have found in the other person's statement. For example: "I agree with you about the decline in product sales in the past quarter. However, if we simply drop the product line before

analysing the reasons for the decline, we might be making the wrong decision."

Specific Assertiveness Techniques

Hints for making requests assertively

1. *Don't apologise profusely.*

2. *Be direct.*

3. *Keep it short.*

4. *Don't justify yourself.*

5. *Give a reason for your request.*

6 *Don't 'sell' your request with flattery or tempting benefits.*

7. *Don't play on people's friendship or good nature.*

8. *Don't take a refusal personally.*

9. *Respect the other person's right to say no.*

Hints for refusing requests assertively

1. *Keep the reply short.*

2. *Simply say "No, I don't want to."*

3. *Give a reason for refusing.*

4. *Avoid "I can't" phrases which often sound like excuses.*

5. *Ask for some more time to decide on the request.*

6. *Don't be abrupt in your refusal.*

Ken and Kate Back, Authors of
<u>Assertiveness at Work: A Practical Guide
for Handling Awkward Situations</u>, 1982.

In thinking about how to handle a situation assertively, it will be handy to be able to bring to mind the following basic assertiveness techniques.

1. **I-Language.** Basic assertion can be used in situations where someone has trampled on your rights. For example: "I am very angry that you did not consult with me as to which school our son will attend."

2. **Broken Record.** This easy-to-use technique is helpful in the face of someone making an unreasonable request. You simply speak like a broken record making the same point each time the person asks you to do something you don't want to do. For example: If a colleague repeatedly asks you to attend a meeting at a time when you have other important things to do, you can simply repeat as often as he requests your attendance, "Sorry, I've made other plans."

   To be really effective, you should use this technique without getting emotional. You need to make sure your non-verbals appear calm and composed.

3. **Fogging.** Fogging is used as a way of dealing with criticism. Fogging allows you to cope with personal criticism in a way that protects your self-esteem. It allows you to receive the criticism without becoming defensive or anxious. In fogging, you calmly acknowledge the possible truth in the criticism without confirming that it is right or wrong. By 'apparently' accepting the criticism without being aggressive, you are able to maintain face. Ways in which you can use fogging to deal with criticism that you were late to an important meeting are:

   - Agree with any truth in the criticism. "Yes, I was late."

   - Agree with the logic of the other person's argument. "Yes, I can see why you think I am inconsiderate."

   - Allow for improvement. "Yes, I could make a bigger effort to get to class on time."

   - Empathy. "Yes, I can see your point and understand you'd be feeling that way."

In using fogging, offer no resistance or counter-argument. By doing so, the person will find it difficult to continue the criticism. Try to understand their point of view and acknowledge any part of the criticism that you agree with.

4. **Defusing.** When someone is getting upset with you, you can assertively divert their train of communication by ignoring the content of someone's anger and putting off the discussion until he has calmed down. Say something like: "I can see you're very upset. Let's discuss this later on this afternoon."

5. **Assertive Agreement.** Another way to handle criticism is to respond by admitting that you made an error (if you did) and expressing the idea that you are generally not like that. For example: "Yes, I did forget to attend the meeting, but I usually keep my promises."

6. **Assertive Delay.** If you find yourself getting emotionally upset when having a discussion, rather than responding to a point of criticism emotionally, you can put off responding until a later time when you're calmer. For example: "Yes, I hear what you're saying. Let me think it over and get back to you."

There are a variety of situations you will encounter in which you will have a choice in terms of the degree of your assertion including when you make a request, refuse a request, disagree with someone else's opinion, express your own opinion in a group and when you're dealing with an aggressive person. In preparing yourself for acting assertively in these situations, the following steps are advised.

Step One   Determine whether the situation warrants assertion.

Sometimes, even though you might find the situation could be handled assertively, you might decide it is not important enough to be assertive. Keep in mind that assertion often results in the other person becoming hostile and aggressive or sullenly submissive.

Step Two   Decide how you want the other person to change and behave.

Step Three   Select the type of assertive technique you will employ to achieve the change.

Step Four   Develop beforehand and rehearse assertive self-talk which you will use in the situation.

Step Five   Make sure your non-verbals communicate a sense of calm and control. Practice with a mirror to insure you maintain direct eye contact, have an erect body posture, speak clearly and firmly, avoid using a whiny or apologetic voice, use facial and hand gestures for added emphasis.

Step Six   Assert yourself.

Step Seven   Evaluate the success of your assertive approach. Make a note of what you did well and which skills you have to improve.

It was Tuesday morning and as Helen poured herself a cup of coffee she was was still fuming. "That bastard! He's so impressed with being the big capitalist that he can't lower himself to call little me. I guess being 'just' a student puts me way down on his totem pole. That's not where I want to be. On top. That's where I want to be. Never mind about him. That's the last time I'll lose any sleep over him. I couldn't even do any study last night I was so churned up."

Helen finished her breakfast, got dressed and gathered her books. "I certainly am not going to wait around for his call. I'll study at the library. He probably won't call today and if he does, I really don't care!"

As Helen dashed out her apartment she had to put on the brakes. Sitting just outside her door were a huge bunch of yellow roses - her very favourite - and a bottle of French champagne. Helen could feel herself going bright red as she started to open the accompanying card.

"Roses are red.
I feel so blue.
You are so sweet
Sorry for not having called you."

Helen laughed out loud. "He might be a top electrical engineer but I bet he flunked English Lit."

Just then, she heard her phone ring and she sprinted back inside.

"Hi there! Didn't wake you up did I?", asked Larry a shade sarcastically.

"Are you kidding. I've been up for hours. Already put in two hours of work. And plus the four I did last night. Hey, I'm ready for lunch. What about some French champagne?"

"Love to but it's a bit early for me. Listen. Sorry about not calling. I didn't finish up until 11 pm last night and I didn't want to wake you."

"Hey. No problem, Larry. I had too much to do anyway. Quite frankly, I hadn't even thought about your call," said Helen not quite so convincingly. "I love the flowers!"

"Any chance you'll want some more positive reinforcment for getting all that studying done?".

"Cool down, tiger. Remember, what Bill says: 'There's no gain without pain.' You put up with the pain of not seeing me and I'll gain the benefits of straight A's." Helen was flying. "This time, I'll call you after work!".

Actions Speak Louder Than Words

See if you can identify any activity you are procrastinating at because of your hostility. Then, look at the disadvantages of remaining angry and procrastinating and the advantages of getting a job done despite your anger. Also try to reduce your anger using rational attitudes.

Write down a list of situations where you would like to behave more assertively. Then rank begining with "1", the situation you would find easiest to be assertive in. Develop an Assertive Plan of Action for this situation as previously described in this chapter. Do this for the next easiest situation and then the next until you have worked through your list.

9

Managing Stress and Fatigue

Doc, I don't need much endurance. I work at a desk all day, and I watch television at night. I don't exert myself any more than I have to, and I have no requirements for exerting myself. Who needs larger reserves? Who needs endurance?

You do. Everyone does. Surely you know the usual symptoms caused by inactivity as well as I do. Yawning at your desk, that drowsy feeling all day, falling asleep after a heavy meal, fatigue from even mild exertions like climbing the stairs, running for a bus, mowing the lawn or shovelling snow. You can become a social cripple, too tired to play with the kids, too tired to go out to dinner with your wife, too tired to do anything except sit at your desk or watch television, and maybe you're even getting tired of doing that. And the final clincher, 'I guess I'm getting old.' You're getting old all right, and a lot sooner than you should.

Dr Kenneth Cooper, Aerobics, 1977.

How many times have you been too tired and stressed out to get to a task you've wanted to do? Perhaps, you've decided to update the family photo album. Maybe, its having a swim early in the morning. Frequently, it will be a favourite hobby you've been putting off. Or it might be that you are not attending cultural events such as a gallery opening or music recital. I'm sure I can think of many activities you would have already accomplished had it not been for your low level of energy.

If stress and fatigue are the negative magnetic forces which are diverting you from achieving your goals, then there are two ways in which you can neutralise their effects so that you actually get to what you want to do:

Increase your tolerance of stress and fatigue

Lower your level of stress and fatigue

This chapter will start off with some practical ideas for increasing your will power in order to increase your tolerance of stress and fatigue. The majority of the chapter will revolve around a discussion of stress and how lifestyle management can increase your resistance to stress and fatigue.

Will Power

Will opens the door to success, both brilliant and happy.

Louis Pasteur, Scientist.

People vary quite a bit in their ability to get things done even when they are tired. I have a good friend, Mary, who is the mother of five children the youngest of whom is 17 years of age. For the past 10 years, Mary has not only provided wonderful mothering care, but has completed her masters and doctorate degrees. Further, she has played an active role in her church, sung in the choir, and coached her children's rowing team. Existing sometimes on five hours of sleep or less, Mary has, over the years, demonstrated a phenomenal capacity to perform a variety of tasks while feeling - as she puts it - "close to death". I guess you could call what enables her to function so well 'mental toughness' or 'will power'. I like the term 'will power' because it clearly communicates the idea of Mary willing herself to have the power to do what is difficult and very tiresome to do. At the same time, she also demonstrates what I have referred to already in Chapter 6 as high discomfort tolerance.

Another good friend of mine, Sally, gave up her job several years ago to stay at home and look after her newborn son and soon-to-be daughter. And at this task she does a magnificent job providing what seems to me to be optimum amounts of love, stimulation and security (along with her husband). However, Sally gets more quickly tired and stressed out than Mary. By 5.00pm she feels totally spent and has little energy left over for anything else but watching television and reading the newspaper. By 9.00pm she is in bed sound asleep. You could describe Sally (through no fault of her own) as lacking in native will power. It's not that she sets out to feel so tired and lethargic, its just that as a combination of her personality and the demands on her life that's the way she is. She would like to function better when she's tired as well as have more energy.

The interesting question is; what enables Mary to function so well over such a long haul while experiencing high amounts of stress and fatigue? What gives her stamina? No doubt her native constitution helps her hold herself together even when she feels like falling apart and giving up. Her whole attitude of life is oriented to making the most of herself and putting up with the discomforts along the way in order for her to achieve what she wants from her life.

Sally is cut from a different cloth. She finds she does not have the internal resources to battle on when stressed. Believing that she needs to feel comfortable and that she can't stand it when she starts to feel very stressed, Sally's attitude towards her own stress is partly responsible for holding her back. Her need for comfort turns stress into distress.

Is it possible to develop stronger will power? Yes, it can be done although it is accomplished slowly over several years. You can, however, see the benefits of the learning process almost immediately.

To develop will power, you need to start slowly increasing the amount of time you spend on activities when you are tired and stressed. So, if you have been putting off studying or other work after dinner because of feeling too stressed and tired, you should schedule ahead of time to start to do some work after dinner whether you feel like it or not. For example, for the next week, you could schedule no less than 30 minutes of work after dinner. Unfortunately, you will have to forgo any alcohol with your meal as alcohol will relax your system and deplete whatever energy you have to apply to the task. Have a glass of wine or can of beer only when you've finished your 30 minutes.

What you will find using this approach is that often, once you have worked for 30 minutes, you will feel like doing more. As well, you will have begun the slow process of re-programming your body's threshhold level at which it cuts off functioning. Its like re-setting your internal thermostat to stay on at higher temperatures.

The other means for increasing your will power is to re-program your thinking about what you can and cannot do when you are tired and stressed. Sally tells herself: "I'm too tired to do any more. I need to relax. I can't possibly do these things the way I feel." On the otherhand, Mary tells herself: "In order for me to do what I want, I'll have to continue to work even though I don't feel like doing so. Even though I'm tired, I know I can still operate. I've done it before, I can do it again."

Another technique which you can use to bring about a desired result is visual imagery. In visual imagery, you practice ahead of time imagining yourself performing the task you've been procrastinating at. You might at first practice seeing yourself getting started and working at the task for some time. Over time, you can change your image so that you see yourself successfully performing the task. For example, to get started jogging in the early morning, in the weeks before you actually try out your exercise program you should imagine yourself performing all the steps you will have to take in getting started. You will need to picture yourself in bed getting woken up by the alarm, getting out of bed, changing into your jogging gear, doing warm up exercises, and starting to jog for a minimum of 10 minutes. Once you actually start to jog, you can increase your will power to continue jogging by using visual imagery of yourself jogging at faster rates for longer periods of time. You will always want to include in your images how good you feel after you've completed the task.

From the above examples, it will be obvious that will power is eminently learnable. To increase yours, follow these steps.

1.   Identify a task you've been putting off because of feeling too tired or stressed.

2. Break down the task into smaller components or sub-tasks.

3. Schedule yourself to work on the task at a specific time and place.

4. Set a minimum goal for the amount of time you will work on the task.

5. Practice beforehand self-talk about having to put up with fatigue and stress and use this self-talk when getting started and persevering.

6. (optional) Visualise yourself accomplishing the part of the task you've set for yourself and the positive after effects.

7. Get started and monitor the success with which you accomplish what you've set out to do.

8. Use positive self-talk to pat yourself on the back when you are successful.

This strategy needs to be flexible. If you find that you are not getting to do what you've set out to do, then you may have to adjust either the goal you've set for yourself or the time and place you've elected to perform the task. And most importantly, you need to allow for your own lapses. If you get started and are doing great guns, don't be over-alarmed if for a brief period of time you sink back into the old habit of not finding enough energy to work. Give yourself permission to be less than totally perfect. Then, as soon as possible, get back to the program you've set out for yourself.

What Is Stress?

(Stress is)....the speedometer of life...the sum of all the wear and tear caused by any kind of reaction throughout the body at one time.

Hans Selye, Stress Without Distress, 1976.

A simple definition of stress is that it is the way you adapt and react to demands and threats in your life. To understand stress, you need to look at the demands and threats in your life which are called 'stressors', how you react to these demands physiologically, psychologically and behaviourally (stress reactions) as well as examine aspects of yourself such as your attitudes, coping skills and lifestyle which often determine how much stress you experience.

It is important to distinguish between stress and distress. As Hans Selye, the pioneering researcher in the area of stress, has said "Without stress you'd be dead." Up to a certain point, stress is manageable, enjoyable, motivational and beneficial and is referred to as "positive stress." It is only when stress becomes uncontrollable and overwhelming and you start to experience physiological damage, physical problems and self-defeating behaviour that stress becomes distress or "negative stress."

From the discussion which follows you will see that stress and fatigue are byproducts of your outside world and yourself. Distress is most likely to occur when your outside world is lousy and your inside world is functioning poorly. Said another way, to understand your stress, it is important not only to identify those stressors in your world which are noxious, obnoxious, threatening and demanding, but also to identify those aspects of your internal functioning which are contributing to your stress.

The effective management of your stress depends upon modifying both aspects of your outside world and aspects of you. This chapter focuses on changing your life style as a way to control the negative effects of stress.

Stress - and Fatigue-Creating Stressors

The demands or challenges of life can come from people and events around us, as well as from our inner thoughts and struggles. When these demands increase, people often feel that they are under excessive stress.

Edward A. Charlesworth, Ph.D. and Ronald G. Nathan, Ph.D., Stress Management: A Comprehensive Guide to Wellness, 1982.

An extensive amount of research has shown that there are different types of stressors which can lead to extreme stress and fatigue. I have grouped examples of different stressors into the following six categories:

1. **Major Life Event Stressors:** death of a loved one, major illness to you or a loved one; bankruptcy; changing jobs and marriage.

2. **Community Stressors:** crime, threat of war, street violence, AIDS, racial unrest, economic down-turn.

3. **Physical and Chemical Stressors:** noise, over-crowding, ergonomic factors (poor design of office and factory space, machinery, furniture); extremes of temperature, dust, fumes and physical health hazards, shift-work, jet lag.

4. **Work Stressors:** quantitative overload (too much to do, time pressures, repetitous work flow); qualitative underload (too narrow job, little content, lack of variety, no demands on creativity); lack of control (over planning, work pace, work methods); machine pacing of work rhythm, machine control of work methods; your own poor work performance, negative evaluations of your work by others; lack of recognition; difficult people, lack of possibilities for contact with people; financial disadvantage, unemployment.

5. **Home Stressors:** relationship conflicts (over finance, sex, sex-roles, child discipline); time/work load pressures; problems with children (illness, educational, personal); in-law problems, parent-child problems.

6. **Lack of Support:** unavailability of people to provide emotional support, self-esteem enhancement, advice, solve problems, and assistance in the way of time and doing things for you.

While it is generally the case that the greater the number of stressors the greater your stress, it is also true that people react to stressors differently and, therefore, for example, you might be as stressed out about one major life event or problem with your child, as is somone who is confronted with many different individual stressors at home and work.

It is also becomming increasingly clear from research into the nature of stress that daily, repetitive hassles are one of the main sources of fatigue. It is apparent that feelings of fatigue and being overwhelmed can be due to the many small daily things you have to do.

As well, the lack of support can be seen as a stressor. With the break-down of the extended family and the isolation of the family unit, it is clear that fewer people are around to help support you when the going gets tough. And the workplace of western industrialised cultures has been characterised for some time by a 'dog eat dog' and 'survival of the fittest' ethos. The more you have to do without support, the more likely you are to experience fatigue. In these circumstances, it is vital for you to have a healthy lifestyle to delay fatigue as long as possible as well as being able to operate while fatigued.

Stress Reactions

In twentieth century modern-day society, and, in particular, in our schools, there are no dangerous dinosaurs and cavepeople out to do us in (or are there?). We have the same stress-arousal physiological system designed for 'flight' or 'fight' with no real outside physical threats (except in extreme circumstances), and, moreover, given our basic sedentary existences, we do not tend to 'work off' by vigorous exercise the increases in bodily chemicals circulating throughout our system in response to stressors.

Michael E. Bernard, Taking the Stress Out
of Teaching, 1990.

It is not always easy to know when you are actually experiencing stress. One of the reasons is that the signs and symptoms are often, especially in their milder forms, subtle. The everyday strain experienced as a result of different daily and major life stressors is something you most probably accept as normal. Sometimes, it is only when you reach the more advanced stages of stress that you may notice you are not feeling your normal (strained) self.

Stress is also hard to detect because your body and mind can absorb and sustain a lot of stress without you being consciously aware of it. For example, you might be able to work for extended hours during the day, on weekends, for weeks on end without being aware of how stressed you are. It is only when you start yelling at your loved ones or drinking excessively to reduce your discomforts that stress is apparent. And drinking and its after effects can distract you from the signs that you are under stress. Furthermore, many of your physiological reactions to stress are not detectable. It is, for example, impossible to notice directly your elevated cortisone levels. You are, however, quite capable of noticing the effects of sustained high levels of cortisone and the weakening of your immunity system as you experience colds, infections and allergy reactions.

Another reason stress is sometimes hard for you to detect is that you may not frequently label the actual physical, psychological and behavioural manifestations of stress such as exhaustion, anxiety or aggression as stress reactions. You might think to yourself "Gee, I feel crummy ... have a sore throat ... feel run down ... I wanna go to Hawaii!", but not draw the conclusion that you are experiencing excess stress or distress. I'm not saying that all unhealthy bodily and psychological reactions are related to stress. You can strain your back while doing the gardening and experience the blues because of events which have nothing to do with teaching. However, research and experience clearly shows that ill-health and injury are far more likely to occur when you are under sustained and negative job demands and threats.

In this section, I will discuss three separate types of stress reactions which interact with one another and can result in you feeling stressed and fatigued.

Physiological stress reactions

There are two main physiological systems responsible for your stress reactions. There is the **sympathetic nervous system,** that part of your autonomic nervous system responsible for arousing ourselves initially for flight or fight. There also the **endocrine glands** which help support the arousal efforts of your sympathetic nervous system and which carry out the important function of supplying you with the energy needed for action. The main endocrine glands involved in your physiological stress reaction are the adrenal glands, located near your kidneys.

While your physiological system was designed to ward off the many physical dangers which your ancient ancestors confronted be they animal or human, such a system seems ill-equiped for helping you deal with the non-life threatening demands you encounter in twentieth century life.

Hans Selye has identified a three-stage physiological response system to threats and demands you encounter which he termed the "general adaptation syndrome" (GAS). It is called a general syndrome because his research has shown that your body responds in a similar way to all demands and threats regardless of the specific identity of the stressor. Your body 'turns on' when your brain interprets a situation as threatening regardless of whether you are faced with a wild animal or a wild student.

During the Alarm Reaction (Stage 1) the hypothalmus, that portion of your brain responsible both for much of your emotion and motivation as well as for activating your central nervous system and endocrine system receives a signal from your brain's cortex that a situation is physically demanding or psychologically threatening. Your sympathetic nervous system reacts rapidly to the threat or demand by sharpening the alertness of your body to flight or fight in the form of changes to your senses (hearing, vision), heart rate, respiratory and digestive systems and increased muscle tension.

In order to maintain your body's alertness and preparedness, your sympathetic nervous system also directly stimulates your **adrenal medulla,** the interior part of the adrenal gland which produces **adrenaline**, a hormone responsible for mobilizing extra energy in the form of glucose. Adrenaline provides you with a burst of energy but this response tends to be rather short-lived.

The other part of the adrenal gland involved in the stress response is the **adrenal cortex** located on the exterior part of your adrenal gland. The adrenal cortex is also activated by your hypothalmus but through a different route. The hypothalmus activates the **pituitary gland**, located within the deep recesses of your brain which sends many hormones throughout your body. For example, the pituitary gland stumulates the **thyroid gland** which raises your level of metabolic functioning at times of stress. The pituitary also produces a hormone called ACTH (adrenocorticotrophic hormone) which, in turn, stimulates the adrenal cortex to produce a wide range of chemicals. Selye believed that ACTH was the most important hormone for studying your physiological stress reaction. The adrenal cortex produces **cortisol** or **cortisone** which helps your body in the short-term to ward off pain and the invasion of foreign substances. (In the long-term, elevated cortisone levels reduces your body's resistance to cancer, infection and illness.) **Mineral-corticoids** also produced by the adrenal cortex influence the mineral balance of your body and, in particluar, convert food into energy.

If you have been unable to neutralise or remove the outside stressor, the General Adaptation Syndrome will advance to **Resistance** (Stage 2). During this phase, the alarm bells of the initial stage have ceased ringing and your body runs at a higher rate in an effort to cope with the stressor. In particular, your endocrine system supplies increased minerals and chemical hormones needed to maintain the extra energy and effort. Until fairly recently, you dealt with outside stressors relatively quickly. You didn't spend a great deal of time in the Resistance Stage and you would have generally resolved the outside stressors with some sort of strong active and physical response.

When you are able to successfully deal with the outside stress, your physiological systems begin shutting down as your body returns to a previous level of rest and equilibrium. Your **parasympathetic nervous system** takes over from the sympathetic system and helps restore your organs and yourself to a stress-free state.

Unfortunately, in our twentieth-century society, the outside stressors are seldom dealt with quickly. Some of your stressors may well be with you forever. Moreover, the way you now handle stressors is more in a passive than active mode, making it more difficult for you to rid yourself of the negative effects of the chemicals which have poured into your system to deal with a demand or threat. The repeated and prolonged exposure to stressors and your inability to recover sufficiently between episodes leads to the most damaging of Selye's stages of stress.

Exhaustion (Stage 3) occurs when you have been unable to deal with the stressors in your world and you do not have the energy to put into resisting any longer. It is during Stage 3 that we are most vulnerable to stress-related physical and mental illnesses. While your body's chemical-hormonal and central nervous system response to an outside stressor is seen as being very necessary and useful, the prolonged 'turn on' of your system without it being able to restore itself is when all the damage occurs.

In a nutshell, your communication system is telling you you are still in danger, but your arousal and energy producing physiological system is 'on empty'. And worse still, you have a much reduced immunity system. Your bodily organs are at risk for injury due, in part, to elevated cortisone levels, and you are extremely vulnerable to the invasion of noxious foreign substances which bring with them illness and disease. At worst, if you do not respond to your body's signals which suggest that you are physiologically spent, physical (and nervous) breakdown may be imminent. At best, you will begin to manifest a variety of physical and psychological stress-related symptoms.

Psychological stress reactions

Psychological stress reactions most commonly refer to your emotional reactions to the outside stressors you encounter; in particular, your feelings of **anxiety** (and panic), **anger** (and rage), and **depression**. Included within emotional reactions are feelings of apathy and alienation, feeling out of control, emotional exhaustion, lack of self-confidence, excessive guilt and moodiness.

Psychological stress reactions may also include disturbances in your ability to think clearly. You may lose concentration easily, fail to remember important details, be mentally confused and indecisive, and lose your capacity to solve problems easily. I think you will agree that when you feel extremely stressed about a person or event in your life it is very difficult to think objectively about the situation and figure out the best thing to do to manage the outside threat or demand.

Have a look at the list of psychological symptoms below and see if you can recognise those which you experience when under extreme stress.

Emotional symptoms of stress

- extreme anxiety or panic lasting more than a few days
- explosive anger in response to minor irritations
- feelings of doubt, poor confidence, insecurity, and depression
- feeling unable to cope
- not feeling in control
- frequent or prolonged feelings of boredom
- feeling desperate
- feeling tired, listless and emotionally exhausted

Cognitive symptoms of stress

- poor memory and forgetfulness
- poor concentration
- poor problem-solving ability
- indecisiveness
- mental confusion

- irrational thinking
- negative self-image
- racing thoughts
- difficulty falling and staying asleep

Emotional and cognitive stress reactions go hand-in-hand. The more upset you get, the more your thinking goes down the drain - and the more likely that your behaviour will suffer.

Behavioural stress reactions

Now, let's have a look at a few common behavioural patterns we observe in people under stress. See if you can recognise your typical pattern of reacting when you get towards the end of your stress tether.

- rushed speech
- withdrawal, non-assertion
- yelling
- throwing things
- hitting someone
- overactivity
- procrastination
- sleeping more than usual
- increase in alcohol or drug consumption
- lack or drive
- disorganised and untidy
- poor use of discipline techniques
- absenteeism
- tardiness

This list of behavioural stress reactions is somewhat small. This is because the variety of specific behavioural stress reactions are literally endless.

There are basically two types of behavioural methods which you typically use when confronted with stressors: Direct Action and Inactive methods. Direct Action methods involve you in doing something actively to modify the stressors or in dealing with your own emotional stress reaction. Direct action methods would involve you using one of your coping skills (e.g., assertion, classroom management) to modify the stressor. Direct action methods for coping with excess emotional stress reactions when you haven't been able to neutralise the outside stressor include seeking support, relaxation, exercise and modifying your attitude towards the stressor.

Inactive methods involve you doing very little to take control of the situation or your emotional reactions. Commonly, you might simply ignore the situation and resort to alcohol or food to combat bad feelings.

Research is pretty clear in pointing to direct action as the method which can minimize the effects of the stressor as well as helping you maintain good physical and mental health.

Your behavioural stress reactions can also be differentiated in terms of whether you tend to employ aggressive, submissive or assertive behaviours. Once again it is possible to identify assertive behaviour as an interpersonal style which will minimise the effects of stress.

How You Influence Your Stress and Fatigue

Things are neither good nor bad but thinking makes them so.
William Shakespeare, <u>Hamlet</u>.

There is little question that people differ considerably in their ability to manage stress and ward off distress. It is now possible to profile some of the things inside of you which help make you more or less susceptible to experiencing stress and fatigue.

Attitudes

It is quite clear that your attitudes towards what goes on in your outside world influences your stress level. As I've shown in previous chapters, certain irrational attitudes involving your need for approval, achievement and self-depreciation can substantially add to your stress (anxiety) brought about by criticism, rejection, mistakes or failure. The stress which accompanies high levels of anger and rage is dramatically influenced by your attitudes towards other people and, in particular, the extent to which you demand that other people act in certain ways and whether you condemn them for their bad behaviour. The stress which accompanies high levels of frustration is similarly effected by your attitudes towards life's difficulties and having to do without short-term pleasures and, in particular, the attitude that life shouldn't be so hard and unfair and that you need your life to be pleasant, comfortable and free of difficulties.

So you can add to life's miseries if you bring with you stress-creating attitudes such as those I've described. Sustained anxiety and anger brought about by negative stressors and stress-creating attitudes will gradually grind you down.

Coping skills

The coping skills you have to confront different stressors will also greatly influence their effects on you. For example, if someone makes an unfair request of you, if you are able to use assertive skills and live with the person's negative reaction to you for saying "No," then your assertiveness will remove the stress of having something additional to do and, hence, you will feel less stressed. Being able to relax after having faced a difficult person or situation will also help lessen the amount of stress you experience. Discomfort tolerance will enable you to face up to anxiety-provoking and frustrating situations the result of which will, over time, be the removal of stressors.

I have already presented a number of coping skills which not only will help you procrastinate later, but also will be of help to you at times to take direct action in controlling outside stressors or controlling your own stress reactions.

Major stress-reducing coping skills are: anxiety management, self-esteem enhancement (rational self-acceptance), discomfort tolerance management, relaxation methods, anger management and time management.

Lifestyle

Your lifestyle plays an important part in your ability to manage stress and, especially, fatigue. By lifestyle, I refer to recreation, exercise and diet. If you do not take time out to rest and recreate, if you are 'out of shape', and if your diet is poor, then you will be much more vulnerable to outside stressors. You will experience distress sooner than if you have a good lifestyle.

One main reason why lifestyle is strongly related to stress and fatigue is that stress is largely your body's physiological reaction to difficult and demanding situations which continue over extended periods of time. We humans are particularly skilled at finding ourselves in highly demanding situations and, further, we have an even more developed skill in thinking about the situation and thereby maintaining the stress even when we are far away. A problem we are having with a loved one can produce heightened stress at work and we often take our work problems home with us. At some point, everyone under the influence of ongoing work and home demands and emotional pressures will experience high levels of stress. The more outside and inside demands we encounter, the more our physiological system is required to provide us with the energy to deal with these stressors. A bad lifestyle will result in your physiological system packing it in much sooner than if your had a healthy lifestyle. The result? Earlier onset of physical stress symptoms (e.g., muscular, cardiovascular, gastrointestinal), emotional breakdown and behaviour disorders (e.g., poor sleep, tantrums, withdrawal, drinking).

The remainder of this chapter provides an overview of lifestyle enhancement methods for innoculating you against the physiological wear and tear of our modern-day living.

Life Style Management

If your body is out of tune, it burns up unnecessary fuel, and it runs roughly, which increases wear and tear. It does not run efficiently or economically, and it is more likely to break down eventually....Similarly, if your body is 'out of tune', meaning unfit, it will not run efficiently, and its struggle to keep up with your stress load will also lead to increased wear and tear. You become more likely to 'break down' in the exhaustion stage of the General Adaptation Syndrome.

Dr. Bob Montgomery and Lynette Evans, Psychologists
and Authors of You and Stress, 1984.

Much of the following material you will find familiar. You'll have either heard about it from parents and friends or read about it in newspapers or magazines. For many different reasons including the popularity of the fast food industry and your own innate tendencies to do what's easy and not good for you, you can fall into unhealthy life style ruts. It is quite common in the face of stress, to act against your better judgement and in order to secure relief from stress eat a chocolate bar or get "stuck into" alcohol. The fatiguing aspects of stress can also take away your energy and the motivation which is required to maintain a good lifestyle. I shall now briefly present the basic principles of lifestyle management in the areas of diet, exercise and recreation. If you believe that your lifestyle is pretty good in one or two of the areas, then just read the area which has relevance to you.

Diet

Early in most people's education, a teacher stood in front of the class pointing to charts of fruit, vegetables, breads, meats, milk and other nutritious items. The teacher talked about the importance of the food groups and recommended the number of servings that should be eaten every day. That same teacher probably failed to eat breakfast, and gobbled a sandwich and a cup of coffeee for lunch.

Sheldon F. Greenberg, Author of Stress and the
Teaching Profession, 1984

There are two aspects of your daily nutritional intake which can effect your stress. The first, inadequate diet, refers to the absence of certain nutrients your body requires for healthy functioning especially when faced with demands associated with high stress. Second, excessive diet, involves you including in your diet unhealthy foods and drinks such as excessive caffeine, alcohol, sweets, fatty foods, and foods high in sodium (salt) content. A third aspect of your diet does not involve what you include in your diet, but rather has you skipping meals and, generally speaking, having an irregular or inconsistent dietary intake. Let's briefly look at some examples of the effects of a poor diet on your ability to tolerate stress.

When you are under stress, your need for essential nutrients increases including, for example, calcium and B-Vitamins. A diet low in milk and leafy vegetables can lead to a chronic calcium deficiency. When your muscles produce a high level of lactic acid, which they tend to when they are tense, there isn't enough calcium in the body to counteract the effects of the lactic acid. As a consequence, you may feel more fatigued, anxious and irritable than if you maintained a balanced diet.

Excess coffee can also exacerbate the effects of stress. Caffeine stimulates the release of stress-producing hormones (e.g., adrenaline) which results in an initial burst of energy. Such energy bursts have the effect of draining your system and, in the case of caffeine, causing low blood sugar levels.

It is estimated that 60 percent of people have systems which are sensitive to changing sugar levels. Eating foods high in sugar while under stress has the effect of stimulating your pancreas to produce insulin which after awhile depresses your blood sugar level to a level lower than before you consumed the sugar, resulting in a variety of physical and emotional stress symptoms including drowsiness, anxiety and irritability.

Under these physiologically and emotionally stressed conditons, you can easily start the cycle again with another cup of coffee, chocolate bar, etcetera. The effects? A constant state of emotional and physiological irregularity which itself can be an additional source of stress.

In order for you to stay reasonably healthy, your body needs 40 to 60 nutrients including 10 essential amino acids, 20 different minerals and 30 vitamins. These nutrients are available in a well balanced diet containing the following elements:

1.   **Proteins.** Proteins provide the anti-bodies to fight disease and are essential to the make-up of your muscles, bones, blood and bodily organs. As a society we tend to consume far too much protein relative to our bodily requirements. Proteins which store approximately four calories per gram should make up between 15 - 20 percent of your caloric intake. Protein is found in most food - especially, meat, fish and poultry.

2.   **Fats.** Fats come in two forms, animal and vegetable. As they are the basic building blocks to your immune system and are involved in energy storage, you should make sure that fats make up between 30 and 35 percent of your caloric intake. Fats store approximately 9 calories per gram. Fats should be mainly polyunsaturated.

3.   **Carbohydrates.** The important ones are the complex carbohydrates (e.g., starches, wheat, fruit vegetables) with the simple carbohydrates (empty calories), found in refined sugar, flour and alcohol, to be avoided. Complex carbohydrates are the easiest source of energy for your body to assimilate. They can be found in whole foods including wheat, beans, grains, fruit and vegetables. Carbohydrates which only store four calories per gram should make up about 50 percent of your total calories.

4.   **Fibre.** Fibre, commonly called roughage, is a vital and still under-rated part of your diet. Fibre, the cell material of plant foods, is not digested and passes

inchanged through your bowels. There are many benefits of eating fibre including slowing down your eating which can help reduce the quantity of food you consume. In the stomach, high fibre food takes longer to process thereby leaving you with a sense of being full for a longer period of time. Eating lots of fibre also will result in more calories being lost in your stool of undigested food. It has been reported that 50 grams of fibre can carry out 100 undigested calories in every bowel movement. Fibre also slows down the rate of absorption of sugar into your blood stream which can be of enormous benefit for people with diabetes. Fibre can be found in all plants, whole grain breads and high fibre biscuits. It is recommended that you obtain your fibre from a variety of foods.

In order for you to obtain the necessary nutrients found in the above elements, you need to include in your diet food in all five of the following basic food groups.

1. **Vegetable and Fruit Group** (citrus fruits, leafy green vegetables, potatoes).

2. **Bread and Cereal Group** (breakfast cereal, bread, foods made from cereals and bread).

3. **Milk and Dairy Food Group** (600ml children for teenagers, pregnant and nursing mothers; 300ml for adults; 250ml can be replaced by 1 x 200ml container yogurt or a 3cm/35g cube firm cheese).

4. **Meat Group** (beef, mutton, lamb, veal, pork, poultry, rabbit, fish, eggs, organ meats, dried peas, beans and nuts).

5. **Butter and Table Margarine Group** (30g butter daily on bread and in cooking).

In the average week, your healthy diet should contain approximately 33 percent vegetables and fruit, 33 percent bread, cereal and grain products, 16 percent dairy products and 16 percent meat, poultry and fish.

Stress-related dietary recommendations

In addition, a number of more specific recommendations related to diet and stress can be made.

1. **Eat a variety of foods.** Select foods each day from the major food groups.

2. **Maintain your ideal body weight.** Consult a weight chart which shows what you should weigh given your sex and height. Here's a stressful thought. If you are 25 percent over your ideal weight, you are two and a half more times likely to have a heart attack. For most of us, your weight should be not much more than it was when you were 20 to 25 years of age.

3. **Avoid too much fat, saturated fats and cholesterol.** This recommendation is especially important if you have high blood pressure, smoke, or have a family history of heart disease. The fats you should first remove from your diet are the saturated ones found in fatty meats, butter, hydrogenated margarines, whole milk and ice cream. Non-fat, low cholesterol food includes lean meat, fish, poultry, dried beans and peas. Also, limit your intake of eggs, organ meats (e.g., liver), and shortenings. Trim fats from meat, remove the skin from chicken and avoid frying your food.

4. **Ensure adequate fibre.** Whole foods deliver to your system fibre which aids digestion, reduces chronic constipation and other gastrointestinal disorders. Whole foods which contain complex carbohydrates include raw or lightly cooked vegetables, fruits, whole grain cereals, bread and biscuits, brown rice, nuts, beans, peas, seeds and nuts.

5. **Avoid too much sugar.** It is estimated on the average that Australians consume more than 130 pounds of sugar a year. To avoid excess sugar: use less of all sugars, including white, brown and raw sugars, honey and syrups; eat fewer foods containing sugar such as sweets, soft drinks, ice cream, cakes and chocolates;

select fresh fruits rather than canned fruits in a sugar syrup; read food labels for clues on sugar content, being on the lookout for ingredients such as sucrose, glucose, maltose, dextrose, lactose, fructose or when syrups are listed first.

6. **Avoid too much sodium.** While an 'unsupervised' daily diet can include up to 50 grams of sodium, the recommended level of sodium consumption is around 5 grams. Table salt contains 40 percent sodium. Other foods to be on the lookout for are sandwich meats, sauces, pickled foods, sauces and food cooked with monosodium glutamate (MSG), and even many medications (e.g., antacids). To avoid too much sodium: learn to enjoy the unsalted flavours of foods; cook with only small amounts of added salt; add little or no salt at the table; limit your intake of salty foods; read food labels carefully to determine the amounts of sodium in processed foods and snack items.

7. **Keep alcohol consumption to a minimum.** We all know the negative effects of alcohol on our well-being, social relationships and driving. And hangovers are, perhaps, the worst antidote for coping with a stressful situation at work the next day. If you drink, especially during the week, limit yourself to one to two drinks per night. On weekends, you should drink in moderation.

Vitamins

The evidence on whether vitamin and mineral supplementation can assist you to function better under stress is equivocal. Some experts argue that when you are under stress you require more of all vitamins and minerals and that deficiencies in the B vitamins, Vitamin C and calcium/magnesium are linked to stress-related symptoms such as insomnia, irritability and depression. Some nutritionists will argue that a balanced diet supplies all the nutrients you need while others argue that today's supermarket foods are nutritionally inadequate.

A common regimen of supplements to combat stress includes a high protein diet supplemented by 500 milligrams of Vitamin C, 100 milligrams pantothenic acid, 2 milligrams each of vitamins B2 and B6. An all-purpose multi-vitamin supplement can do no harm and may provide needed nutritional support.

The following foods can increase your intake of natural vitamins and minerals: brewer's yeast, cod liver oil, raw wheat germ, wheat germ oil, rose hips, bone meal, kelp, lecithin and whey powder.

If you have been feeling stressed and run down and are considering a high-intensity vitamin program, consult your physician. Self-prescribed vitamin programs should be avoided.

Losing weight

Without going into the many ins and outs of dieting, there are a few basics to keep in mind. To lose one pound of body fat, you must take in 3,500 calories less than you expend. To know how slowly you will lose weight without some form of exercise, take an estimate of how many calories you need to maintain your current weight. Subtract your calorie intake on a diet from that weight and what's left over is your calorie loss per day. If your weight maintenance level is 1,600 calories and you consume 1,100 calories per day, you should by the end of the week lose one pound.

There are two basic components to any successful weight reduction program: calorie reduction and exercise (discussed in next section). Cutting back on high calorie foods and starting up an exercise program will get you heading in the right direction. Specific suggestions include:

1.   Don't go on a crash diet. Try to lose weight slowly by reorganising your lifestyle.

2.   Set small, achieveable goals for yourself. The one I use is the 'one pound a week plan'. When I have to lose some weight, I plan on losing at least one pound a week. That minimizes the pain, increases my chances of success, allows me to have some 'non-diet'

food and, if I fail to lose a pound, I can discipline myself to lose two pounds the following week.

3. Weigh yourself once a week.

4. Change your diet to reduce calories and increase your intake of fruit and vegetables.

5. Keep alcohol intake to once or twice a week.

6. Eat smaller portions of food.

7. Eat slowly.

8. Don't eat when you're anxious, angry or tired. Find another competing activity.

9. Eat regularly. Don't starve yourself. Have low calorie snacks planned for periods between meals.

10 Monitor weekly progress and reward yourself for achieving your goals.

Let's now examine an equally important way of making sure you are in shape to combat stress at school and in the rest of your life: exercise.

Exercise

The human body was designed to be exercised. That is why research studies show the following: that longshoreman with lifting and carrying jobs live longer than fellow workers with desk jobs; that among 17,000 graduates of Harvard over a 34-year period, those who vigorously exercised several times each week had fewer heart attacks and a longer life span than those who did not exercise; and that middle-aged men who began to regularly walk, run or swim lowered their chlosterol, blood pressure, weight, anxiety, and depression.

W. Schafer, Author of <u>Stress Management</u>
<u>for Wellness</u>, 1987.

The one stress management technique which seems to me to offer the greatest promise in preventing and reducing physiological distress symptoms is physical exercise. I know it's not for everyone and by that I mean that you, because of age or circumstances, may not find it feasible to exercise. I would hope, however, that before coming to that conclusion, you search in yourself and examine your environment to see if there isn't room for exercise. It seems to be that if you experience a great deal of stress (e.g., fatigue, physical ailments, emotional ups and downs) then exercise offers you great promise for symptomatic relief.

Vigorous physical exertion is the natural outlet for your body when it is in the flight-fight state of arousal. It provides a way of releasing a great deal of the muscle tension and general physical arousal accumulated in response to stress. After exercise, your body returns to normal equilibrium and you feel relaxed and refreshed. Exercise seems to clear your thinking providing you with new insights into the problems which you might find stressful. Its beneficial effects on your body weight and physical well-being leads to an enhanced self-image. And an increased self-images does wonders for your ability to cope with the variety of hassles. Recent research also is showing that exercise can augment the effects of vitamins in fighting off disease.

Many people, including yours truly, do not take to exercise naturally. We have to exert a fair amount of will power to get started and to continue. This is especially the case if we get injured or sick. We find it hard to get started again. Why? It's what Pogo referred to when he wrote: "We have met the enemy and it is us." Something inside us - call it need for comfort if you like - creates an oppositional force to exercise. That force we can reduce by starting; it does get easier.

Exercise has an additonal benefit to stress management. It will reduce your risk of heart disease and, as previously discussed, help you manage your weight.

No, I'm not suggesting that you immediately start to jog around town or power walk. I am encouraging you to move from a completely sedentary lifestyle to one where you start exercising. You can start off with simple walking for 20 minutes or so combined with a little muscle stretching and conditioning. A program of graduated exercises will help prevent muscular atrophy due to inactivity and will help eliminate your fatigue.

Aims of exercise

When you exercise, your aim is to gain physical fitness which can be broken down into three areas. Cardiorespiratory endurance involves using your large muscles by engaging in certain activities such as walking, swimming or jogging for long periods of time (20 - 30 minutes). This type of endurance relies heavily on your heart and lungs. Flexibility involves having an extended range of motion about a joint such as when you bend to touch your toes. Muscular function refers to strength, power and endurance of your muscles.

Guidelines for exercise

1.   Your exercise program should be designed to develop all parts of your body.

2.   Particular attention should be placed on building up your weaker areas.

3.   For adults, cardiorespiratory endurance is considered the most important fitness component. The material on aerobic exercise is particularly designed to improve cardiorespiratory fitness.

4.   Include exercises specifically designed to strengthen stomach muscles.

5.   Pick activities which are fun and practical for you.

6.   Exercise on alternate days. For example, Monday, Wednesday and Friday. As you progress, you may choose to add a session on the weekend.

7.   Get into an exercise program gradually and take it easy. This is especially important if you are past 35. Your body ain't what it used to be when it was 20. So, for example, if you are deciding to take up jogging, start with a short distance and a slower pace.

8.   Keep cool. Don't overdress.

9.   Warm up. Use a variety of warm up exercises (e.g., arm circling, toe touching, jumping jacks) for at least 5 minutes before getting into muscle conditioning and aerobic exercises.

10   Drink plenty of water. Water will help your body remove the waste products generated by your exercise. Drink a glass of water before starting off jogging in the morning.

11.   Allow a 5 minute cool down period. End your exercise with five minutes of slow walking. Move your head from side to side and swing your arms gently.

Aerobic exercise

The most popular form of exercise to increase cardiovascular efficiency has been popularized by Dr. Kenneth Cooper and his work on aerobics. Aerobics are basically activities in which you use oxygen to produce energy. They involve sustained, rhythmic activity of the large muscle groups - especially the legs. Aerobic activities use lots of oxygen through increasing your heart and respiratory rates. This in turn leads to a relaxation of the small peripheral blood vessels which allows more oxygenated blood to reach your muscles. Common aerobic activities include walking, running, swimming, bicycling, swimming and dancing.

The key to aerobic exercise is insuring that your heartrate reaches its 'aerobic range' for at least 20 minutes. Your 'aerobic range' involves you working at 70 to 85 percent of your maximum heart rate. Your maximum heart rate can be estimated as follows: 220 minus your age = maximum heart rate. For example, if you are 40 years old, 220 - 40 = 180 heart beats/minute. Your target 'aerobic range' is 70 to 85 percent of your maximum heart rate. Using the above example: .70 x 180 = 126 beats per minute; .85 x 180 = 153 beats per minute. Therefore, your 'aerobic range' would be between 126 and 153 heart beats per minute. If you are beginning your exercise program, it is good to exercise in the lower part of your 'aerobic range' so that you will be able to exercise comfortably for between 20 and 30 minutes.

There are definite benefits of aerobic exercise which can help you modify your stress level. Physical stress-related benefits include release of muscle tension; burning off adrenaline; production of endomorphs (the body's natural pain killer and mood elevator); reduction of cholesterol, tryglycerides, blood sugar, body fat, blood pressure; post-exercise quieting of your sympathetic nervous system and reduction of adrenaline output; more energy and faster recovery from acute stress. Psychological stress-related benefits include: release of pent up emotions; enhanced self-image and self-esteem; greater sense of personal control; clearer thinking and better concentration ; feelings of well-being and comfort.

Muscle conditioning

Calisthenic and isotonic exercises can increase your flexibility and muscle strength, power and endurance. Exercises centre on your major muscle groups including abdomen, trunk, thighs, hips, buttocks, lower back and arms, shoulders and chest. Strength exercises include weight lifting, knee bends, push-ups and side leg raises. Flexibility exercises include toe touching, body stretching, single leg raises, calf and achilles tendon stretches, side bends and head rotations.

In summary, a good exercise program should contain four parts: warm up, muscle conditioning, aerobic exercise and cool down. If you are interested in starting to exercise regularly, acquire some of the many fine exercise books now on the market.

Recreation

So, if you think you do have a job that's a source of distress to you, that does not offer much relaxation, amusement or refreshment, then you will have to accept your personal responsibility to look after yourself, by making sure you do have sufficient recreation in your life.

Dr Bob Montgomery and Lynette Evans,
Stress and You, 1984.

The third area of your lifestyle which can buffer you from stress is recreation. You would think that recreation would come naturally and that everyone would know how to recreate. Surprisingly, many of us are extremely poor recreators. We tend to limit ourselves to a very few inactive activities such as watching television or going to the pub. As I'm sure you're aware, educators concerned with preparing our youth to cope with the fewer number of jobs and work hours projected to characterize our work in the 21st century are targeting recreation as a topic which needs to be introduced in the school curriculum. Recreation as a self-management skill offers the promise not only of stress-reduction but also, perhaps, as an area of personal endeavour apart from your job which can bring you sastisfaction in the future.

I think of recreation as time out from stress where you are able to relax your mind and body. You get away in time and space from those constant demands which you experience as stressful. What you do when you are away from the madding crowd can and should vary considerably. At times, you may wish to simply curl up with a good book, take a long bath or go for a walk. These more solitary recreational activities are generally motivated out of your need to be alone, away from people, so that you can collect and take charge of yourself, rather than react or serve the desires of others.

Recreation may also involve others such as friends or family. Time with friends offers companionship and support as well as amusement and stimulation. Friendships offer a great deal. Unfortunately, when you are under stress you can actually ignore your friends thereby losing out on one of the main resources for stress-reduction. Friendships need to be worked on.

Another type of activity which can relax and refresh you surrounds your hobbies. Too many of us, when we get heavily involved in our work and have family commitments, put our hobbies and interests on the back burner. We give up playing squash, bush walking, walking at all, taking photographs, fixing old cars, collecting and renovating antiques, etcetera. Aside from distracting us from work, hobbies also offer the additional good feelings which go along with the intrinsic satisfaction of doing something well which you have chosen to do.

So laughing, playing, going on a short walk, taking a brief holiday, getting involved in a hobby, playing sport, taking a class or just relaxing can cut your stress. Why not have a little check-up on your recreational habits to see what you are and are not doing and then, move on to expanding your recreational options.

How to Develop a Good Recreational Lifestyle

Adapted from Montgomery and Evan's Stress and You, 1984

Step One: Examine your present recreational activities

For the next month, make a written record of all the recreational activities you engage in both inside and outside of school. Make a note of exactly what you were doing, who you were doing it with, how much time you spent doing it, and how much enjoyment you received from the activity. You may want to use a diary, calendar or note pad for such a record.

Step Two: Evaluate your present recreational activities

For some, this step will take very little time as their recreation is very limited in time and scope. If you have recorded different recreational activities, consider each one in terms of what it achieves for you. Use the five criteria of recreation (relaxation, amusement, re-energising, relationships, time alone). Try to draw some conclusions as to the nature of your recreational pursuits. See if you are failing to engage in certain activities which might help satisfy more of your recreational requirements.

Step Three: Select new recreational activities

In identifying gaps in your recreational program, you will be orientated towards activities which would be a good addition to your life style. For example, you may see there is an absence of any self-development hobby or interest and elect to take one up. Or you may realise that you are exercising far less than you thought and want to expand your exercise program. Or you may notice that the time you spend with friends is far shorter than the priority you hold for friendships.

Step Four: Get organised

Before charging into a new recreational activity, get yourself organised. Decide when you are going to do it. Get a hold of any material or equipment you might need. Investigate different options about where to go for a short holiday.

Step Five: Put it into action

You've heard the expression 'Paralysis through analysis'? Don't over-analyse what you are going to do, just get a bit organised and get into it. Sure you might not like it and have to modify it accordingly. The main thing is to make the committment to trying out some new activity for awhile, giving yourself a full chance to judge whether its for you. You may have to try many different activities to come up with a few that really suit you, that you enjoy, and which can give you the relief from stress you desire.

Barriers to recreation

There are a few little devils which can prevent you from trying out new things. One is your own attitude about taking time out for yourself. You may be so used to doing things for others that the thought of doing something for yourself only increases your guilt and stress. Remind yourself that everyone is entitled for some time in their own day to day life for themselves. As well, by taking the time, you will have more to give to others and provide it more generously.

Another barrier is simply time. You believe there is no time. As you'll see shortly, one of the keys to finding more time is by learning to monitor, plan and manage it better. By scheduling events in your hectic life - especially during your peak periods - you will find time to recreate.

Finally, you may want to recreate and think you deserve it and will perform better once having had it, but you might feel anxious about asking your significant other (if you are in a relationship) to support you by assuming some of the household responsibilities. The chapter on assertion offers you basic skills in how to stand up for and assert in a pleasant way your basic rights.

It was 10pm at night and Bill could hardly keep his eyes open. "I thought a bit of exercise and good diet was supposed to energise me. I'm exhausted," he complained to Denise, who did not appear to hear him.. She was totally immersed in doing something at the desk in the study. "Darling, what are you doing? And how come you've got so much energy? Your usually dog tired by 8.30pm. What's gotten into you, anyway?"

"For your information, I am finally writing my book. And I'm finally getting my self together. Like you, darling, I've been pigging out on the wrong foods which have been slowing me down. No more after-noon cakes for me. Increased my fruit intake - in moderation, Bill. And I've scheduled myself to work for a half hour starting tonight. Now excuse me. It's time for a break and a few sit-ups. I also want to look good for your party in two weeks."

"Denise, honey. You're not having an 'affair' with anyone? How come you were so long at the dry cleaners?"

"Don't be stupid. I actually was delivering your pants to have them taken in like you asked. You just might lose enough weight for your party. How much more to go?"

"Eight pounds. I think I'll make it. You still haven't told me what your book is about."

"Well if you must know, the title is "How to Live with A Neurotic Husband.""

"Hey, that's a bit close to home. And who is neurotic? I'm the most stable man you know."

"I am taking literary license in parts. Especially with the part about you having an affair with your graduate student to compensate for a mid-life crisis you're going through as you approach 40."

"Are you out of your mind! What will our friends and our colleagues think? Anyway, if anyone's having an affair with a graduate student it's Larry, not little ol' innocent me."

"Don't worry darling, nobody would believe it about you!"

"Wouldn't they?" Bill started to feel a bit miserable and decided to go to the kitchen and sneak a butterscotch lollypop. He promised himself to run an extra 10 minutes in the morning

---

Actions Speak Louder Than Words

Write down a list of 5 things you could do to improve your daily diet including minimising stress-increasing foods. Select two that would be easiest for you to implement and do so for one week. Gradually make other changes to your nutritional plan and add other improvements to the list.

List a variety of types of exercises (e.g., walking, jogging, tennis, stretching, bowling) which would be possible for you to engage in. Try to schedule at least three sessions of exercise per week.

From a list of solitary recreational activities to ones involving friends and family, select one activity from each list which would be the easiest to do and most pleasureable. Schedule each activity over the next month. Slowly schedule other recreational activities.

10

How to Get Others to Procrastinate Later

It is very important to build employees up, make them feel important and let them get the credit for things they have accomplished....While being free with your praise, never let people rest on their laurels, become complacent and feel that a good accomplishment one week allows them to get away with almost anything in the future. Sometimes you can motivate good employees to be better by pointing out their minor shortcomings and urging them to greater heights. This is what I call negative motivation.

Mark H. McCormack, <u>What They Don't Teach You at Harvard Business School</u>, 1984.

Not only can your procrastination be a problem for you, others' procrastination can also prevent you from achieving what you want at home, in work and from life.

At work, you may find yourself becoming increasingly exasperated with one or more people who promise to do things, but do not deliver on time. If your work is dependent on their contributions, then their procrastination can be severely harmful to your work efficiency and success. You may end up having to do their work, thereby neglecting other of your important tasks. For example, suppose your colleague has agreed to take responsibility for the marketing of a joint venture. You spend your time putting the project together, be it a sales seminar or new product line. As the time approaches to launch your product or service, you might find that your colleague has done little in the way of advance promotion. The result is that not only do you have to take over marketing, but the probability of the enterprise being successful is greatly reduced.

Or you might be a manager which, by definition, involves you getting things done through other people. If you have one or more people who chronically fail to carry out courses of action which you believe are vital for you to accomplish company objectives, then you will have, as a consequence of their procrastination, failed in your role as manager. Your failure would be seen as the 'bottom line'. Additionally, you could be viewed as the person having minor or major responsibility for staff induction, training and performance.

On the home front, almost all parents see part of their role is to ensure their children are studying and performing to the best of their ability. Unfortunately, the serenity of home life can be severely disturbed by the issues of study and homework. I know of too many parents whose relationships with one or more of their children have been reduced to conflict and tension simply because their child procrastinates at doing homework. You might be a parent who is extremely disturbed and stressed by your own inability to get your youngster to work more and play less.

You may also have to bear the cross of your significant other being a procrastinator. You may be used to having discussions about what your mate will do to help your domestic economy run smoothly only to find that at crunch time they haven't fulfilled their part of the bargain. While they may well have the best of intentions to do more housework, pay bills on time, fix things which are about to or have broken down, unfortunately for you, their talent for procrastination overrides their desires to co-operate with you!

Indeed, life would be much easier for all of us if important people whom we count on in our various roles were not so skilled at procrastinating. In retrospect, you might have even decided that if you had to do it all over again, you might not get involved with or hire someone who so easily qualifies for the Born Procrastinator's Club. At work, you might be able to encourage them to move on to more satisfying jobs. At home, it is much harder to fire a husband, wife or child.

This final chapter is devoted to providing you with some ways of better managing someone who procrastinates. A word of advice. Be realistic in what you can expect of yourself in being able to modify someone who chronically procrastinates. While getting others to become more motivated isn't as hard as getting a leopard to change its spots, the difficulty of your task can come close.

Self-Control: Without it You Will Fail

The key to managing others is self-regulation.

Albert Ellis, Ph.D., <u>Executive Leadership</u>, 1972.

One of the almost inevitable consequences of working or living with someone who procrastinates at doing tasks you've decided are important is that, over time, you develop a large amount of negative emotion towards the person. In many cases, their continued procrastination has coloured your overall relationship with them to the point where many of your interactions and communications are imbued with discord. Not only are you frustrated with the employee who constantly hands in reports late, you are getting to the boiling over level. At home, the school's report of your adolescent's lack of progress and, in particular, the comment that he/she has the potential if only they would work harder leads you not only to feel angry with your child, but frequently anxious about the future.

However, while it is human to experience a great deal of anger, anxiety and other emotions towards a procrastinator, these emotions in their extremes will make it much, much harder for you to motivate them to action. Why? For two main reasons.

First, when you get overly upset about someone's procrastination, you will find it much harder to solve the problem at hand. This is because extreme emotional upset interferes with your problem-solving ability and results in you employing the old methods such as shouting, threatening or ignoring which haven't worked. Second, when the procrastinator confronts your being upset, your upset often provokes in them an equally strong negative emotion which makes it even more unlikely that they will get on with their tasks.

This second reason illustrates why it is vital for you to have self-control before you try to manage them and their problem. Extreme anger on your part towards the procrastinator will often result in the procrastinator feeling very angry with you for what, in their mind, is your unreasonable attack. They may also feel that you are de-valuing them as people and, as a consequence, feel rejected and hurt. Or rather than feeling angry, if your predominant emotion is high anxiety, then be aware that if the reason for their procrastination has to do with fear of disapproval or failure, that your upset will be adding to theirs. Extreme negative feelings on the part of the procrastinator will only make it less likely that they will feel like doing what they already do not feel like doing.

So, if you have a procrastinator in mind whose behaviour you would like to see modified, ask yourself how emotional you have been in discussing their procrastination with them and the need for them to change. If you have been very uptight, ask yourself how they feel as a consequence. It may well be that the way you have handled them in the past has made it tougher for them to change. Here are a few suggestions for gaining emotional self-control.

Controlling Anger. To reduce your high levels of anger, remind yourself that they are procrastinating because that's the way they are. For whatever reason (anxiety, low discomfort tolerance, poor time management, hostility), they are the type of person who finds it difficult not to procrastinate. Remind yourself that while it is bad for them and for you that they are procrastinating, it is hardly the very worst thing that they could be doing (they could be on drugs, stealing or murdering someone!) Remind yourself that while you do not like their procrastination, you certainly can stand it; that is, it's not going to kill you. Recognise that, while their procrastination in some areas of their life is a bad characteristic, they most certainly have other more positive qualities. While their behaviour might be bad, they are not totally hopeless. And finally, remind yourself that getting very angry with them does little to help improve the situation. (Other techniques for managing anger are reviewed in Chapter 8).

Controlling Anxiety. If you are feeling very anxious about the consequences of their procrastination (e.g., failing a course), then it is likely you are telling yourself that it is 'terrible' and 'awful' that they are procrastinating. As well, you might be taking their procrastination too personally, evaluating it as a sign that you have failed. To keep your anxiety under check, ask yourself on a scale of real life catastrophes, how bad is it that this person is procrastinating and might not succeed at what they are doing. Most of the time you will see that you are blowing the badness of the procrastination out of proportion. Also, dispute the idea that it is your fault they are procrastinating and that you, therefore, are a failure. Remind yourself that there are many other reasons for their procrastination than you and that, many times, their procrastination is under the influence of other factors which you have no influence over. (Other techniques for managing anxiety are reviewed in Chapter 5).

Controlling Frustration. Certain people have the personal qualities to successfully modify the procrastinating behaviour of another. One vital characteristic is *high frustration tolerance*. That is, you have to be prepared to put up with the hassles and frustrations of not getting what you want from the other person. In particular, you will have to be able to accept that, even with your best of efforts, change will be very slow. Indeed, you will have to accept that sometimes, the person who you are trying to change is actually going backwards and procrastinating more rather than less. Ways to boost your frustration with their slow progress and with having to put in so much of your time and effort is to remind yourself that in all probability you are working with someone who is not like other people in the respect that they have personal qualities which make it harder for them to respond to your inspirational efforts. Remind yourself that you are dealing with a 'hard case' and, after all, what would you expect from a 'hard case?'. If they

responded quickly to your efforts, it's unlikely they would
be procrastinating so often in the first place! (Other techniques for increasing your tolerance for frustration are
reviewed in Chapter 6).

Let's be crystal clear on what I mean by self-control. In your
efforts to get someone to procrastinate later, make sure that
you are reasonably cool, calm and collected. And be
prepared to stay calm for some time until they begin to
change. Don't be impatient and don't let anger and anxiety
influence the skill with which you manage a difficult problem.

Work on Changing the 'Real Reasons' for Another's Procrastination

*performance = f (aptitude level x skill level x understanding of
the task x choice to expend effort x choice of degree of effort x
choice to persist x facilitating and inhibiting conditions not
under the control of the individual).*

Campbell and Pritchard, <u>Motivation Theory in Industrial
and Organisational Psychology</u>, 1976.

As I have written, there are many different reasons why
people procrastinate. If you want to modify another's behaviour, it is often useful to try to analyse for yourself the
reasons they are procrastinating. It may then be possible
to directly tackle those reasons thereby bringing about a
change in the desired direction. Let me illustrate how you
can work on three of the main reasons people procrastinate:
low frustration tolerance, anxiety and poor time management.

Low frustration tolerance

Laziness is a shorthand way of saying that someone is easily
frustrated by tasks they find boring and which require
sustained effort. In this sense, laziness is synonomous with
low frustration tolerance. The attitude which drives laziness can be represented by the phrase "I can't be bothered".
And there are great numbers of people who can't be
bothered doing things which they don't enjoy doing. The

reasons for these attitudes have to do with their basic temperament, the ways they were disciplined while growing up and other social or cultural factors which might encourage an "I'd rather be sailing" attitude.

You can pick someone's low frustration tolerance by examining what sort of task they are putting off. You need, however, to get inside their head a bit to determine what sorts of tasks they find boring and frustrating. Some people find filing and paperwork dull while others simply can't be bothered getting out of bed on time. If you believe a person is putting something off because they find it too hard and unpleasant to do, then it is likely they have low frustration tolerance.

To deal with someone's procrastination which is motivated by low frustration tolerance, you have two basic options. One is to see if you can relieve them of your expectations and give them a job they will enjoy more than the present one. For an adolescent, you might find that shifting subjects or schools invites an improvement. At work, rather than expecting everyone to participate in every aspect of every job, you might find that allocating jobs differently might produce the trick.

And keep in mind that although your procrastinator might seem to be totally hopeless in getting certain things done on time or at all, they might have other talents which they could be using for the betterment of your organisation. For example, I know of a surprisingly large number of people who, while procrastinating at the dull and dreary jobs which have to be completed on schedule, are fantastically creative and innovative thinkers. While you wouldn't want everyone in your company to be a thinker rather than a doer, you may want to consider whether the person you are wishing to motivate possesses certain talents which could be better employed in other ways.

The other main way of motivating someone with low frustration tolerance is using one of the motivational systems which I will describe shortly.

Anxiety

You'll remember that people put off doing certain activities due to their fear of failure and/or disapproval. People who can be described as operating in their comfort zone might well be doing so because they simply can't be bothered putting in any additional effort. This we refer to as low frustration tolerance. However, they might be avoiding more challenging activities due to their anxiety.

Again, you will recognise procrastination which is motivated by anxiety by the type of task or activity the person is putting off. If it is one which is clearly threatening and where there is a good chance (at least in their mind) of failure and/or criticism, then you might be faced with having to address anxiety as an issue rather than low frustration tolerance. Examples of tasks which people may put off due to anxiety include applying for a new job, enrolling for a very demanding university course, entering a competition, asking for a raise and taking on new and more challenging aspects of one's job such as the selling of new products, the offering of new services or the promotion of a service provider to a manager.

Some organisations actually foster an atmosphere of anxiety as a way of ensuring top quality performance. Not too long ago I consulted with senior executives of a top governmental agency employing hundreds of people which instilled in its employees the idea of perfectionism and the requirement that everything be done without mistakes. While this agency's ethos did produce very smart looking reports which were always submitted on time, unfortunately many senior executive officers were putting off making important decisions in the future planning of their divisions because of a collective fear of failure and fear of criticism from 'up top.'

If you are trying to help someone to procrastinate later at anxiety-provoking tasks, then it is vital you tap into their fears of failure and criticism. Highly anxious people can be reminded that it is sometimes good to perform tasks less than perfectly to discover what they can and cannot do. This type of person can also be reminded that all people learn by trial and error and that without trying and making mistakes, they will find it much harder to get ahead. As well, in helping people deal with their fear of other people's negative evaluations of their work, remind them that, while it's definitely nicer to have approval, they don't *need* approval. They can accept and enjoy themselves without it and still be successful.

In addition, see if you can dispute their negative forecasts of the future. You can anticipate that if they are delaying doing something out of fear, they are predicting negative outcomes for themselves. If there is evidence from their past performance that when they try something they generally do reasonably well (even if it takes a bit of time), encourage the person to make more positive forecasts. Keep in your mind what Denis Waitley, the internationally known motivator and psychologist has written: "Your mind is the best forecaster of the actions of your body."

Poor time management

Sometimes people put things off which you want them to do or believe they need to do for their own good because of their inability to manage their time better. You'll be able to recognise this person easily by their frequently vocalised complaint: "I just don't have enough time to get to it."

As a manager, co-worker or even a parent, you need to do an analysis of all the different committments of the person who is putting things off because of time constraints. On your own or with their help, write down everything they are expected to do during a day and for a whole week. Then see if they really do have too much work to do and not enough time to do it.

If you find that they are over-committed then, if possible, in order to help them get to what you consider important activities, see if you can relieve them of some of their committments. At home, it might be relieving your child of some chores during their peak study period. (You might even have to insist they give up one or more of their lower priority recreational interests). At work, you might be able to modify some of the deadlines in which other work is due or simply make more time available to them by relieving their workload.

You can also help a person whom you find very committed to many different activities to think about the relative priority of the activity. Some people who procrastinate fail to discriminate the most important tasks in front of them from those less important. Getting people to ask themselves which activities are the most important (e.g., writing a book) in helping them achieve their long-term objectives and which are of less importance (e.g. sitting on committees) can often help them to focus their energies in more productive ways.

A technique I've already discussed in Chapter 7 is "scheduling". People who are often late and fail to keep deadlines have great difficulty in scheduling their time. For younger people at home, helping them fill out a weekly time planner where they write down all their committments and specify exact times at which they will plan to carry out their activities can be useful in helping them make better use of their time. With adults and people you work with, sometimes spending your own or your company's funds on diaries and time management planners can be of similar assistance.

Let's now turn to four basic procedures designed to reduce the extent to which someone else procrastinates.

Behaviour Modification: Rewards and Penalties

One reason managers often fail to motivate subordinates is that the reinforcements they offer are far removed from the subordinate's actions. For example, informing subordinates during the annual performance appraisal interview that they have done a good job is probably less motivating than praising them each time they perform a task particularly well.

James A. F. Stoner, Ph.D., Roger R. Collins, Ph.D. and Philip W. Yetton, Ph.D., Management in Australia, 1985.

Behaviour modification is a set of principles and procedures which you can use to bring about a change in someone else's behaviour. Behaviour modification can help you to increase how often someone does what you've asked them to do as well as reduce how often they procrastinate.

The two behaviour modification procedures which, if employed thoughtfully and consistently, can help you to get someone else to procrastinate later are: positive reinforcement and punishment. Both procedures are based on a simple principle of human behaviour; namely, that human behaviour is greatly influenced by the consequences which immediately follow the behaviour. Let me define these two important procedures as follows:

Positive Reinforcement: Giving someone a positive reinforcer (reward) immediately after they have performed a behaviour will result in an increase in the frequency of that behaviour.

Punishment: Giving someone a penalty immediately after they have performed a behaviour will result in a decrease in the frequency of that behaviour.

Simply stated, if you want someone to start working on and completing a particular task on time, then every time they work on and complete the task on time, immediately reward them for their efforts. Similarly, to decrease their procrastination, every time they fail to work on or complete a task on time, immediately penalise them for their failure.

Now you might be thinking that this is so obvious that it is something we would ordinarily think of and do. Wrong! Many times you can find yourself reacting inappropriately towards someone who procrastinates. At work, people frequently deal with another's procrastination in unhelpful ways. When you encounter someone not doing what they said they would do, you often do not say or do anything, but rather just get angry inside and at a later time let loose. Or you might opt for giving the person what amounts to a lecture on what they've done wrong and insist that next time they improve. Or given the number of courses on the benefits of an assertive interpersonal style, you might state how their procrastination effects you, how you feel and what you want.

At home, you might resort to similar unproductive methods with your child or mate. For example, as your child demonstrates a great reluctance to do their homework or clean up their room after agreeing to do so, being an enlightened parent you spare the rod and lecture your child on the wrongs of their actions and ask them to reconsider their committments and to take greater responsibility for their actions.

Behaviour modification is a system designed to promote an increase in positive behaviour rather than a reduction in negative behaviour. As such, it orientates you to paying more attention to instances of non-procrastinating behavior than to instances of non-compliance. The reason behaviour modification works is that most of us take for granted when someone does something positive and only tend to respond to them, albeit negatively, when they haven't done the right thing. People who procrastinate need to be taught to get things done. They will not learn from seeing you taking their accomplishments for granted. Rewarding them for completing tasks will motivate them to complete the task the next time.

To use behaviour modification effectively, you will need to start with a concrete description of what you want the other person to do. At home, it might be spending at least 60 minutes on homework each night. Or at work, it might be handing in a fully completed report on time. Having defined what you want and communicated your desires to the other person, the key is to closely monitor the person and, as soon as they have complied with your request, to reward them with something they find positive and pleasurable. And the success of your behaviour modification program will hang on selecting a reward which the person will enjoy.

At home, it is important for you to pre-identify a range of rewards to give to your child or mate after they have worked on or completed what it was they agreed to do. Examples of rewards which can work can be as simple as a statement of praise for the effort they put in or the quality of the result. Examples of verbal praise include:

"Good work."

"I really appreciated what you did."

"Champion effort."

"Thanks for getting that done."

Other examples of rewards which you can use with family members are tangible rewards such as money, special treats and prizes, edible rewards (especially effective for use with younger children) such as favourite foods, and activity rewards where you make available to your child or mate a special privilege such as attending a special event or watching a favourite show on television. A reward can also involve allowing your child or mate to 'get out of' having to do something they don't like doing after they've accomplished their work, such as not having to help do the dishes.

If you think that positive reinforcment sounds a bit like bribery, that's because it is. The main difference is that in this case the end justifies the means.

You can also use rewards at work to encourage someone to get work completed on time. Rather than being relieved that someone has finally done what they've set out to do, you need to praise and acknowledge them as soon as they have finished the task. One of the most powerful rewards at work for some people is verbal praise. Telling a procrastinator how much you appreciated what they've done is the primary means for motivating them to do it again the next time.

In his book How to Motivate People Michael Le Boeuf, the internationally renowned management educator, advises managers to ask themselves three basic questions if they want to motivate an employee:

1.   What behavior do I want?

2.   How will I recognise it?

3.   How will I reward it?

He offers the following 10 'best' rewards which you can use to motivate people at work.

Reward No. 1: Money. Companies that give monetary rewards based on performance get performance.

Reward No. 2: Recognition. Some of the more popular ways to make people feel appreciated and important are: employee-of-the-month awards; certificates and citations for achieving important goals; clubs with special privileges for high achievers; favourable publicity such as a write-up in the company newspaper; change in job title; public praise; a congratulatory letter for special achievement which goes into the employee's file; status symbols such as rings, better office, private parking space; charts showing how well a group or individual is doing the job.

Reward No. 3: Time Off. If the job permits, give people a job deadline and specify the quality you expect. If they finish before the deadline, the extra time is their reward.

Reward No. 4: A Piece of the Action. Those who own a part of the company and have a stake in its success are less likely to procrastinate.

Reward No. 5: Favourite Work. Give people more of the tasks they enjoy doing as a reward for good performance.

Reward No. 6: Advancement. If goal accomplishment is linked to job advancement, people are more likely to put in the effort on tasks which they may not feel like doing.

Reward No. 7: Freedom. You may decide to reward someone for being self-disciplined by getting rid of time clocks and rigid working hours. Not only will they be motivated to successfully execute different tasks to continue to earn their freedom, but others at work may vicariously start to work harder in the hope of winning more freedom for themselves.

Reward No. 8: Personal Growth. The two basic ways personal growth rewards can be given is by providing people with new tasks that challenge their creative ability and by providing further educational and training opportunities.

Reward No. 9: Fun. People are much more likely to put in the effort on boring, frustrating and unfulfilling aspects of their jobs if they have opportunities at work to enjoy themselves. Examples of ways to increase the fun at work include having recreational facilities on the premises, parties, a bulletin board for jokes and piped music.

Reward No. 10: Prizes. There are a large number of prizes at your disposal to reward another's efforts, including tickets for recreational events, company products and gift certificates.

While the list of rewards provided by Le Boeuf were selected as appropriate reinforcements to increase motivation, I think you'll see the range of options avialble to you to reward someone for reducing their procrastination and getting the work done.

Penalties can also be combined into a behaviour modification program designed to decrease procrastination and increase effort on different tasks. When you employ penalties, it is important that the other person is quite clear beforehand what he or she has to do to avoid them. For example, if you are trying to motivate your child to spend more time on study, you might have the rule that on those nights they spend less than 60 minutes on their work, they will lose the privilege of staying out late on the following Friday night and the weekend. At work, you can inform your 'delinquent colleague' that unless they fulfill their obligations on time, they will lose out in terms of sharing profits or other projects you might have in store for them down the line.

There are a few additional behaviour modification principles for using rewards and punishments effectively with someone who is procrastinating. During the early part of introducing the program, reward **successive approximations.** That is, do not expect the person you are trying to motivate to go from an unacceptable level of performance to 100 percent success over night. Be prepared to accept and recognise behaviour which begins to look like what you expect down the line.

The principle of **small sequential steps** involves your breaking down the overall tasks you want the person to perform into smaller, more manageable parts, if at all practical. Rather than expecting your child to complete an extended essay, have them work on the different parts of the assignment (e.g., outline, introduction, first half, second half, conclusion). Reward them for accomplishing each small part.

Catch them in the act so you can reward them while they are performing what you desire. For example, 'peek' into your child's room and when you catch them studying, reward them. At work, if someone is in the process of getting to the job they've been putting off, reward them at the time you catch them at it.

And finally, make sure your **rewards and penalties are given to the person immediately following their behaviour.** Do not wait until later in the day to say thankyou or withhold privileges for good performance. People need to be told immediately as to the consequences of their successful or unsuccessful behaviour. (You can wait until later to actually carry out some forms of rewards or punishments).

Contracting

Contracting is a process used to make the necessary elements of a behavioral change program so clear and explicit that they may be written into an agreement that is understandable and acceptable to everyone involved. It is also a means of scheduling the exchange of positive reinforcements (rewards or desirable elements) between two or more persons.

William J. DeRisi and George Butz, Writing Behavioral
Contracts, 1975.

Contracting is a more formalised way of instituting a program designed to reduce someone else's procrastinating behaviour. Contracting involves you negotiating an agreement with someone else which provides something for you and provides something for them. The exchange of rewards involves the other person agreeing to do what you want them to do while you agree to reward the other person for their efforts. Contracting is more often used to combat the procrastination of people you live with at home and, most particularly, with your children. It can also be used by teachers and school counsellors with students who are putting off doing their work (as well as breaking rules). If you want to use a contract to increase someone's effort on accomplishing tasks they tend to put off, it is important to follow these steps:

1. Select the behaviour you want to change.

2. Describe the behavior so that it may be observed and isolated.

3. Identify the rewards that will help provide the motivation to do well.

4. Find people who can help keep track of how often the behaviour is being performed and who can, perhaps, issue rewards.

5. Write the contract so that everyone can understand it.

6. Record how often the behaviour is performed.

7. If no change is observed in the behaviour, problem solve to see how to improve the system, paying particular attention to finding better rewards and whether the amount of change expected is too great, too soon.

8. Rewrite the contract.

9. Continue to record, problem solve and rewrite until there is a positive change in the behavior.

In negotiating a contract, it is important that you are negotiating rather than simply imposing your way. The more say the other person has in the contract, the more likely it is that they will be committed to keeping to it.

There is a standard way of getting a contract on to paper once everyone has agreed to terms. Here is an example of a standard contract I negotiated with a 13 year old boy and his parents.

1. **Date agreement begins.**

    March 12 (renegotiation date: April 12).

2.   **Behaviour to be increased.**

60 minutes of homework each night and 120 minutes on the weekend.

3.   **Amount and kind of reward to be used.**

Each day (and weekend) that goal is achieved, Eric can use the family computer for 60 minutes.

4.   **When the reward is to be given.**

Immediately after the homework time is completed.

5.   **Signatures of all those involved including your own.**

6.   **Schedule for review of progress.**

In 2 weeks.

7.   **Bonus clause for sustained or excellent performance.**

Computer game of Eric's choosing. Movie of Eric's choice.

8.   **Statement of the penalties that will be instituted if the specific behaviour is not performed.**

No computer time or television viewing on the night that goal is not achieved.

The above contract produced a rapid decrease in Eric's procrastination and definite improvements in his school work. One of the reasons for its effectiveness was Eric's absorption in computers. Eric was only allowed to use the computer after he had fulfilled his end of the bargain. Had Eric access to the computer at other times, the reward of extra computer time would have had less impact due to Eric possibly reaching what is called satiation level. Make sure that whatever rewards you incorporate in your behaviour modification program are not readily available. Otherwise, the person you are motivating may have already had their fill and may find your reward less appealing.

The 'One Minute Manager'

Goals begin behaviors, consequences maintain behaviour.

Kenneth Blanchard, Ph.D. and Spencer Johnson, M.D., The One Minute Manager, 1983.

One of the most popular procedures for managing the behaviour of another was initially developed for business and industry by Kenneth Blanchard and Spencer Johnson. Coined the 'One Minute Manager', this method is based on principles of behaviour modification and assertion. It is designed specifically for managers to help bring out the best in employee performance in as pleasant and efficient way as possible. The three steps involved enable you to go about motivating others in a systematic way. An additional benefit for the person who is procrastinating is that, by being exposed to the technique and witnessing its effectiveness, they learn to apply the technique to themselves, leading to self-discipline. The 'One-Minute Manager' has been applied by parents as an aid to their becoming better managers (rather than slaves or dictators) at home. The three steps to becoming a one minute manager are as follows.

1. **One minute goal setting**

    * Agree on your goals.

    * See what good behaviour looks like.

    * Write out each of your goals on a single sheet of paper using less than 250 words.

    * Take a minute out of your day to re-read your goals.

    * See whether or not your behaviour matches your goal.

2.   One minute praising

- Tell people right from the start that you are going to tell them how they are doing.

- Praise people immediately.

- Tell people what they did right.

- Be specific.

- Tell people how good you feel about what they did right and how it helps the organization and the other people who work there.

- Stop for a moment of silence to let them 'feel' how good you feel.

- Encourage them to do more of the same.

- Shake hands or touch people in a way that makes it clear that you support their success in the organization.

3.   One minute reprimand

- Tell people beforehand that you are going to let them know how they are doing in no uncertain terms.

The first half of the reprimand

- Reprimand people immediately, telling them what they did wrong.

- Be specific.

- Tell people how you feel about what they did wrong, stopping for a few seconds of uncomfortable silence to let them know how you feel

The second half of the reprimand

- Shake hands or touch them in a way that lets them know that you are honestly on their side.

- Remind them that you think well of them and value them but not their performance in this situation.

- Realise that when the reprimand is over, it's over.

To use the one minute manager method with a subordinate who has promised to finish a report and get it to you in the afternoon, but only gets it finished and to you the next morning would have you using a 'one minute reprimand.' You might say something like: "You know, Bob, you promised to get this report to me yesterday afternoon so that I could use it to prepare for my meeting later on this morning. I am angry that you are late with this report and that I will not be able to be fully prepared for this important meeting ... [pause for a few seconds] ... I know that you are much better than this. Let's see what both of us can do to prevent this from happening again ..." [shake hands].

The Quarry Method of Performance Appraisal

Based upon the inherent conflicts in performance appraisal, it is vital that the person giving the appraisal not only be very skilled in the various aspects of the interview process, but, more importantly, be in control of themselves in order to handle negative reactions in the part of the subordinate.

Peter Quarry, Australian
Organisational Psychologist.

Recently, performance appraisal has become the catch-cry of those seeking a mechanism for ensuring greater worker accountability. As you'll most probably know, performance appraisal involves managers of varying levels of seniority periodically meeting with those less senior to review their past work accomplishments in light of goals which have been spelled out at an earlier time. Weekly, monthly, six monthly and yearly performance appraisals have become quite common in certain sectors of private enterprise although it has been slower to take in the public service.

Performance appraisal is ideally suited as a formal process for helping others you work with to procrastinate less.

Carried out the right way, performance appraisal will in- crease the likelihood that you will motivate the hard to motivate. You'll understand, of course, that there are no guaranteed outcomes in this area of human endeavour.

Unfortunately, the promise of performance appraisal has gone largely unrealised. Why? Because many people who give performance appraisals are not very good at giving them. They may give them only with the greatest reluctance or dodge the whole affair. If they attempt to give them, they flounder and fluster. To give a good performance appraisal requires the right attitude and set of skills. Without being prepared, it is very likely that you won't do it well.

Once again, strong negative emotions can interfere with giving a sound performance appraisal. As already dis- cussed, becoming angry with a subordinate inefficient performance will make it almost impossible for your per- formance appraisal to be constructive. You'll be more than likely to ram your subordinates failings down their throat, resulting in them feeling quite put down and antagonistic towards you.

Another main barrier to giving honest and accurate perfor- mance appraisals is a high need for approval. If you feel a fair amount of anxiety about what the person who you are giving negative feedback thinks about you, you will be less likely to present the negative side of their performance. Your concerns for their approval will heighten your anxiety to the point of you procrastinating at being honest with them. After all, if you only stress the good, they will be much more inclined to think well of you. Negative feedback from you, no matter how constructively expressed, will never be greeted by someone else like an old friend.

In order to give good performance appraisals, it is vital you are not overly preoccupied with what others think of you. If they temporarily do not like you, that's tough. You'll have to live with it. Often, if your appraisal is perceived by another as being fair, they'll be able to cope with the negative.

Peter Quarry, one of Australia's leading organisational psychologists, has developed the Quarry Performance Appraisal Method which has been used very successfully in the training of managers. The Quarry Method is based on a problem-solving approach to performance appraisal. It offers an alternative to the 'tell-listen' methods which have characterised managers' attempts to motivate under-performing employees in the past. The Quarry Method consists of six steps which start with making observations of your employee before giving any feedback. Another distinguishing characteristic is that after you have gained agreement with the employee that there is a 'gap' between what is expected and what you have observed, then you allow the employee (along with input from you) to identify the reasons as to why they have not achieved a given standard. A summary of the Quarry Method is now presented.

Step 1   **Monitor and assess employee before talking**

- Describe specific expectations and goals you have for the employee including a 'standard'.

- Obtain clear and objective evidence of the employee's actual work performance.

- Determine that a gap exists between expected standard and actual behaviour.

Step 2   **Give feedback**

- Focus on work behaviour and not the person.

- Give examples of gap.

Step 3   **Gain agreement as to gap between expected standard and actual performance**

- If agreement is not achieved, clarify standard expected, how it can be monitored and then go back to Steps 1 and 2.

Step 4   **Identify cause of the gap**

- Unclear standard communicated to employee.

- Lack of employee skill.

- Work overload.

- Equipment problems.
- Work relationship problems.
- Outside problems.

Step 5 **Problem-solving solutions**

- Generate a list of alternative solutions.
- Examine positive and negative consequences of each and select the best.

Step 6 **Formulate action plan**

- Who is going to do what, when and where?
- Review date for next meeting.

Step 2 of the Quarry Method is a particularly vital one as poor feedback can prevent you from successfully completing future steps. In their book "Personnel/Human Resource Management in Australia" Randall Schuler, Peter Dowling and John Smart provide the following list of characteristics of effective feedback.

1. Feedback is most effective when an employee believes he/she wants or needs it and voluntarily enters the situation where feedback is given.

2. The feelings of the employee should be taken into account. Rather than making you feel better by cutting the employee 'down to size,' make your feedback helpful.

3   Focus your feedback on the employee's behaviour rather than on the person. "You have been late three times", rather than "You are irresponsible".

4. Make your feedback specific rather than general. "Just now you were not listening to what I said", rather than "You are too dominating".

5. Immediate feedback is better than delayed feedback.

6. Don't overload the employee with too much information.

7.   Focus your feedback on what or how something has been done, not why. Telling an employee what their underlying motivations are tends to alienate them.

8.   Have the employee paraphrase your feedback to see if it was what you intended.

An example of using the Quarry Method to get an employee who works in the mail room to complete assigned tasks on time would involve you collecting data and verifying that their is a gap between what has been expected of the employee and actual performance. The second step is to give feedback to the employee as to the positive and negative aspects of their performance. The third step involves you getting agreement with the employee that they, in fact, have been late in getting things accomplished. The fourth step involves you in a discussion with the employee to find out what they think the causes of the gap are. In this case it might be that the employee is uncertain as to what the priorities are of the various tasks he's been assigned and that he does not have a proper work station. Step five is to discuss with the employee various ways in which the causes can be remedied (e.g., clarification of people's roles at work; new desk). The final step is to review what you are going to do, what the employee will do, and to make arrangements for the next meeting to see how things are going.

"Well Bill, your party was phenomenal!" That is, what Larry could remember about it. On the night, he was not only celebrating Bill's 40th, but Helen had finished her exams that same day and was in a partying mood. The only problem was that Larry couldn't remember anything past about 10 pm. The champagne just kept slipping down. The next thing he knew was waking up the next day, alone, with a crashing headache and with Helen's watch in his bed. And what's worse, Helen wouldn't say anything about the night and how her watch ended up in his bed.

"Yeah Larry. You sure seemed to have a wild time," smirked Bill. "Over did it a bit on the old champagne. Never seen you look so bad the next day. As for me, Mr. Moderation, I felt fantastic the next day. Went for a jog and then had a hit of tennis with Denise." Bill couldn't help but gloat. He was just 2 pounds over his weight when he graduated from college and probably fitter. He really surprised himself as to his will power.

"That's the last party I'm going to with you, Larry" said Helen winking at Denise. "Not only did I have to drive you home, I had to carry you to your house and put you to bed. Broke my watchband in the process."

"Er, can't you remind me what we were exactly doing when your band broke?" Larry was determined to get at the truth once and for all.

"It's no wonder you don't remember. Denise, he was so off his face he didn't see me to the door!"

"Alright you guys," said Denise stepping in to protect Larry, "Larry was just having a good time. Nothing wrong with that is there? Anyway, you're all invited to another celebration. I've just got an advance for the book I'm writing."

"Advance?" Bill started to look worried. "You mean you are really going to write that book?"

"Don't look so happy, Bill," said Larry. "What's this book about, Denise?"

"It's a self-help guide...It was going to be called 'How to Live With a Neurotic Husband' but I can't write that now. Bill isn't as neurotic as I thought. No, this one will be called "How to Have Great Sex with Your Mate After 40". And guess what? I'm dedicating it to you Bill!"

"Hey, that sounds fantastic", exclaimed Helen. "We can have a bit of a double celebration. I got three A's and a B for final grades."

Bill looked a bit dubious.

"In fact," chimed in Larry putting his arm around Helen, "We can make it a treble celebration. Helen and I are ...you're the expert Denise. What do you call it when the 'oldies' go steady?"

"You'll have to wait and read about it in the new book."

"And what besides my beautiful new look body do I have to celebrate?" whined Bill.

"Why, Bill, " smiled Denise. "You'll have a wife who will be an international celebrity touring all over the world talking about your beautiful body, that's what!"

Bill took another bite of his watercress sandwich and frowned.

Actions Speak Louder Than Words

Set up a behaviour modification program to motivate someone else to procrastinate later. Pick something which you think should be relatively easy to change in another. Remember to have as your goal an increase in some behaviour. Follow the steps outlined above. Once successful, pick another more difficult behaviour to change.

See if you can use the Quarry Method of Performance Appraisal to motivate someone at work or at home. Remember to be self-controlled and to invite the other person to seek causes and solutions to their procrastination.